NEGOTIATING RESPONSIBILITY
IN THE CRIMINAL JUSTICE SYSTEM

The Elmer H. Johnson and Carol Holmes Johnson Series in Criminology

Negotiating Responsibility in the Criminal Justice System

Edited by Jack Kamerman

With a Foreword by Gilbert Geis

SOUTHERN ILLINOIS UNIVERSITY PRESS

Carbondale and Edwardsville

01 00 99 98   4 3 2 1

Library of Congress Cataloging-in-Publication Data

Negotiating responsibility in the criminal justice system / edited by
Jack Kamerman ; with a foreword by Gilbert Geis.
   p. cm. — (The Elmer H. Johnson and Carol Holmes Johnson
series in criminology)
   Includes bibliographical references.
   1. Criminal justice, Administration of—United States.
2. Criminal liability—United States. 3. Criminal behavior—United
States. I. Kamerman, Jack B. II. Series.
HV9950.N44 1998
364.973—dc21
ISBN 0-8093-2211-0 (alk. paper)   98-5414
ISBN 0-8093-2212-9 (pbk. : alk. paper)   CIP

To the late Edward Sagarin,
the only true Renaissance man I have ever met,
whose ideas still guide our thinking
and whose spirit still enriches our lives

Contents

Contents

viii

Foreword

Gilbert Geis

In terms of criminal justice, the last decade of the twentieth century might well be labeled the Period of Perpetrator-as-Victim. The Menendez brothers, cold-blooded killers, maintained in court that their death-dealing should be excused because they had been beaten and molested by their father. Governors and legislatures throughout the United States have been scrambling to reexamine the cases of women convicted of killing husbands who they claimed had subjected them to merciless physical abuse. The "perpetrator-victims" have sought—and often received—the endorsement of a *nol-pros*, an acquittal, or, on later review, release from prison, even though the murder might have been carried out calculatedly, while their mate was asleep. In California, O. J. Simpson's defense lawyers would persuade a jury that their client was the victim of race prejudice, manifest through a conspiracy of the law enforcement establishment against his interests, and that he deserved to walk out of the Los Angeles courtroom a free man. To turn Simpson loose, it was insisted, would teach "whitey" a lesson.

There is an argument contrary to the Perpetrator-as-Victim thesis. Thomas Szasz, a renegade psychiatrist, has insisted in a series of feisty tracts—most notably *The Myth of Mental Illness* (1961)—that the only decent way for human beings to respond to the actions of their fellows is to hold them completely accountable for what they do. To adopt any other policy, Szasz maintains, is to deprive people of their dignity and self-respect. Insanity should not be a legal excuse, since the state of mind that elicits such a diagnosis is only another adaptation that some of us make to the exigencies of existence. We all do foolish and self-defeating things to varying degrees, and we will only do them less often if we are inexorably persuaded that the consequences will be unappetizing.

Szasz further argues that the public reaction that malefactors anticipate often triggers their actions. Assassins, for instance, would not kill famous people if they could not anticipate that thereafter they would be transformed into celebrities, garner vast news media attention, and in many other ways obtain relief from the life of monotonous unimportance that typically marks their previous existence. Sirhan Sirhan was a stable-boy at the Santa Anita race track. He put a bullet into Robert Kennedy's head and his name became indelibly engraved in the nation's history.

At the core of Szasz's ideology is the view that we should all be obligated to play the cards that we are dealt at birth and those that we draw thereafter. Szasz understands that each of us starts life with very different hands—some have all aces, others have jokers—although I heard him say during a lecture some twenty or so years ago, rather to my surprise, that he would be willing to make exceptions to the rules for juveniles, on the ground that youth is a transient condition and in due time everyone who survives outgrows it.

The Perpetrator-as-Victim school is rooted in Anatole France's well-known aphorism from *Le Lys Rouge* (1927:91) that "the law, in its majestic equality, forbids both the poor man and the rich man to sleep under bridges, to beg in the streets, and to steal bread." But for Szasz this is just so much fol-de-rol. For others, the fundamental question is whether the slogan that all persons are equal under the law camouflages—even perverts—true justice. Should the unequal resources, the unequal statistical likelihood of committing crime, and the unequal personalities and experiences of those who violate the law be factored into the judgments they receive?

Michael Weisser in *Crime and Punishment in Early Modern Europe* (1979: 143) argues that the doctrine of "equal justice under law" first developed as a response to efforts to eliminate brutality and arbitrariness without jeopardizing the safeguards that favor the bourgeoisie and the wealthy. The doctrine, he notes, "assumed equality of social circumstances" and thus "invented a social fiction to disguise its legal fiction." Eugene Erlich (1936:84), a legal sociologist, summarizes the point well: "The more the rich and the poor are dealt with according to the same legal propositions, the more the advantage of the rich is increased."

But the views of France, Weisser, and Ehrlich only provide details about something that most of us know, that justice is not equal and that those who possess particular kinds of resources can work the system to their advantage. Alan Dershowitz (1996), granting that O. J. Simpson had bought his way out of a prison sentence, noted as a justification that if any of us had a great deal of money and a serious medical problem, most assuredly we would hire the best doctors we could find. So what else is new? he rather cavalierly asks,

romping by the obvious point that because something is true does not necessarily make it right. The very difficult issue remains: What kinds of circumstances, such as race, ought to diminish full responsibility for actions? And
how can such exculpatory policies enhance justice for perpetrators while at
the same time adequately protecting those innocents who have been and
might be victimized?

The search for sensitive and sensible policy responses to the oppositional
viewpoints of the Perpetrator-as-Victim school and that of Szasz and his followers lies at the core of the chapters in *Negotiating Responsibility in the Criminal Justice System*. The fascinating series of essays that make up this book
confront, each in its own way, questions of responsibility and accountability
as they bear upon the substantive matters that the chapters address. These
issues include the future of juvenile and family courts, prison suicides as they
impact on the custodial staff, the privatization of prisons, terrorism, crimes
as part of organizational behavior, and tactics for inculcating personal responsibility.

There is also, in the epilogue, a gripping account that responds forcefully
to the tormenting question of why prisoners in the German concentration
camps did not rebel against the utter degradation to which they were subjected by their captors and did not strike out at the guards when they humili-
ated them. The chapter's answer is that the prisoners thoroughly understood
that such action was pointless, uselessly suicidal. This compelling analysis
recalled for me the similar passivity among conscientious objectors to the
Vietnam War who, after they were imprisoned, soon abandoned their protests
against what they saw as intolerable institutional injustices because they came
to appreciate that nobody was listening and that rebellious actions accomplished nothing except the prolongation of their incarceration.

In this book the analytical stage is set for us by Charles Fethe, who looks
at some of the fundamental philosophical issues associated with responsibility
and accountability, most notably questions concerning the conditions that
might abrogate full responsibility. Fethe's essay pinpoints the powerful conflict between the moral and legal world and that of science. Science assumes
that when something happens, behind it lies a causal pattern that led to the
occurrence. Things don't just come about; they are the consequence of earlier
events and circumstances. But if behavior is caused by deterministic forces,
how can the person who is merely responding to those forces be held responsible for the behavior? Religions, of course, must assume that human beings
are personally responsible for what they do; otherwise, there is no justice in
declaring that evildoers have defied God's commandments and will be punished by divine judgment unless they repent.

Similarly, the legal system cannot operate without an assumption of free
will rooted in the premise that virtually all of us have the ability to engage in

rational conduct. Supreme Court Justice Oliver Wendell Holmes noted in his classic study *The Common Law* (1881:3) that laws "do not require that every man should get as near as he can to the best conduct possible for him. They require him at his own peril to come up to a certain height. They take no account of incapacities, unless the weakness is so marked as to fall into the well-known exceptions, such as infancy and madness." Thurman Arnold in *Symbols of Government* (1935) grudgingly endorsed that principle, observing that the means of imputing responsibility used by the criminal justice system are scientifically indefensible, but that nonetheless they are an essential piece of "folklore" that serve as a basis for integrating social values and maintaining a stable moral order. His view is similar to the belief of the seventeenth-century scientist and philosopher Blaise Pascal that even if free will did not exist, it would be necessary to invent it in order to maintain human balance.

Tied to such ideas, two major themes run through the chapters in this book. One group of contributions rests on the belief that equality under law is a make-believe construct; suggestions are offered by the authors regarding how justice might better be achieved. In contrast, the other chapters start from the assumption that people need to take responsibility for their actions if we are to deter undesirable acts, and they offer analyses of how and why such assumption of blame often does not occur and how it might be encouraged.

In the first category, which seeks to address issues of different levels of responsibility, Mark Moore, as an example, makes a provocative call for transforming juvenile and family courts, now under severe attack, into civil tribunals that regard youthful waywardness as an indicator of some possibly remediable deficiency in surrounding circumstances. Moore argues that "the offenses they [juveniles] commit are less theirs than is true for adults, and therefore they are less blameworthy." For Moore, responsibility for much juvenile crime comes to rest on the state, which has allowed families to sink into emotional bankruptcy. In his blueprint, which he grants may prove to be too utopian or even counterproductive, the state is to be charged with the task of rearranging family or other aspects of the wayward juvenile's life so that the undesirable behavior will cease.

Terrorists are used by Robert Kelly to demonstrate the manner in which those who commit fearsome criminal acts avoid introjecting feelings of responsibility and thus "morally disengage." Kelly seeks answers to the question "How are they able to do what they do?" and provides an insightful inventory of tactics that are employed for this purpose. Although they accept "tempered" responsibility, terrorists totally deny accountability for their actions. They tend to operate in political isolation, to mask their reprehensible activities by the use of sanitized vocabularies.

The other chapters offer equally astute insights into the extraordinarily important developments that now are coming to the fore in the administration of criminal justice as the search for equality under law increasingly tilts toward a kind of courtroom "affirmative action," in which those defendants who come to be defined as socially beleaguered demand to be rendered less personally responsible for their crimes.

Ultimately, it seems to me, persons are most likely to assume responsibility for their behavior when they perceive that there will be some reward for doing so. The Salem Village witch trials of 1692 offer a striking illustration of how the process of assuming responsibility operates. In his revisionist analysis of the witchcraft trials, based on a painstaking review of original sources, Bernard Rosenthal demonstrates in *Salem Story* (1993) how those accused of being witches, their lives in fearful jeopardy, responded to their growing awareness that confession to diabolic deeds would lead the judges to spare their lives. Many thereupon enthusiastically took full responsibility for acts that they could not conceivably have committed: attending sabbats, putting curses on cattle, tormenting their accusers, or signing the devil's book with their own blood. Accepting blame meant staying alive. Nonetheless, many of those who "confessed," although severely and often mercilessly pressed by their inquisitors, shrewdly restricted the roster of coconspirators, typically naming persons already accused or, better yet from their viewpoint, already hanged.

Those among the accused who were more deeply devout, whose reference point was not the here but the hereafter, could not bring themselves to lie. "I dare not tell a lie if it would save my life," Susannah Martin responded to the judges' insistence that she confess her diabolic deeds. She was hanged on July 19, 1692, along with three other women who also proclaimed their innocence, and their bodies were stuffed into an unmarked hillside grave.

The Salem Village story, of course, offers an unusual, although illuminating, twist on the issue of responsibility. Those among the accused who assumed responsibility were actually inventing tales; those who truly took responsibility by denying the accusations condemned themselves in the belief that what awaited them in heaven was so inestimably important that it should not be jeopardized on earth. For both groups of accused, it was the anticipated outcome of the position they took that marked their response to their interrogators. The lesson seems clear. If people are to be persuaded to behave well or, failing that, to agree that they had the chance to do so and failed, they must see some benefit in doing so.

Since fear of a life of torment in hell no longer suffices, some compelling contemporary rationale, be it mythic or mundane, seems essential. Or, perhaps, we ought to abandon the premise of global responsibility and introduce a formula that holds those more responsible who appear to be least pressured by social forces to commit an offense. After all, very few people who own two

BMWs steal a third: It is the slum kid, without transportation, who understandably lusts for a car of his own.

Perhaps an answer lies in what John Braithwaite in *Crime, Shame and Reintegration* (1983) calls "reintegrative shaming," a process in which offenders are confronted by those they love and respect—and perhaps the victim as well—and are told in no uncertain terms that what they have done is totally unacceptable, but that they themselves otherwise remain an essential and valuable part of the group. Braithwaite argues that successful reintegration through intrafamily negotiations by the use of tactics of shaming will implant a conscience that will remain on duty, in effect delivering an immediate punishment for every transgression, as opposed to the relatively remote prospect of being caught and dealt with by the criminal justice system. His ideas may be utopian in contemporary metropolitan areas that are characterized by relativistic moral codes and abiding cynicism, but they may offer some hope in more integrated and isolated communities.

Readers will reach their own conclusions about the most effective manner with which to deal with issues of accountability and responsibility that are raised in the chapters of *Negotiating Responsibility in the Criminal Justice System*. None can fail to be challenged by the intricacies of this profoundly important issue or to be caught up in the questions raised by the book's contributors.

References

Arnold, T. W. (1935). *Symbols of Government*. New Haven: Yale University Press.

Braithwaite, J. (1983). *Crime, Shame and Reintegration*. Cambridge: Cambridge University Press.

Dershowitz, A. M. (1996). *Reasonable Doubt: The O. J. Simpson Case and the Criminal Justice System*. New York: Simon & Schuster.

Ehrlich, E. (1936). *Fundamental Principles of the Sociology of the Law*, trans. W. L. Moll. Cambridge: Cambridge University Press.

France, A. (1927). *Le Lys Rouge* [The Red Lily], trans. W. Stevens. New York: Dodd, Mead. (First published 1894.)

Holmes, O. W., Jr. (1881). *The Common Law*. Boston: Little, Brown.

Rosenthal, B. (1993). *Salem Story: Reading the Witch Trials of 1692*. New York: Cambridge University Press.

Szasz, T. S. (1961). *The Myth of Mental Illness: Foundations of a Theory of Personal Conduct*. New York: Hoeber-Harper.

Weisser, M. R. (1979). *Crime and Punishment in Early Modern Europe*. Atlantic Heights, N.J.: Humanities Press.

Preface

The chapters in this book examine how the issue of responsibility for one's actions is worked out in the criminal justice system. Although the focus is on the United States, the contributions by Alison Liebling, Paul Neurath, and William Rentzmann describe situations in other countries that are in turn recognizable and unrecognizable to Americans.

The analysis of responsibility can be done on several levels: psychological (for example, how individuals manage to distance themselves from their horrific actions); organizational (for example, how bureaucracies function to cloud the assignment of responsibility); occupational (for example, how professional ideologies support the dodging of responsibility); and societal (for example, how changes in values color the social construction of responsibility). These sectors of life are so deeply intertwined that separating them requires a justification; in this case, analytic convenience. The essays in this book focus on the three macrolevels, although their implications for understanding the psychological lives of individuals should be obvious.

The foreword by Gilbert Geis, rather than offering the usual opening remarks, is in itself an important statement on the subject of responsibility. The rest of the book is divided into three parts. The two essays in part 1 delineate different frameworks for understanding the acceptance and denial of responsibility and include a discussion of the relationship between the various levels of analysis: psychological, organizational, occupational, and societal.

The essays in part 2 focus not only on criminal justice institutions charged with the care and control of inmates but also on the societies, organizations, and occupations that support those institutions. Criminal justice institutions are housed in organizations, populated by people in particular occupations, and embedded in societies that give them their specific character. The privatization of corrections, for example—the subject of Jess Maghan's paper—is a wave in the tide that is sweeping across the United States, carrying with it functions that have traditionally been assigned to agencies of government. In the same way, William Rentzmann's paper, which describes one of the few programs that specifically focus on the issue of responsibility, situates the program in the context of Danish society.

The essays in part 3 focus on offenders and how they define their own involvement in the acts they commit. Offenders operate in the same societies as the criminal justice institutions that handle them. They sometimes conduct their activities with occupational ideologies analogous to, and within the same organizational forms as, those of the institutions that process them. On a psychological level, the devices they use to own and disown their actions are presumably the same as those in general use.

The conclusion focuses on the societal context of responsibility, delineating an underlying theme of the chapters in this book: that contemporary society is structured in a way that encourages the denial of responsibility and, in fact, discourages its acceptance. In the epilogue, Paul Neurath examines inmate status from inside and outside the experience, suggesting that it is only from the outside that certain myths about inmates' motives, actions, lives, and worth can be propagated. It is on the basis of this wicked mythology, the product of social distance, that the great atrocities in history have been committed. Through this process the motivation to commit these atrocities is transmuted from psychopathology and evil into duty and calling.

Neurath's paper is an example of a frayed tradition: a sociological analysis with moral weight. This tradition is also exemplified by the work of the late Edward Sagarin. Ed was teacher and colleague and friend to many of the contributors to this volume, including myself. When Bob Kelly suggested that I edit a book in connection with the Edward Sagarin Institute, the purpose was to honor Ed's memory by addressing a social issue that we thought he would have found significant, in a collection of papers to which we hoped he would have liked to contribute.

On the long and sometimes rocky road to publication, a number of people have deserved special thanks. I want first to thank the contributors to this volume, who did their fine work on the simple basis of my invitation and who never once wondered out loud why the book was taking so long to be published.

I am grateful to Bob Kelly, president of the Edward Sagarin Institute, for asking me to develop the idea for a book.

I want to give special thanks to my friends, colleagues, and fellow Sagarin students Jess Maghan and José Sánchez for their ideas, their support, and their humor. They shared with me their optimism and strength when my will faltered. Jess knew from the beginning that this book would happen, and, as usual, he was right.

Without realizing it, Paul Neurath, by the example of his grace, reduced my frustration with this project to its proper level of pettiness.

My friends Charles De Fanti, Barry Pearl, and Ronald Wolf listened to my complaints with the appropriate mixture of sympathy and sarcasm.

I owe thanks to Rick Stetter of Southern Illinois University Press for seeing this book as a book and for grasping immediately what it was about. He is rare in academic publishing, a field awash in people who would probably see the Bible as a textbook for Religion 101. His assistant, Mona Wilson, is the model of equanimity he deserves.

Three editors from Southern Illinois University Press deserve special thanks: John Gehner, for handling the early phases of the editorial process with sense and good humor; Carol Burns, for helping to revise the overall organization of the book; and John K. Wilson, for steering the book toward publication with flexibility and editorial clarity.

And, as always, my overriding gratitude is to my family: my children, William, David, and Anne, who answered impatience with affection, and Connie Munro, my wife, for her editorial gift, her patience, and her love— "but the greatest of these is love."

PART I

FRAMEWORKS

1

The Social Construction
of Responsibility

Jack Kamerman

The Negotiation of Reality

In the sociological view, our view of reality is never a given but rather is something that needs to be explained. Its meaning changes in the course of interaction with others through a process of negotiation. This negotiation is sometimes formal and explicit (Strauss, 1978), but more often it is an implicit element of an interaction. An example of the former is the attempts of defense attorneys and prosecutors to work up the "facts" of a case in order to portray a defendant in antithetical ways (Scheff, 1968). This particular negotiation of identity is a conscious effort to do what all people do as a matter of second nature in the course of their everyday lives. The negotiation of identity very clearly underlies the assignment and denial of responsibility for acts inside and outside the criminal justice system.

On a larger scale, the meaning of the basic notions we take for granted, such as right and wrong, human nature, and time, emerges through a process of negotiation and interpretation and is never settled for all time. (In fact, ironically, seeing society as unchanging is the outcome of this fluid process of negotiation.) This notion of the social construction of reality is the most basic concept in sociology (Berger and Luckmann, 1966).

The changing interpretation of the law is negotiated by incumbents in the judicial system who argue their positions and align themselves in part based on social and economic factors such as social class, race, and religion. Yet, at the same time, they maintain the position that their interpretations come from what inheres in the law itself—that is, that they discover the meaning of the law rather than invent it.

4

A notion such as responsibility is an excellent example of a social construction. Who is defined as responsible when something goes wrong or goes right, or whether Fate is seen as the force that powers human actions, varies according to factors like culture, social class, occupation, and generation.

Responsibility as an Issue in the Criminal Justice System

In ways that have rarely been examined and even less often understood, ideas about responsibility affect the operation of the criminal justice system. The assignment and denial of responsibility are among the hottest legal, moral, and political issues in contemporary American society. But for all of the recent talk in politics and business about accountability, the United States remains a one-sidedly no-fault society: People take credit for their accomplishments but disown their mistakes. If Harry Truman were president today, the sign on his desk would probably read: If you play your cards right, the buck never stops.

Just as societies have characteristic styles of crime (Durkheim, 1964:64–75; Erikson, 1962), these trends in American society are reflected in the criminal justice system. Blame is negotiated on both sides of the law. Trials often play off the absence of a defendant's guilt against the underlying fault of the criminal justice system and society, with some defendants depicted as victims of the American Dream. White-collar criminals are simply casualties of the drive to succeed, and corporate crime becomes an almost patriotic defense against the vagaries of the global economy and the overriding goal of economic viability. Corruption and police violence are explained away by the pressures on law enforcement agencies, by budget cuts, and by an all's-fair-in-the-love-of-justice-and-the-war-against-crime mentality. Expediency becomes the engine that drives the justice system, neutralizing the culpability of the guilty through plea bargaining and, at the same time, convicting the innocent by making pleading guilty to a lesser charge preferable to being steamrollered into conviction on a more serious charge.

The assumptions that criminal justice institutions make about offender responsibility underlie their conviction and acquittal decisions. The increasing use of medical and psychological explanations of behavior in both society at large and courtrooms in particular to explain and, in effect, to explain away responsibility for what would otherwise be seen as criminal acts illustrates the seepage of societal changes into a specific societal institution.

Conrad and Schneider (1992) have called this trend *medicalization* and described its effects on the assignment of responsibility as the shift from "badness to sickness." It is not simply in the "insanity defense" that this shift is seen. Crimes in general are explained in psychological or sociological terms as functions of the biographical details of a defendant's upbringing, or the socioeconomic circumstances in which that upbringing took place, more often than they are explained in moral terms as acts of good and evil.

Some defendants may try to recast their "crimes" as "revolutionary acts" whose etiology lies in the inequalities of society rather than in the calculus of personal gain. The extent of this social change lies not only in the increasing frequency with which criminal acts are explained in this fashion but also in the very fact that, whether honored or not, these explanations are comprehensible. The fact that this phenomenon has remained virtually unstudied is in itself an interesting comment on to what degree this explanatory strategy is taken for granted.

The "medicalization defense" represents one strategy for explaining away responsibility for criminal acts. The process of distancing oneself from the victims of crime is another important strategy for negotiating guiltlessness. Social distance has more benign functions, such as in the case of physicians, who distance themselves from patients in order, in part, to establish the atmosphere in which strangers are willing to undress, share intimate details of their lives, and so forth. However, the extreme form of social distance, dehumanization, has usually preceded the most horrific atrocities in human history. (See, for example, those described in Paul Neurath's chapter in this volume.) Dehumanization is a major precondition for allowing people to commit atrocities against others without seeing themselves as responsible for their acts. Again, these are trends and processes in a society at large that affect all of the institutions in a society, including the criminal justice system.

Levels of Analysis

The assignment and denial of responsibility may be studied on three levels of analysis: psychological, organizational-occupational, and societal. There is, of course, overlap between these three levels. Some concepts cross over lines—for example, bystander apathy or doubling (Lifton, 1986). Consequences may filter down from the societal through the organizational level to the individual level. Societal values affect the way organizational structures will operate. The emphasis on individual performance and gain, endemic to American society and American corporations, is in sharp contrast to the emphasis on the good of the larger entity—in this case, the corporation—that is at the center of both Japanese society and the Japanese style of management. Because the approach here is sociological, large-scale factors will be emphasized even in the case of the psychological level of analysis, because the influence of these factors on psychological processes is often neglected.

All of the factors discussed below operate at the same time, at the same moment of history, so their interaction is a given. Nonetheless, it is useful for analytic purposes to separate these three levels of analysis.

Psychological Factors in the Assignment and Avoidance of Responsibility

The most obvious example of a psychological device for disowning one's actions is the defense mechanism of denial. The questions that need to be raised to situate this mechanism sociologically include the following: Are there eras in which denial is more common or easier to pull off? Before the psychoanalytic revolution, for example, denial, if spotted, would have been seen as simple lying and punished rather than dealt with therapeutically. In that sense, denial as a defense didn't exist before psychoanalysis. Denial involves a judgment that one version of reality is better or more accurate than another. The version that prevails sometimes has more to do with power than validity.

Another personal but nonetheless socially grounded mechanism for distancing oneself from one's actions and the responsibility for their consequences is identity disavowal. People make the claim that they are not who others think they are, as in the amateur shoplifter's incantation from the 1960s: "You think I am a thief, but I am really a revolutionary doing my part to undermine exploitive capitalism."

Identity disavowal is easier to carry off in a large society or community, in which people live among strangers and don't know most of the people they interact with in the course of their day. It is also easier in a rapidly changing society in which blossoming ideas compete with fading ideas for the mantle of truth.

Another example of a psychological process that allows people to distance themselves from responsibility for their actions is what Robert Lifton (1986: 419–65) calls "doubling." Doubling entails "the division of the self into two functioning wholes, so that a part-self acts as an entire self" (418). The constraint of conscience is not eliminated but rather shifted from one self to the other. "The requirements of conscience were transferred to the Auschwitz self, which placed it within its own criteria for good (duty, loyalty to group, 'improving' Auschwitz conditions, etc.), thereby freeing the original self from responsibility for actions there" (421). Doubling is not a common adaptation. Rather, it is reserved for cases in which the crime is particularly heinous or the work particularly horrible, when the career of the criminal or the worker is ongoing, and when, because of other, more respectable statuses the person occupies, conscience might otherwise be problematic in performing a criminal or occupational role.[1]

Doubling may also be seen as one end of a continuum, with lesser degrees represented by the adaptations of respectable people who do, as Everett Hughes (1958:70–73) puts it, "dirty work." Lifton (426–29) points out that doubling may be linked to larger-scale variables such as culture (to explain why it shows up more frequently in some places than in others) and occupation (to explain why some occupational groups are particularly prone to use it).

Organizational and Occupational Factors in the Assignment and Avoidance of Responsibility

Although the traditional model of bureaucracy (Weber, 1958:196–244) has undergone changes in the past twenty or so years with the infusion of organizational models from Europe and Asia, it is still safe to say that work in the criminal justice system is overwhelmingly done in traditionally defined bureaucratic settings. This is true whether the organization is in fact large scale or whether a small police or sheriff's department simply tries to emulate that organizational form. That means that the ways in which bureaucracies undermine responsibility will certainly operate in large organizations but will also, to one degree or another, operate in smaller ones.

The very structure of bureaucracies provides camouflage for those who work in them when blame is assigned. The division of labor and the hierarchy of authority, in particular, function in this way, making the following lines recognizable to all: "That's not my department"; "You'll have to speak to . . ."; and "I don't make the rules. I only work here."

Geller and Silver (1978) claim that in large organizations responsibility is diffused by fragmenting the tasks that the organization performs and assigning them to different departments. The division of labor operates to make no one officer or office wholly responsible for organizational actions, nor, as a result, for the ultimate consequences of organizational actions. They point out that this exemption from responsibility is aided by the dehumanization of the objects of organizational actions. This dehumanization neutralizes feelings of guilt and also makes difficult to impossible the assignment of responsibility for damage, say, that customers may suffer from the use of inferior products an organization manufactures. (See José Sánchez's chapter in this volume for an explication of these themes.)

Occupational ideologies function in part to justify the work people do and in part to explain away mistakes. These ideologies are learned in formal training and in informal socialization. For example, teachers may believe that the failure of their students to learn is a function of the environment their students come from or some other factor that puts success, and by implication the responsibility for failure, beyond the teacher's control. As with all ideologies, the point is not as much whether these self-serving ideas are true as whether they work to neutralize guilt and to shift or dilute responsibility.

Police officers may believe that people are basically corrupt. The cynicism and suspiciousness that are claimed to constitute part of the police officer's "working personality" (Skolnick, 1975)—and that of many other occupations in the criminal justice system—result from the work that police officers do. These traits are compounded by the increasing civil liability that characterizes police work as well as many other kinds of work in the contemporary United States.

In light of this increasing liability, even the most straightforward encounters with citizens must be subjected to extra scrutiny. This undermining of trust in everyday discourse and interaction is perhaps the most subtle and important consequence of the litigious atmosphere that permeates both personal and professional lives in the United States. Suspiciousness and cynicism are not simply necessary adaptations in a particular occupation; they are features of all occupational lives and basic elements in the contemporary American character.

In police work in particular, the siege mentality that has developed reinforces the idea that no one but another police officer has the right to judge police officers' mistakes (the so-called "blue wall"). In this respect, police work is like medicine and the other professions in which, traditionally, only members of the profession had the right to judge a colleague's work. But, just as the physicians' prerogative has been undermined through consumerism and malpractice suits, civil liability and civilian review boards function to undercut this traditional advantage in police officers' negotiating responsibility. Once again, these changes in police work as an occupation have to be understood in their relationship to trends in the larger society in which police work is embedded.

Societal Factors in the Assignment and Avoidance of Responsibility

The definition and assignment of responsibility are influenced to the greatest degree by history, culture, social trends, and ideas and zeitgeist. While all four are inextricably tied, they are examined individually as a matter of intellectual convenience.

Historical Situation

The historical era influences not only the degree to which members of a society will accept moral responsibility for their own actions and their assignment of responsibility to others but also the very terms in which moral responsibility is defined. Generations within an era, and generation units within a generation (Mannheim, 1952),[2] color the way people work up their interpretations of the world. The dominant generation unit of the 1960s (which, in fact, ran from about 1967 to about 1973) was empowered by the abdication of the generation that preceded it; it came to believe that the privileges of a privileged childhood would go on forever. The line between childhood notions such as "this is for pretend" and "this is for real" was blurred. The notion "this doesn't count" was transmuted from a street game amenity into a generational exemption from the consequences of one's actions.

The PATCO air traffic controllers' strike in 1981, during the Reagan administration, is a good example. The legal line that forbade the strike and spelled out the penalties was clear, but no one seemed to believe the penalties would be enforced. After they were, people thought that they would surely be rescinded. After all, the air traffic controllers had "learned their lesson." There was general disbelief when the penalties were made to stick.

If "nice" people don't expect laws to be enforced, what is the likelihood that criminals, who have experience with plea-bargaining and who also presumably have less respect for the law, will have a different attitude?

Other examples of the legacy of the 1960s, compounded by the general American de-emphasis on the past, include a resurgent generational blindness among homosexuals to the problem of HIV contagion and the growth of heroin use in some sectors of the middle class. The general inattention to the experiences of those who have come before is simply applied to these scourges in particular.

Culture

Ironically, the view that one will not suffer the consequences of one's actions exists side by side with the idea that others will inevitably be held responsible for the consequences of *their* actions. The view that one will be compensated for one's losses is predicated on the notion that the world is a rewarding place (Rainwater, 1970), while the notion that one *should* be compensated for one's losses is predicated on the notion that losses are not a natural part of life. What started out as an idea of the "first team" of American morality—the middle class—has trickled down to lower socioeconomic levels. Lawsuits, like lottery games in American states and bullfighting in Spain, are seen in part as a chance for a poor kid to make it big—that is, as an avenue of upward mobility.

In civil suits, judgments quantify responsibility in dollars, sometimes dividing responsibility precisely according to some explicit formula. Lawsuits fix responsibility on someone who *isn't* you, in effect both supporting and undermining a sense of responsibility at one and the same time.

Criminal guilt is also based on notions of responsibility. Conviction is based in part on the idea that defendants are responsible for their actions. The law sometimes explicitly defines the meaning of responsibility. In the case of the New Jersey law making it an offense to serve a drink to someone who leaves your house drunk and then causes an automobile accident, the circle of those held responsible is enlarged to include the host. (See also William Collins's chapter in this volume.)

Societal Trends

Several trends have undermined the sense of control that people felt they had over their lives and, consequently, the feeling that they are responsible for what happens to them. Mills (1959:3–5) pointed to the pace of social change as an underlying factor that explains the feeling people have that they have lost control over their lives. Part of this process is the rapidity of change in the social structure of society.

Just as changes in the leadership and staff of an organization shake the ground under it (Kamerman, 1996:27), changes in the composition of a society's population may mean that consensus erodes and behavioral expectations are no longer met. As a consequence, the social foundation shakes under that society. The more diverse a society becomes, the easier it is to distance oneself from what happens to other people, because one is not like "them." The ease of establishing social distance is certainly a requisite for the kind of dehumanization that in turn is a requisite for atrocities like genocide. As Edward Sagarin (1975:168) has written: "In a heterogeneous and pluralistic society, there are overwhelming forces that militate against conformity. It is not so much . . . that various groups come with different norms; rather, it is that they come with competing sets of loyalties and identities and with relatively lesser demands on the individual for his loyalty to the greater society."

Urbanization and the coming of mass society meant that people lived more and more of their lives among strangers. The sense of community (commonality) that characterized rural areas and small towns, particularly at the turn of the twentieth century, became more and more an accomplishment in the largely impersonal arena of urban life. Georg Simmel (1950) in his 1902 essay "The Metropolis and Mental Life" described this effect by saying that people in cities, flooded by sights and sounds too numerous to take in, develop the blasé attitude that allows them to effectively block out much of what they see and hear.

Another trend, mentioned earlier, that impinges on the definition of responsibility is the medicalization of deviance (Conrad and Schneider, 1992). Among a number of consequences of medicalization is the banishment of evil—that is, the ascendancy of the notion that no one is evil but that the criminal is rather just sick. Motivation and character became the proper subject of clinical not moral judgments. An empirical—certainly not a logical—consequence of this is the commonly held notion that to explain the etiology of a criminal act is also to excuse it.[3]

Ideas and Zeitgeist

This century has seen the growth of deterministic theories of behavior and their considerable popularity in the United States. In psychology, theories such as traditional psychoanalytic theory and behaviorism have been latched onto, in part because of their function of exempting people from responsibility. Their use, of course, has nothing to do with their validity. In any case, the ideological utility of psychoanalytic theory lies in the idea that basic character sets (like cement) early in life, before children are usually held responsible for their character or its consequences.

Behaviorism makes it easy to see behavior as the outcome of an inevitable chain of events, consequently leaving the actor blameless. One reason behaviorism caught on in the United States is that it rests on a mechanistic metaphor for human behavior that is basic to American culture in this century: the notion that people are passive recipients of the effects of outside forces. This mechanistic view reinforces an exemption from responsibility.[4]

Psychological determinism has its counterpart in the social determinism of some macrosociological theories (such as functionalism) that focus on the largest-scale level of analysis, the social systems of whole societies, in which individuals are notable by their absence (Homans, 1964). One attraction of systems theory is that it sees the individual as an almost invisible part of the societal engine, like Charlie Chaplin in *Modern Times*, slipping and slithering through the machinery of a factory production line.

The Restoration of Responsibility

Understanding the circumstances under which people either distance themselves from or embrace responsibility is the first step in making grounded recommendations both for reordering responsibility in the criminal justice system and, more generally, for restoring a sense of responsibility to organizations, occupations, and society. Clues to a plan for restoring responsibility are scattered throughout the papers in this volume. (For example, see William Rentzmann's chapter for the description of one already existing program. See John Rakis's chapter for an analysis of strategies for instilling a sense of responsibility in offenders.) Programs must be specific to specific organizations and situations, but it is possible to make some overall comments on the building blocks of these programs. Strategies developed to address these issues must be geared to the appropriate level. Solutions may be appropriate at one level but not at another. What is also obvious is the most effective direction of these changes: Large-scale changes must be instituted before changes at the lower levels can be effected. However, societal changes are the most expensive, meet the most resistance, and so are the most difficult to bring about.

A more pragmatic, if less effective, approach is to address organizational and occupational change. If "changing society" is a grandiose and unrealistic goal, on a smaller scale, organizations can be geared to encourage the development or at least the emulation of responsible styles of behavior in their employees. If the threat of swift and certain punishment has an important place in the criminal justice system, the same is also true within organizations. When people are not afraid of losing their jobs, either because they don't believe it will happen or because they don't care whether or not it will happen, control is virtually impossible. One consequence of civil service protection is the virtual inability of government to fire workers. An analogous effect of unemployment insurance is to neutralize the sting of being fired. In the organizational climate these conditions create, employees have little motivation to do their jobs well, because they won't be held accountable for their mistakes. Similarly, organizations that fail to reward initiative have the same effect from the opposite direction.

The fragmentation of responsibility can be diluted by making inroads in the traditional division of labor inside organizations. That is precisely the value of recent innovations in organizational structure, such as the "flattening" of organizations and the development of work teams and quality circles.

In the absence of a societal work ethic, for another example, organizations can be restructured to cultivate a work ethic in their employees or, as already mentioned, to demand that employees act as if they have one. This "ethic" can be made a central part of recruitment and training. Recruitment can be done in sectors of the work force whose work styles retain vestiges of the traditional work ethic—for example, the tack already taken by some companies to recruit farmers who have lost their farms and to retrain them for precision work that requires discipline, consistency, and commitment.

Measures that work from the lower levels up, from individuals to organizations and occupations to systems within a society and then to societies as a whole, tend to be ineffective, although they appeal to the American sentimentality about grass-roots movements and programs. But while they may be inconsequential in the larger sense, they may be worthwhile nonetheless because we all live at local addresses and because, in a world that appears to be largely out of our control, they are a welcome consolation.

Notes

1. Of course, these two categories may overlap. It is useful analytically to see some crime as an occupational pursuit, in order to differentiate it from what might be termed recreational criminality. The professional thief is a good example of the former category. See Kamerman, 1979.

2. A generation unit is a sector (and, only a specific sector) within a generation that, because of its particular vantage point, works up its interpretations of the events of its era in a specific way. A generation unit often comes to stand for the entire generation. For example, the so-called generation of the 1960s, who protested the Vietnam War, used psychedelic drugs, wore tie-dyed shirts and flowers in their hair, and so on, were, in reality, a generation unit of people who were mainly middle and upper middle class, college students or college dropouts, and white.

3. I am certainly not trying to make the judgment that this should not be done, nor am I applauding its use. I am simply pointing out that explanation as a defense was a concomitant of the medicalization of deviance. (See, for example, the parade of explanations of untoward behavior in the song "Officer Krupke" from the Broadway show *West Side Story*.)

4. The widespread use of drugs, both legal and illegal, to solve problems of all sorts is in part an outcome of this basic metaphor. When your engine is speeding or dragging, the proper additive makes a convenient solution, less expensive and laborious than solving any underlying problems or making any significant changes.

References

Berger, P. L., and T. Luckmann (1966). *The Social Construction of Reality: A Treatise in the Sociology of Knowledge*. Garden City, N.Y.: Doubleday.

Conrad, P., and J. W. Schneider (1992). *Deviance and Medicalization: From Badness to Sickness*. Philadelphia: Temple University.

Durkheim, E. (1964). *The Rules of Sociological Method*, S. A. Solovay and J. H. Mueller, trans., and G. E. G. Catlin, ed. New York: Free Press.

Erikson, K. T. (1962). "Notes on the Sociology of Deviance." *Social Problems* 9:307–14.

Geller, D., and M. Silver (1978). "On the Irrelevance of Evil: The Organization and Individual Action." *Journal of Social Issues* 34:125–36.

Homans, G. (1964). "Bringing Men Back In." *American Sociological Review* 29:809–18.

Hughes, E. C. (1958). *Men and Their Work*. Glencoe, Ill.: Free Press.

Kamerman, J. (1979). "Thievery as a Profession: A Footnote on the History of a Curious Idea." Pp. 294–306 in *Legality, Morality, and Ethics in Criminal Justice*, N. N. Kittrie and J. Susman, eds. New York: Praeger.

——— (1996). "Correctional Officer Suicide and Stress." *American Jails* 10 (3):23–24, 27–28.

Lifton, R. J. (1986). *The Nazi Doctors: Medical Killing and the Psychology of Genocide*. New York: Basic Books.

Mannheim, K. (1952). "The Problem of Generations." Pp. 276–320 in *Essays in the Sociology of Knowledge*, P. Kecskemeti, ed. London: Routledge and Kegan Paul.

Mills, C. W. (1959). *The Sociological Imagination*. New York: Oxford.

Rainwater, L. (1970). *Behind Ghetto Walls*. Chicago: Aldine.

Sagarin, E. (1975). *Deviants and Deviance: An Introduction to the Study of Disvalued People and Behavior*. New York: Praeger.

Scheff, T. J. (1968). "Negotiating Reality: Notes on Power in the Assessment of Responsibility." *Social Problems* 16:3–17.

Simmel, G. (1950). "The Metropolis and Mental Life." Pp. 419–24 in *The Sociology of Georg Simmel*, K. H. Wolff, ed. New York: Free Press.

Skolnick, J. H. (1975). *Justice Without Trial: Law Enforcement in a Democratic Society*. 2d ed. New York: Wiley.

Strauss, A. (1978). *Mirrors and Masks: The Search for Identity*. San Francisco: Sociology Press.

Weber, M. (1958). "Bureaucracy." Pp. 196–244 in *From Max Weber: Essays in Sociology*, H. H. Gerth and C. W. Mills, eds. and trans. New York: Oxford.

2

Philosophical Perspectives on Responsibility and Excuse

Charles Fethe

It is by now a commonplace observation to note that contemporary American society is characterized by a peculiar tendency to use the judicial system to promote public morality and settle private disputes. Not only do we go to court much more often than in the past but we also stay there longer: In nineteenth-century America, trials generally lasted no more than a day and often only a few hours, but now even minor cases can remain in the judicial system for months or possibly years, especially if they involve criminal behavior. If the rates of litigation continue to increase, it may well be that someday Americans will be able to recall the face of a judge as well as they can now recall the face of a teacher.

Commentators and theorists have proposed a number of explanations for this increase in judicial proceedings. Some have suggested that it reflects an increase in crime and a general deterioration in social relations. Others interpret it as merely a product of more careful reporting and record-keeping on the part of the police and the judiciary. It is difficult to find a single explanatory cause of a phenomenon of such size and complexity, but I believe one underlying factor that certainly must be taken into account is a slow but steady broadening of our concept of responsibility and the concomitant increase in the legal and moral strategies used to prevent it from being applied.

In simpler times, if you came home from carousing with your drinking buddies and drove over your neighbor's prize azaleas, you—and you alone—would face the court, pay the penalty, and, it could be hoped, walk away a wiser person. But today responsibility casts a larger net, and others may find themselves standing at your side in the dock—your spouse perhaps, your drinking buddies, the friendly bartender, the president of Anheuser-Busch.

And your lawyers, if they are skilled enough, need not rest their defense simply on your generally upright character. They might invoke your addictive personality, your unfortunate upbringing, or any of the determining chains of causes that made you what you are today.

Making sense of the modern concept of responsibility is no easy task, and it would be a vain hope to seek a simple moral or legal formula for determining when we are justified in holding people responsible for their behavior. But since this act of holding people responsible is such a pivotal element in our system of law and morality, it is important that we have at least a basic grasp of what we are doing, why we are doing it, and where we have been mistaken in our judgments of responsibility in the past. In this paper, I should like to examine some recent philosophical arguments on some of these issues and see if they can be of use in helping us to recognize not so much the essential features of the concept of responsibility but at least some of its dominant outlines and pitfalls.

Types of Responsibility

The concept of responsibility has a number of meanings, and confusion can easily result if we ignore the distinctions. One common use of the concept, for example, is to attribute causal agency, as when we say that dry weather was responsible for crop failure or that inflation is responsible for a weakening in the value of the dollar. But in this essay I shall be concerned with a different sense of responsibility, the sense it has when we discuss moral and legal issues; and so it might be helpful in our attempt to understand this use of the term if we take a quick view of the function of moral and legal judgments.

Moral and legal judgments are primarily tools for evaluating and guiding behavior. This applies to both positive and negative judgments, although it is the negative examples that show the point more clearly; I shall restrict my discussion to them. When we say that an act is wrong, we are doing more than merely classifying it as an instance of a violation of some kind of rule or principle; we are providing the basis for a response that will express our condemnation and suppress the reoccurrence of the act. This point was made well by John Stuart Mill (1957:60) in his comments on justice, law, and morals: "We do not call anything wrong unless we mean to imply that a person ought to be punished in some way or other for doing it—if not by law, by the opinion of his fellow creatures; if not by opinion, by the reproaches of his own conscience."

The act of holding people responsible is an essential step in putting into effect this system of distributing blame and punishment, for it functions as a guide to locating the recipients: The person we should blame or punish for an immoral or illegal act is the person who is held responsible for it. A theory of responsibility is basically an explanation of how this rule works; it provides the directions and explanations for recognizing the proper targets for approval and disapproval, for praise and blame.

In their efforts to develop a general theory of responsibility and trace the guidelines for determining where blame should be directed, legal and moral theorists have often found it useful to distinguish two ways in which we use the concept of responsibility, one associated with duties and obligations and the other serving to direct blame for wrongful actions. We would, for example, be using the concept of responsibility in the first sense when we speak of assigning the police the responsibility to maintain public order or of holding parents responsible for educating their children. This sense of responsibility is often referred to as "role responsibility," since the assigning of duties and obligations can be seen as related to one's position within a network of social relations or institutions. The second sense of responsibility occurs when we identify a person who we believe deserves punishment or blame for wrongful behavior, and so it is sometimes called "act responsibility." Unlike role responsibility, which deals with actions a person is expected to perform, act responsibility concerns actions that have already been performed. It is retrospective rather than prospective, and it is often expressed in the form of a judgment or an accusation: "You are the one responsible for ruining my car by driving it with no oil!"

It should be obvious that there are intricate connections between these two uses of the concept of responsibility, and the courts have spent many long hours examining how judgments of responsibility in one sense affect a judgment of responsibility in the other sense. The results of many of these court decisions often seem at variance with natural intuitions. So, for example, most of us would think that people who hold role responsibilities cannot be blamed unless they actually perform (or fail to perform) an act of some kind that falls within their realm of responsibility. But that is not always the case in the law. A corporation might be found legally guilty of failing its public responsibilities, and the people in the organization who must pay the penalty may not have in any way engaged in the guilty act. Or, to take another example, the United States Supreme Court, in its decision on *Pinkerton v. United States*, introduced the concept of "vicarious responsibility," under which a coconspirator can be found guilty for substantive violations of the law performed not by him but by his cohorts. A rather dramatic example of the separation of role and act responsibility is the case of General Yamashita, who was put on trial for war crimes committed by his troops when the Japanese were being forced out of the Philippines. Yamashita had no knowledge of the atrocities his troops were committing, and, given the breakdown in lines of communication and authority, he was in no position to monitor or control his soldiers. His American prosecutors nevertheless charged him with responsibility for the acts under the doctrine of *respondeat superior* ("let the superior answer"). He was found guilty and hanged.

The intricacies of legal judgments in cases of this sort fortunately need not detain us. Instead, I would like to examine a few philosophical issues that the concept of role responsibility raises, and then turn to the more extensive concerns surrounding act responsibility and the assigning of blame for wrong behavior. I shall take examples from both law and morals, but it is the moral view of responsibility that I believe deserves the priority, not because I follow the thesis that law is simply a reflection of the moral code but rather because I think it is the system of morals that first introduced the notion of responsibility and that at least serves to limit the more complex legal development of the term.

Issues in Assigning Responsibilities

As people go through life, they assume various social roles and are held responsible for the performance of actions associated with these roles. This observation, so commonplace and seemingly unremarkable, has been the source of a number of intriguing philosophical puzzles. For we are not born with responsibilities; an infant has no duties, no obligations, nothing placed under his or her care. So how do responsibilities get attached to us as we get older? Is this simply a matter of raw social fiat, of simply putting a burden on someone and demanding that he carry it?

In the case of many responsibilities and the obligations associated with various social roles, the mere act of voluntarily accepting the role, with full knowledge of all that it requires, justifies the assignment of the responsibility. You agreed to take the job, so now you must take the responsibilities that go with it. Simple as that.

Of course, difficulties might arise if there are responsibilities you were not aware of, but that seems to be easily handled by proper notification. A more problematic situation occurs if you did not voluntarily choose your role. Perhaps you are a conscript or an inmate in a prison: You will certainly be expected to have responsibilities in those roles, but what is the justification for this? Society may have the right to force you into these positions and even compel you to behave in certain ways, but does it thereby have the right to impose responsibilities on you too? Can society assign responsibilities as it chooses?

A long tradition in Western political philosophy, beginning with Hobbes and Locke and continuing up to the think-tank philosophers at Harvard, holds that responsibilities cannot be incurred without consent. One major exception to this rule, accepted by many but certainly not by all philosophers, concerns moral responsibilities; for it seems that simply by being a moral agent and a member of society, a person necessarily can be held responsible for performing a wide range of actions. Suppose, for example, that while hiking in the woods with a child and her parent, I discover that the parent has abandoned the child and vanished. Like it or not, I have a responsibility not to leave the child in a dangerous situation like this, and the fact that I did not consent to be in this situation does not nullify my obligations. But if the same parent left his valuables at my feet and then vanished, I certainly have no responsibility to look after these goods, for there is no moral rule that requires me to look after other people's belongings unless I consent to do so. If I did watch over his property, it would be an act of kindness but not the fulfillment of a responsibility.

If this line of argument is correct, then it seems that even conscripts and inmates in penal institutions do have responsibilities, for they are certainly moral beings. And so there is no problem in holding conscripts and prisoners responsible for behavior that might endanger others or violate other people's rights. But what about those responsibilities that do not seem to have a moral character? A conscript is held responsible for saluting any officer he passes while on the base. What justification is there for thinking that the army has the right to hold its conscripts responsible for this practice? Suppose a warden in a prison decided to impose a similar obligation on prisoners and held them responsible for saluting the prison guards—would this be justified? Can responsibilities be created by the fiat of authority?

In his discussion of civil disobedience and legal obligation, John Rawls (1992) offered a view that might be helpful to us in answering these questions. Rawls argued that if people have benefited by the existence of certain social institutions and if those institutions meet the criteria for justice and fairness in a democratic society, then people have a general responsibility to maintain those institutions. A conscript and an inmate may feel that their personal interests are being harmed by the army or the prison system, but this should not cancel out obligations of support; for the conscript and the prisoner have both enjoyed the benefits of the protection offered by those institutions: As long as the institutions accord with the idea of justice in a democratic society, we have a right to hold everyone responsible for supporting them.

If we follow this way of thinking, it would seem that the argument that must be given to justify imposing institutional responsibilities in conditions of nonconsent is that the responsibilities are necessary for maintaining the functionality of just institutions. How this argument would be made in specific instances is a matter we cannot go into here, but it is easy to see how one might make the case for requiring saluting of military officers but not of prison guards. The conscript is being trained for war, and so we may well hold him responsible for practices that will prove necessary to maintain military discipline under chaotic conditions and thus enhance the chances for military success. Being quick to recognize and acknowledge military authority may be such a practice, and saluting is one way to show it. But the inmate is in a very different situation, and so there is surely less justification for imposing obligations on him to demonstrate a recognition of authority. His responsibilities fall in a narrower range and are primarily based on duties of noninterference and duties required for maintaining the functionality of the institution.

Before we turn to a consideration of the way we hold people responsible for wrongful actions, I think it important to note here that imposing responsibilities is only one way to get people to act as we think they should, and there are quite a number of other strategies for getting the same result. Perhaps the most common such strategy is to point out to the person the advantages that will accrue if he acts as we want him to act. This technique requires no responsibility-imposing authority nor does it raise any problems about justifications or the right to impose responsibility. So, for example, a teacher may, by virtue of her position, announce to her class that she is holding everyone responsible for handing in assignments on time, but she may get the same result simply by offering a reward of some kind for everyone who meets all the deadlines. Deciding which strategy should be used in particular situations is, as Aristotle well noted, a matter of common sense and practical wisdom.

Responsibility for Wrongful Actions

Assigning role responsibility is an important feature of any society, but perhaps even more fundamental to social life is the practice of holding people responsible for the wrongful acts they have committed—what we earlier called "act responsibility." It is this very complex practice that I should now like to examine. The practice is pervasive in all forms of social engagement, but I shall restrict my attention primarily to its use in moral relations and criminal law.

Under a doctrine of strict liability, a society could hold responsible and thus blameworthy anyone who performs a wrong or prohibited action; but although strict liability may at times be necessary, it seems to most people to violate a sense of justice and fairness. And so we have introduced a number of conditions that we use to decide when a wrongful action is also one for which the agent will be held responsible. For the sake of simplicity, we can classify these conditions under two broad headings: The first requires that the agent performed the action and thus played a causal role in bringing about a prohibited state of affairs, and the second condition requires that the agent performed the action with a "guilty mind"—the doctrine of *mens rea*. These two conditions have raised a number of serious legal problems, but I shall try to restrict our examination to the central philosophical issues they pose.

Causal Responsibility

In discussing the first condition, we must carefully keep in mind the fact that an agent may be said to be "causally responsible" for bringing about a prohibited state of affairs without being "act-responsible." Act responsibility involves a moral or legal judgment of the agent, and the agent's causal role is at most a necessary and certainly not a sufficient condition for making such judgments. Our language often obscures this point. So, for example, the statement "Hamlet is responsible for the death of Polonius" can be interpreted in two ways, as either a statement of fact about what or who killed Polonius, or as a judgment indicating who should be blamed or punished for the deed.

Failure to pay attention to this distinction has vitiated many recent sociological and psychological studies concerned with how people assign blame. In their paper "On Causality, Responsibility, and Self-Blame," Shaver and Drown (1986) reviewed a number of research projects that attempted to correlate a subject's blaming himself or herself for an unfortunate occurrence with the subject's recognition of other factors that played a role in the event. They concluded that a large number of these studies were methodologically defective because in interviewing the self-blamers and asking them what they thought "was responsible" or "to blame" for the event, the researchers did not distinguish between moral and simple causal responsibility. For example, in one study, counselors in rape centers were asked what percentage of their clients blamed themselves for the rape because of their behavior prior to the crime; they were then asked what percentage of their clients blamed themselves because of some character trait or flaw they believed they had. The counselors reported that 75 percent of the women engaged in self-blame, with behavioral self-blame predominating by a ratio of four to one. But the answers to these questions should not have been pooled as evidence for self-blame, because the questions were asking about two different forms of responsibility: The question that asked about behavioral blame was inviting the women to speculate about their causal role in bringing about the attack, while the second question, dealing with character flaws, was asking for a moral assessment of their role.

Recognizing causes is no easy task, and the courts have often spent long hours trying to decide what causal role an agent may have performed and whether his behavior supports a judgment that he is morally or legally responsible. The agent's behavior may, for example, have been only indirectly connected to the action, linked to it by a series of intermediary causes. Or the agent's behavior may have been passive: The event occurred because the agent failed to act. Unweaving the causal strands and finding a strong enough link to support the judgment of moral and legal responsibility is thus no mean feat.

It should be noted that today our greater understanding of the complexity of the chain of causal links explains why the net of moral and legal responsibility is taking in more people than it used to, for we can see connections between our social actions that we never appreciated before. So, for example, an addict's crime is now often thought to be not simply produced by the addict alone but to involve all the social agents that led the addict to be in that situation in the first place.

Mens Rea *and the Need for Excuses*

Suppose, now, that we have worked our way through the links of causality and we know that the person before us is indeed causally responsible for a wrongful act. Our second condition requires that we must next determine whether the agent acted with a "guilty mind." The doctrine of *mens rea* has been interpreted in many ways, but there seems to be general agreement among those who support the doctrine that the judgment of responsibility must take into account the following factors: agents' awareness of the consequences of their action, their appreciation of the wrongfulness of what was done, their intent, and their voluntariness or freedom to choose whether to do the act.

A full theory of moral or legal responsibility would provide an analysis of each of these conditions, but such a project is obviously beyond the scope of this paper. I should like, therefore, to take a different route to gaining some perspective on our topic, one suggested by the British philosopher John Austin in his influential essay "A Plea for Excuses" (1961). Austin noted that when we are faced with difficult and complex terms in areas such as philosophy or law, terms like "responsibility" or "freedom," we can often understand the concept best if we avoid trying to define it directly and instead concentrate on the cases in which we agree the term should *not* be applied. If I cannot understand what makes my engine run well, at least I can learn something about it by noting what brings it to a dead stop. Now, what brings a judgment of responsibility to a stop is an excuse, and so, following Austin here, I would like to set aside the difficult task of developing an account of act responsibility and instead consider what it is that makes us excuse certain actions. How do excuses work this magic—how do they get me off the hook when it is clear I did it and it was the wrong thing to do?

Austin does not himself provide a general theory of excusing conditions, but he does offer an insightful and often witty account of what excuses are like. Excuses, he notes, rarely wash away completely the taint of the wrongful action: "The average excuse, in a poor situation, gets us only out of the fire into the frying pan—but still, of course, any frying pan in a fire" (1961:125).

And often the excuses we make rely on subtleties in the way we acted. Yes, I did throw the inkwell at you, but I didn't do it knowingly. And even if I did know what I was doing, I didn't do it intentionally. And even if it was intentional, it wasn't done deliberately (it was more like a sudden impulse). As Austin wryly observes, in the realm of excuse-making we can do a lot with adverbs.

One point that Austin insisted on and that has recently been the subject of some dispute among legal theorists is that there is a distinction between excuses and justifications. Both are designed to negate punishment or blame, but they do so in different ways. In offering a justification, I admit responsibility for the act but defend it as the right thing to do. With excuse, I may admit causal responsibility and agree that the act was wrong, but I try to characterize the situation in a way that shows punishment or blame should not be directed at me. In the rest of this paper, I shall assume this distinction is correct and so I shall not be concerned with problems concerning justification and recognition of wrongfulness.

Austin's approach serves as a good antidote to those theorists who are still driven by a Platonic urge to find simple definitions of complex concepts. A good account of responsibility and excuses must, I believe, be guided by an Austinian sensitivity to the complexity and nuanced differences in this field of human behavior, but it must also go beyond this point and help us to recognize which excuses seem to be most effective in their function of weakening the charge of responsibility. Let me offer some preliminary suggestions on how we might go about this.

Excuses and Choice

In discussing excuses, we must first avoid a misinterpretation of what we are doing when we offer an excuse. To some people, making excuses has often been thought of as a deliberate and perhaps unsavory attempt to avoid responsibility. The psychologist C. R. Snyder (1985:36) illustrates this view when he defines excuses as "explanations or actions that lessen the negative implications of an actor's performance, thereby maintaining a positive image for oneself and others." There undoubtedly are many occasions when "making excuses for yourself" is nothing more than an attempt to shirk responsibility and keep one's ego intact, but it would be a distortion of the concept of excuse to think that it should, or even could, be properly defined in such negative terms. Many excuses that people offer for their behavior are perfectly valid and upright, and any account of responsibility that failed to provide a strong place for such excuses would be woefully inadequate. Indeed, we cannot really understand how excuses are misused unless we first understand how they are properly used, just as we could not understand false promises or invalid contracts unless we already had an understanding of true promises and valid contracts. To understand the concept of excuse, we must, then, deal primarily with valid excuses.

In his recent survey of theories of responsibility, Peter French (1991:21) offers a quick and easy concept of excuse to open up discussion: "Excuses are the way we express how unfree our actions were." This seems to fit the classic excuses recognized in criminal law, such as duress, necessity, and insanity. In all these cases, we judge the agents not responsible and refuse to inflict punishment because we believe that their actions, even though wrong, did not reflect a voluntary choice: Given the circumstances, they could not have done other than they did.

But this raises an interesting question: Why do we think it wrong to punish a person who could not have chosen otherwise? What is it about free choice that makes it the clue to deciding when to praise or blame? In philosophy and legal theory, there are two general answers to this question. The first answer reflects a utilitarian conception of the law: We institute laws and punish their infractions because this is a way to affect people's choices and prevent them from engaging in harmful, antisocial acts. Actions that are not the product of free choice, such as the actions of the insane, are not amenable to this process of education and correction and so would not be considered responsible in the utilitarian view.

The second general answer to why we use free choice as a guide to excuse and responsibility is based on a different conception of the law. It follows a more retributive view and contends that the function of law is to express social condemnation of actions that reveal immoral character. It would thus, in this view, be a mistake to hold the insane responsible because their actions are the product of disease and not a reflection of vicious or immoral character.

The utilitarian and retributivist theories of law and responsibility have both been subject to much criticism and debate, but I do not wish to assess their relative merits here. Instead, I would like to concentrate on a philosophical and scientific theory that threatens both of these views of responsibility. It is the theory of causal determinism, and if it is correct it would then be difficult to see how any theory of moral responsibility or accountability could possibly survive. For causal determinism provides an excuse not for some but for all actions.

Determinism

Determinism, stated simply, is the claim that all behavior is the product of causal conditions and so, in principle, explainable and predictable by science. It is thus incompatible with popular conceptions of free will. Determinism is often considered a paradigm example of a philosophical theory, but a number of psychological and sociological studies indicate that beliefs about free will and determining causes are part of most people's behavioral assessments and often influence their views about responsibility and punishment. Stroessner and Green (1990), for example, showed a positive correlation among a group of American undergraduates between strength of commitment to various forms of determinism and libertarianism and a willingness to punish. In their article "Free Will, Determinism, and Criminality" (1990), Holbert and Unnithan suggested that prison inmates' views of where they themselves fell in the "free-determined" division reflected how the inmates interpreted the way prison authorities classified them on this scale, and the authors suggested that this correlation could be useful in developing educational and rehabilitation programs. But the serious effects of determinism lie not in how it changes our psychological perceptions of other people's behavior: Its significance lies in the way it attacks the basic premises on which our theories of moral and legal responsibility rest.

Although determinism is subject to a wide variety of interpretations, its basic argument as applied to human action can be expressed as a syllogism with two premises. The first premise is that all behavior is the product of causal conditions. The second is that whenever behavior is the product of causal conditions it should be excused from attributions of moral responsibility. The conclusion then follows directly: All behavior should be excused from attributions of moral responsibility.

It is the conclusion that startles, of course; for if it is accepted it would mean that the system of morality and law that we have used for so long has a gross error in its foundations and cannot be justified. I shall discuss the implications of this conclusion toward the end of this paper, but first I would like to pay some attention to the arguments for the two premises.

Causality as an Excuse

To understand the first premise of the determinist argument, that all human behavior is the product of causal conditions, we must clearly understand what we are saying when we state that one event is the cause of another. In everyday speech, to say that "something caused me to do it" is often a way of attributing the action to some force that overwhelmed the agent's own powers of decision. Causal agency is thus viewed as a threat to our own good intentions.

This way of interpreting causality is certainly not the view that determinists adopt. Their claim of universal causality is based on the more scientific view, which interprets a cause-effect relation as simply an exemplification of a universal pattern that can be expressed in the form of a natural law. To say that your aggressive behavior was caused is not to say that you felt forced or compelled to do it; rather, the claim of causality asserts only that the behavior is tied to prior conditions in a way that allows us, at least in theory, to predict that the same behavior will always follow when those same conditions are present. It is possible, of course, that these conditions may enter your consciousness as feelings of force and compulsion, but that is certainly not necessary. If determinism is true, all behavior, even that which is cold, calculating, and performed with a sense of freedom and autonomy, falls within the set of patterns that govern the universe.

Let us now turn to the second determinist premise and its claim that causality negates the ascription of moral responsibility. Why should anyone believe this? Why should the fact that your behavior falls within the realm of natural patterns and is thus subject to scientific explanation and prediction have anything to do with excusing you for what you have done?

It is this second premise that has been the subject of most debate. In a recent paper on the theory of excuses published in the *Journal of Criminal Law and Criminology*, Michael Corrado (1991) examines the two main contenders over this premise: those who believe it is true and that determinism is incompatible with responsibility ("incompatibilism"), and those who believe the premise is false and that determinism and responsibility are logically compatible ("compatibilism"). Those who defend compatibilism rest their case on a distinction among the causes that lead us to act as we do. The compatibilist argues that causes excuse behavior only when they are shown to overwhelm or short-circuit the agent's internal processes of thought and decision, but behavior that is the product of internal causes, of the agent's own thoughts and feelings, should not be excused.

The compatibilist view seems to correspond closely to natural intuitions about responsibility and excuse: If some external circumstance made you do what you did, then we withdraw our attribution of responsibility; but if you knew what you were doing and made a choice to do it, you are responsible. But the problem here is that this seems to be a surface judgment, and the compatibilist has a more difficult time once we look closely at the circumstances surrounding those cases in which the theory holds you responsible.

One immediate problem the compatibilist faces is making a distinction between the responsibility-bearing internal causes and the responsibility-excusing external causes. The compatibilist wishes to hold you responsible when you decide to drink too much alcohol, but he excuses you for the drunken castigations you make while "under the influence"—but aren't your own mental processes at work in both cases? And if we say that the drunken decision to castigate cannot bear responsibility because it is the product of causes, is not the same true of your decision to start drinking in the first place? Aren't you drunk and you sober both the product of causal conditions? The same problem occurs in other cases: Take the insanity defense—are actions that result from paranoia the product of internal or external causation? And if internal—the agent acts out of his own beliefs and fears—must we hold the agent responsible?

Corrado contends that the main difference in the moral and legal implications of these two views about the second determinist premise lies not in their interpretations of generally accepted legal excuses but rather in the way they handle excuses that are still in dispute—such as citing an agent's deprived and abused background as an excuse for criminal behavior. I believe the difference is far more extensive, but Corrado is correct in pointing to the agent's background and upbringing as a key area in which the contrast between the two views is most clearly seen. To the compatibilist, agents' environment and past history are largely irrelevant to the ascription of responsibility, for their behavior is still the consequence of their own thoughts, desires, and decisions. The incompatibilist takes a different stand. It is exemplified in Darrow's (1989:207) successful argument to lessen the punishment for Loeb's and Leopold's murder of Bobby Franks:

> Every effort to protect society is an effort toward training the youth to keep the path. Every bit of training in the world proves it, and it likewise proves that it sometimes fails. I know that if this boy had been understood and properly trained—properly for him—and the training that he got might have been the very best for someone; but if it had been the proper training for him, he would not be in this courtroom today with the noose above his head. If there is responsibility anywhere, it is back of him; somewhere in the infinite number of his ancestors, or in his surroundings, or in both.

Darrow's courtroom rhetoric sounds a bit old-fashioned today, but his basic argument still continues to be used, only now expressed in the colder, more sophisticated language of the sciences of behavior. As our psychological, sociological, and even medical understanding of the causal determinants of behavior increases, there will be more pressure to shift closer to the incompatibilist view and thus to extend the realm of excusing conditions to a much broader base. This shift seems already to have occurred in our judgments concerning insanity, where many courts have abandoned the "wild beast" criterion of legal insanity and adopted instead more encompassing views that recognize that thought and decision can still be products of an excusing mental illness.

Because the incompatibilist view is so extreme in its exculpation of all actions, it has little chance of gaining acceptance; but like extremist parties in pluralist democracies, its effects will lie in its power to shift the central beliefs closer to its own position. But how far should this extension of excusing causes go, and what effect would it have on our fundamental beliefs about morality, law, and responsibility? These are deep and difficult questions, but I should like to make a few closing comments on what is at stake.

A World Without Responsibility

Those who investigate the intricacies of our ideas about responsibility often reach different conclusions, but all would surely agree that it is not easy to determine where the blame must lie and who should be punished and who should be excused. Faced with these difficulties, we might come to wonder whether this whole moral and legal practice is actually worthwhile. Would it be possible to live in a world without responsibilities? This is a strange idea to conjure over.

How could this be done? We noted earlier that there are many ways to get people in institutional structures to act properly without assigning responsibilities: A simple appeal to self-interest is a wonderful motivator. Could we then design institutions based solely on self-interest, with no duties or responsibilities at all?

And as for act responsibility, we already exclude many people from it, so why not follow the incompatible determinist line and exclude everyone? Why not join with those social reformers who find the model for social justice in the juvenile-court system? If a young boy commits a heinous act, we do not ask whether he is morally responsible; we assume that some condition led him to act this way and that our job is not to condemn or blame but to correct the condition and ensure that it does not occur again.

What do we gain and what do we lose if we abandon our concepts of responsibility, blame, and punishment and replace them with a therapeutic or, as Peter French (1991:16) calls it, a "no-fault" system of law and morality? The therapeutic approach has been tried in many advanced countries, and the results have not been encouraging. Often the new therapies are little more than thinly disguised manifestations of the older ways for dealing with violations of the rules. What difference is there, for example, between punishing you with solitary confinement and imposing on you an extended period of therapeutic meditation in an isolated "quiet room"? Does being sprayed on the back with a fire hose really lose its punitive nature if it is called "hydrotherapy" (see Allen, 1973)?

Defenders of the therapeutic model might argue that these examples only prove that their approach has not yet been fully developed, and they may rest their case on hopes for a more advanced system of psychological and psychiatric techniques that will be able to transform criminal nature into a healthier, more law-abiding character without using any punitive measures. That would indeed be an achievement, but it would not come without a cost. On the social level, the therapeutic model would certainly eliminate the democratic element that we find in the criminal justice system, for questions of therapy and cure would not fall within the expertise of a jury of one's peers. Decisions about how to deal with offenders would be made by authorities skilled in the arts of treatment, and the values these social therapists might have could be very different from the common moral values now used to decide guilt and punishment. Our present system of responsibility is based on a moral judgment about how to fit the punishment to the crime and to level a penalty that would constitute a fair repayment of the violator's debt to society. But social therapists would find little need for the scales of justice: Their aim is simply to cure, and the length of the process and the means required cannot be determined at the time of trial and sentencing. The rules of the hospital and the clinic are not the rules of democratic process.

But even more important than the social alterations that the therapeutic model would promote are the changes it would bring about in our personal responses to wrongdoing. Since criminal and immoral behavior would, under the therapeutic model, be considered as simply symptoms of a pathological condition, the normal feelings and attitudes we display toward those who violate the rules would be out of place: Moral outrage, a sense of injustice, a readiness to blame and retaliate would have no appropriate function. Our demand that wrongdoers must show a sense of guilt and shame for what they have done must also disappear: One could regret one's actions but not show remorse—how could one have remorse for the effects of a disease? And it should be noted that these changes in attitude would not be restricted to our evaluation of evil; for if wrongdoing is only a sign of a sickness, then moral and heroic actions would only testify to health, and though a healthy character can be admired, it cannot be respected or honored. Those individuals who sacrifice for others or hold to principles in the face of temptation would deserve their medals and rewards, but the honors would be like those we give to show dogs—best of breed.

I have no clear idea about how a society based on the therapeutic model would actually function. Perhaps its citizens would all be tolerant, compassionate, and highly motivated in their jobs, and everyone would be happy. But the people in such a society would be almost like alien beings. For with us, character counts and character involves responsibility. And our acts of praise and blame, of reward and punishment, are often more than prods to encourage good results or eliminate defects. They are testimony to the way we see ourselves as moral beings. Our responsibility-based systems of morality and law are unwieldy and often ineffective, but they are sure reminders that the way we deal with each other is very different from the way we deal with our pets.

References

Allen, F. (1973). "Criminal Justice, Legal Values, and the Rehabilitative Ideal." Pp. 172–85 in *Punishment and Rehabilitation,* J. Murphy, ed. Belmont, Calif.: Wadsworth.

Austin, J. (1961). "A Plea for Excuses." Pp. 123–52 in *Philosophical Papers.* Oxford: Clarendon Press.

Corrado, M. (1991). "Notes on the Structure of a Theory of Excuses." *Journal of Criminal Law and Criminology* 82 (fall):469–97.

Darrow, C. (1989). "From The Defense of Loeb and Leopold." Pp. 204–8 in *Philosophy and the Human Condition,* T. Beauchamp, J. Feinberg, and J. Smith, eds. Englewood Cliffs, N.J.: Prentice-Hall.

French, P. (1991). *The Spectrum of Responsibility.* New York: St. Martin's Press.

Holbert, F., and P. Unnithan (1990). "Free Will, Determinism, and Criminality: The Self-Perception of Prison Inmates." *Journal of Criminal Justice* 18:43–53.

Mill, J. S. (1957). *Utilitarianism.* New York: Liberal Arts Press.

Rawls, J. (1992). "Legal Obligation, Fair Play, and Civil Disobedience." Pp. 20–32 in *Social and Political Philosophy,* J. Arthur and W. Shaw, eds. Englewood Cliffs, N.J.: Prentice-Hall.

Shaver, K., and D. Drown (1986). "On Causality, Responsibility, and Self-Blame: A Theoretical Note." *Journal of Personality and Social Psychology* 50 (4):697–702.

Snyder, C. R. (1985). "Collaborative Companions." Pp. 36–51 in *Self-deception and Self-understanding: New Essays in Philosophy and Psychology,* M. Martin, ed. Lawrence: University of Kansas Press.

Stroessner, S., and W. Green (December 1990). "Effects of Belief in Free Will or Determinism on Attitudes Toward Punishment and Locus of Control." *Journal of Social Psychology* 130 (6):789–99.

PART II

CRIMINAL JUSTICE INSTITUTIONS

Superintending "Bankruptcies" in Child Rearing

A Family Court Model of Juvenile Justice

Mark Harrison Moore

The Eroding Mandate for Juvenile Justice

Over the last few decades, the nation's juvenile justice system seems to have lost its way. Its legitimacy has been undermined by powerful, diverse criticisms. Some attacks have focused on the court's overreaching intrusiveness and its disregard for the rights of the children who come before it (Platt, 1969). Others have criticized the reluctance of the court to hold juvenile offenders accountable for their offenses, and its failure to dispose of cases in ways that adequately protect society from future juvenile crime (Springer, 1986). Nearly everyone has been disappointed by the court's performance in preventing children who commit crimes from advancing to criminal careers (Silberman, 1978).

The wave of criticism has eroded the foundations of the juvenile court and the juvenile justice system. Indeed, great hunks of its jurisdiction have fallen away. Some states have lowered the age of jurisdiction, exposing more juvenile offenders to the rigors of the adult criminal justice system. Other states have bored holes in the exclusive jurisdiction of the juvenile court by establishing procedures that allow or mandate the bringing of certain kinds of offenses and offenders into the adult court (Feld, 1987). Still other states have "decriminalized" status offenses such as truancy and incorrigibility. Wedged between the adult court on one side and social service systems on the other, the juvenile justice system is giving ground in both directions. Perhaps it will disappear altogether as a bad compromise between the two.

In a series of discussions held at Harvard University's John F. Kennedy School of Government from 1984 to 1986, a group of juvenile court judges, youth advocates, prosecutors, defense attorneys, and academic experts sought to shore up the institutions of the juvenile court and the juvenile justice system by giving it a new platform on which it could stand. We sought a new social understanding about the proper ends and means of the juvenile court—in effect, a more useful, more durable, and more just mandate for the enterprise than then existed.

Predictably, the group was deeply divided about the shape that this new mandate should take. Its divisions reflected the disagreements and tensions of the broader society. Some members were principally concerned with retaining the system's commitment to the goal of rehabilitation, and the recognition and affirmation of children's rights vis-à-vis society and their parents. Others insisted on the primacy of the goal of community protection and the justice and effectiveness of holding children accountable for their crimes. Still others were primarily concerned about the terrible conditions under which many children were being raised in the United States but were hard put to say exactly how the juvenile court or the juvenile justice system could contribute usefully to the solution of that vast problem.

Unfortunately, the group did not reach a consensus. What it did produce, however, was the germ of an idea about juvenile justice that seemed to open some new ways of thinking about the proper and best use of the juvenile court and the other institutions of the juvenile justice system (Moore et al., 1987). It is an idea that seeks to break out of the increasingly confining debates of the past, instead focusing our attention on how the unique traditions and capabilities of the juvenile court and the juvenile justice system might best be used to confront the problem not only of crimes committed by children but also of crimes committed against children, as well as the terrible conditions under which many children are being raised. It is this idea that I would like to present. First, however, it is important to understand in what important ways our thoughts about the juvenile court and the juvenile justice system are limited by thinking of the juvenile court as a criminal court.

The Limiting Analogy of the Criminal Court

Inevitably, most people think of the juvenile court as a criminal rather than a civil court. Its purposes and procedures have to be adjusted to accommodate the fact that offenders who appear there are children, but it is fundamentally a criminal court, and the adult criminal court is its nearest cousin.

People think in these terms primarily because it seems that responding justly and effectively to crimes committed by children is the court's most urgent, most common, and most important task. That much is true. But another reason people consider the juvenile court a special kind of criminal court is that they have never seriously thought about any alternative. That is unfortunate, because once one has decided that the juvenile court is a criminal court, one gets locked into a relatively narrow set of conceptions of how the court might be developed and used.

From this perspective, the only way to answer the question of how the juvenile court should operate is to develop a theory of how juvenile offenders differ from adult offenders in ways that are relevant to the just and effective handling of their cases, and then to trace the implications of those differences for the operations of the juvenile court. Basically, that approach produces three different conceptions of the juvenile court: one that makes a great deal of the differences between adults and children and exploits those differences for practical efficacy—the individualized, rehabilitative court (Feld, 1987); one that makes the distinction but establishes for children many of the same due-process protections that are available to adults in the adult criminal court in order to ensure that the child's liberty interests are not jeopardized—the children's rights court (Feld, 1987); and one that minimizes the differences between adults and juveniles and finds in the principles of accountability not only a purer vision of justice but also a plausibly more effective response to juvenile crime—the austere justice court (Springer, 1986).

The Individualized, Rehabilitative Court

Most people, now and in the past, have seen important differences between adults and children in the adjudication of criminal offenses. In the English common law, for example, children beneath the age of seven could not be found guilty of criminal offenses because they were judged incapable of forming the required criminal intent; those between the ages of seven and fourteen had a rebuttable presumption of innocence. More recently, since the establishment of the juvenile court, society has extended the notion of diminished culpability to older groups of children. The differences between children and adults deserve recognition in the adjudication of cases for reasons of both justice and practicality.

From the perspective of justice, juveniles are arguably less autonomous than adults and therefore less morally accountable for their actions. Compared with adults, juveniles have more fragile characters, with less settled intentions, and with less ability to control their actions. They are impulsive and relatively easily influenced, not only by the urgings of their peers but also by circumstances. Moreover, their actions may be seen as at least partially a reflection of their parents' efforts to instruct and supervise. For all of these reasons, the offenses they commit are less theirs than is true for adults, and therefore they are less blameworthy. In effect, one cannot necessarily see in juvenile offenses the sort of bad intentions and character that would expose them to the moral condemnation that is part of criminal judgment in the adult courts.

The implications of this view for juvenile court processing and adjudication include the following: First, there is a reluctance to hold juveniles criminally responsible for their conduct, symbolized by the fact that the court finds the children "delinquent" rather than "guilty." The second is a willingness to look beyond the immediate circumstances of an offense—the narrow question of whether the juvenile did or did not commit the alleged delinquent act—to the broader social context in which the juvenile is being raised. The aim of such investigation is to bring to light factors that would both mitigate guilt and guide the construction of an effective disposition. The third, symbolized by the privacy of the proceedings and the protection of the child's record, is an effort to insulate children from society's desire for retribution. Fourth, there is a certain casualness about the protection of the due process rights of juveniles, justified at least partly on the grounds that the process is a less adversarial one than occurs in adult criminal court, where the assumptions about moral blameworthiness are quite different and the conflict between society's interests and those of the offender are much sharper.

From the perspective of concerns about practical efficacy, children are seen as being more changeable than adults and with longer futures. Thus they become more promising and rewarding targets for therapeutic intervention. The implications for juvenile court processing and disposition include the following: First, in making dispositions of juvenile cases, a greater weight is placed on rehabilitating the offender than on short-run risks to the community, reflecting the concept of the "least restrictive alternative." Second, there is a greater willingness to rely on and seek to enhance existing ties to family and community, and to invest in rehabilitative services, than would be true in the adult criminal court. Third, there is a greater concern for avoiding the stigmatization and labeling that would handicap children in future rehabilitative efforts. And fourth, there is a greater willingness to view disposition of cases in utilitarian and instrumental terms rather than in terms of justice.

These basic ideas form the core of a vision of the court as an individualized, rehabilitative court for adolescent offenders.

The Children's Rights Court

Recently, those who are primarily interested in the rights of children have been concerned that the paternalistic/instrumental features of the traditional juvenile justice court have given far too much leeway to courts (including the U.S. Supreme Court) to intrude into the lives of children, with too little respect for their autonomy and rights. To limit such intrusions, the children's rights advocates have sought to discipline the individualized, rehabilitative justice vision of the juvenile court through the establishment of greater due-process protections for children (Feld, 1984). In this conception, because children in the juvenile court are subjected to dispositions that are indistinguishable from imprisonment, they are entitled to the due-process protections that adults would have in facing such state action. Anything less would be inconsistent with respect for the constitutional rights of individual children. This has since been used as a justification for insisting on the child's right to counsel, to a jury trial, and to other features designed to protect the rights of children against both the state and their parents (Feld, 1984). This concern for due process protections and the celebration of the rights of children establishes a second view of how the juvenile court, as a criminal court for children, might develop in the future.

The Austere Justice Court

There is, of course, yet another vision of the juvenile court, seen as a criminal court for children—one that makes much less of the differences between adults and children and emphasizes their moral autonomy and accountability rather than their dependency. This view could be called the austere justice court.

This view, too, sees crimes committed by children as the principal focus of the juvenile court. It emphasizes both the justice and practical efficacy of treating juveniles as accountable for their crimes. It sees punishment of children as valuable not only to teach juveniles about their responsibilities to the broader society but also to satisfy the community's sense of justice. It is less willing to risk community security in the interest of rehabilitation or maintaining juveniles' links to family and community. Because this view is more hostile to juveniles, it also includes the notion that children should have adult-like due process protections. In short, this conception holds that if the proper focus of the juvenile court and the juvenile justice system is only crimes committed by children, and if children are to have the benefit of adultlike due process protections that honor their independence and autonomy, then they should also have adultlike accountability and dispositions.

The Dialectic among These Visions

These are the three principal visions that emerge from viewing the juvenile court as a criminal court for children. Not surprisingly, these visions mirror the current liberal/conservative debate about the adult court.

For example, an important liberal idea about the adult court is that it should be guided by the views of human nature that shape the juvenile court's view of crime that is, that we should see all individuals as less autonomous, more capable of rehabilitation, and more likely to be influenced by transient impulses and circumstances than is now routinely acknowledged.

There is much to commend this view. Indeed, it is one of the ironies of criminological research that just as it has become clear that much crime is committed by offenders who seem dangerous (in the sense that they commit offenses frequently and over a sustained career), it has become equally clear that many adult crimes, like juvenile crimes, result from impulsive moments and provocative circumstances (Vera Institute, 1981; Moore et al., 1984). Consequently, many adult offenders (almost certainly the majority of criminal offenders who appear in the criminal justice system) might well be seen as *accidental* offenders, just as juveniles are. To the extent that this is true, the adult criminal court might be better guided by the juvenile court's notions of justice and efficacy than the more traditional images, and the distinction between adult and juvenile courts would thus disappear.

Similarly, there is a powerful conservative idea about the adult court that is closely analogous to the austere justice view of the juvenile court. In this conception, it is proper and just to hold individuals accountable for their actions. Such accountability has virtue not only as a principle of justice but also as a device to protect community security and promote individual rehabilitation. In short, one sees both liberal and conservative ideas shaping these images of juvenile and adult court processing.

If I had to bet on which of these competing conceptions would wax over the next decade and which would wane, I would bet on some combination of the children's rights court and the austere justice court. Indeed, there is powerful evidence to indicate such a trend. There is a palpable increase in the rhetoric of community security and accountability against the rhetoric of rehabilitation and mitigation of guilt. In many states, the juvenile justice system has lost pieces of its jurisdiction to the adult criminal court. In a few states, new legislation for the juvenile justice system has been passed that establishes accountability and just deserts as the dominant principles of the court's operation. These trends have been accompanied by the development of additional due process protections in the operations of the nation's juvenile justice system. The net result of these trends, I suspect, will be something that looks like a version of the adult criminal court for juvenile crime. That development, over the longer run, will gradually raise the question of why we need a juvenile court at all.

An Alternative Conception

There is an alternative to these conceptions of the juvenile court—one that proceeds from radically different assumptions. The alternative conception holds that society should understand and authorize the juvenile court not as a special criminal court for dealing with crimes committed by children but rather as a civil court administering a body of law regulating the conduct of parents, children, and caretakers to advance the public's interest in ensuring that children are decently cared for, effectively supervised, and properly trained for the tasks of citizenship (Moore et al., 1987).

In this framework, crimes committed by children are of interest not only in themselves but more fundamentally as signs of breakdowns in the nexus of care, supervision, and socialization on which the society relies to help produce its citizens. In this context, crimes against children—abuse and neglect by parents, legal guardians, or other public caretakers (including those who run state institutions)—become an important and natural part of the juvenile court's jurisdiction, for these too signal a breakdown in family relations or the nexus of care surrounding a child.

I will advance this alternative conception by setting out its jurisprudential basis and tracing its implications for the current organization and operations of the juvenile court. Finally, I will explain why I think this is a more promising idea than any of its alternatives as well as indicate the many, large issues that remain to be resolved before committing to this alternative conception.

Jurisprudential Principles

The view that the juvenile court should be seen as a criminal court overseeing the conditions under which children are raised—like the conception of the juvenile court as a criminal court for dealing with crimes committed by children—begins with some key assumptions about the status of children in society. The principles I will elaborate here are broader than those presented above because they are not based solely on the question of the ways in which children differ from adults as criminal offenders. They seek, instead, to define the social position of children and their caretakers more broadly—to understand how society views the "offices" of parents and children. Three axioms are key.

Axiom One: Society Has Broad and Final Responsibilities for Child Rearing. The first axiom is that society has a widely acknowledged, broad responsibility for rearing its children. Put more provocatively, child rearing is ultimately a public responsibility.

This may seem startling, for the state, for the most part, does not participate in or interfere with child-rearing practices. Generally speaking, the responsibility for raising children rests with parents, and they discharge their duties tolerably well. This is fortunate, as it allows the state to achieve the dual objectives of protecting the privacy and autonomy of families and ensuring the proper development of its future citizens without conflict. This state of affairs also makes it seem as though the state has few legitimate interests or concerns with the quality of child rearing.

What makes the axiom a plausible one, however, is that when children's private structures of support break down, society, through its legal institutions, must inevitably and invariably step in. When a child lacks a legal guardian, the court appoints one. When parents attack a child, the state steps in to prevent future occurrences. When a marriage with children breaks up, the state decides who will have custody.

One can argue that in stepping into such situations the state is simply adjudicating a private dispute between parents and children. But I think that the state's interests are different from and greater than the mediation of a dispute. The interests extend to substantive concerns about the adequacy of the arrangements for supervising, developing, and caring for the child as a future citizen. The state seeks to help establish a nexus of care and supervision that can transform defenseless barbarians into resourceful citizens.

The state has a practical interest in this process, for if the process of child rearing does not go well, society will pay the price. Future criminal offending is only the most obvious way that neglected or badly treated children might repay society for their mistreatment. They can become ill, refuse to work, bear additional children whom they mistreat, and so on. To avoid these future problems, then, society might be practically interested in doing what it can to ensure that child rearing goes tolerably well.

Alternatively, one can see society's interests in child rearing as a matter of justice. In this view, children are entitled to decent care, effective supervision, and training. It is up to the state to see that they receive it—at least to some minimal degree. (For their part, in exchange for these special protections, children may also be obligated to accept some appropriate level of care, supervision, and developmental assistance.)

In any case, society has a stake in the quality of care, supervision, and guidance offered to children, as manifested in the laws that require all children to have legal guardians and that empower the state to create and transform the custodial arrangements for children.

Axiom Two: Families (and Other Private and Public Caretakers) Have Public Responsibilities. The second axiom is closely related to the first: namely, that in the enterprise of rearing children, parents, legal guardians, and other public caretakers have substantive responsibilities to society. Caretakers are not entirely autonomous (Zimring, 1982). Put more provocatively, the family (and its various substitutes) is at least to some degree the agent of society.

This, too, may seem surprising—even outrageous. We are accustomed to thinking of families as granted autonomy and deference in child rearing. And so they are. Nonetheless, even with this great deference, families remain under some degree of supervision and restraint by the state. Minimal standards of care exist implicitly in the substantive laws defining abuse and neglect of children. These standards are also implicitly present in the standards regulating the conduct of those public agencies that assume responsibility for children. If the standards are violated, the caretakers—whether private or pub-lic—will come under public scrutiny. If the violations are serious enough, the court will seek to reconstitute the arrangements for caring for the children so that the new arrangements meet the minimal standards of care, supervision, and training.

The image of private and public caretakers as agents of society is best ex-emplified by cases of abuse and neglect. But it also inheres in our images of delinquency. To a degree, we see the crimes of juveniles not only as their acts but also as the result of breakdowns in past and present parenting. Even more interestingly, we increasingly dispose of juvenile cases by relying on private and public caretakers to provide adequate levels of supervision to juvenile of-fenders. The principle that a disposition in a juvenile case should be the least restrictive one consistent with public safety, along with the principle that a disposition should be designed to maintain close connections between the child and his caretakers, contributes to turning private and public caretaking arrangements into agents of the court. The only question that preoccupies the court in making such dispositions is whether the caretaking arrangements fulfill the aforementioned principles better than other publicly available alter-natives. If they do, the existing arrangements are used by the court as an alternative to public custody and are explicitly recognized as agents of society for the care, supervision, and development of the juvenile offender.

Axiom Three: The Public Response to Breakdowns in the Existing Arrangements for Child Rearing Properly Includes the Imposition of Responsibilities, the Vindi-cation of Rights, and the Provision of Material Services. Often people imagine that the only proper response to evidence of breakdowns in child-rearing ar-rangements is to provide additional material assistance to the child or to the parents in the form of increased financial assistance, more social work coun-seling, or increased educational services. Such assistance may well be impor-tant—valuable both for its own sake and for reassuring struggling parents and children that society has not entirely abandoned them.

It is worth keeping in mind, however, that society can also respond to such situations by reminding both parents and children of their obligations to the broader society. This response can be described as holding parents or children accountable for the performance of their duties in the process of child rear-ing. Indeed, in Colonial times, when there was little material assistance avail-able in the public larder, the predominant public response to breakdowns in child rearing was "responsibility reminding" (Bremner et al., 1974). Parents of misbehaving children were put in the stocks.

More recently, of course, society has developed a much greater capacity for providing material assistance. We have the welfare system (which was origi-nally understood not as a device for eliminating poverty or redistributing in-come but rather as a way of helping single or widowed mothers to care for their children in their own homes without having them taken away and placed in foster care or state institutions by the juvenile court). We also have an elaborate system of foster care, maternal and child health programs, preschool education, public schools, youth recreation and employment programs, and so on.

Such programs, used voluntarily by parents and other caretakers, have helped to improve the conditions under which children are being reared—at least to some degree. Indeed, one might say that, in the modern world, the task of child rearing requires organizing the provision of these services to one's children, whether the family stays together, falls apart, or has a limited capacity either to provide such services on its own or to acquire them from the agents of society (Golden, 1992).

But this proliferation of differentiated public services to children has created its own problems. Society may have come to a point at which no single person can be relied upon to organize a suitable nexus of care, supervision, and assistance to suit the needs and basic rights of our children. It may be that there is no single parent or agency advocate who can organize the supply of services and insist that each contributing agency meet its specific duties to the child.

The Juvenile Court and Family Bankruptcies

This task—seeing what needs to be done for children in situations in which breakdowns are occurring, establishing obligations, and holding caretakers accountable for the performance of their duties—is quintessentially the work of the courts. No other institution can impose public duties on private and public caretakers. Thus, in a world in which private capacities for child care have weakened to the point of becoming a source of public concern and in which the public provision of services to children has become more plentiful and diverse, the juvenile court may have reemerged as an agency that can help organize the complex task of child rearing by holding both private and public caretakers accountable for their share of that task.

Note that a crucial feature of this idea of the juvenile court is that the court's role in child rearing is never direct or substantive. The court is never the parent or legal guardian of the child nor is itself accountable for the quality of care provided to the child. Instead, the court's role is indirect and regulatory. It holds those who are directly responsible for the care, supervision, and training of children accountable for meeting minimal public standards.

To grasp this image of the juvenile court, an analogy might be helpful. The juvenile court, in this conception, is less like a criminal court that deals with the problem of crimes committed by children than it is like a bankruptcy court that oversees a public institution called a "family" and interferes to protect the public's interest in rearing children tolerably well.

The signs that a family is going bankrupt are present when it declares itself disrupted, or when society has evidence that things are not going well with respect to child rearing. The indications are written into the codes defining the jurisdiction of the juvenile court. They include situations in which parents are neglecting or abusing their children in serious and visible ways, children are attacking other citizens, or children are engaging in conduct that is particularly dangerous for their future development, such as becoming involved in drug use or risking unwanted pregnancies.

Faced with signs of bankruptcy, the court can intervene in two ways broadly analogous to the options facing a bankruptcy court. It can decide to "liquidate" the enterprise and transfer the child to the care and custody of someone other than the current caretakers. Or it can seek to "restructure." It can explain to the victims of juvenile crime or the children who are themselves being victimized that they should not insist that the family be broken apart. Instead, they should understand that their interests would be better served if the family is kept together and allowed to keep going. To ensure that the interests of both crime victims and juveniles are protected, the court should make a flow of services available to the caretakers, as well as insist that they understand and live up to their duties to provide effective care, supervision, and training for the child.

In organizing this set of obligations and services, the court never assumes direct responsibility for the care of children. It merely guides others who have that responsibility by setting out their obligations. In defining and enforcing these obligations, the court might appoint someone to serve in a role analogous to the "special master" in a bankruptcy case. This role could be assumed by a welfare case worker, a court probation officer, or even a youth authority case manager.

Note that this image of the court is not the image of a *parens patriae* court as it has operated over the last few decades. Like that court, it retains a potentially broad jurisdiction including juvenile crimes, abuse and neglect, and perhaps status offenses as well. The difference, however, is that the relationship between the child and the court is a mediated one. The court operates not by assuming direct control over and responsibility for the child but by holding private and public caretakers, and children, responsible for performing their part in the task of child rearing.

Implications for the Constitution and Operation of
the Juvenile Court and the Juvenile Justice System

The image of the juvenile court as a court that superintends bankruptcies in families (or other institutional arrangements for rearing children) has important, concrete implications for the organization and operation of the juvenile court and juvenile justice system.

First, the jurisdiction of the court would remain broad. It would continue to include juvenile crimes, but these would be seen not only as problems in themselves but also as evidence of a breakdown in social arrangements for supervising juveniles. Repair of those arrangements would ordinarily be considered the appropriate response, rather than "incapacitation" or "rehabilitation."

The jurisdiction would also include instances of abuse and neglect. Indeed, in the context of a family bankruptcy court, the jurisdiction over juvenile offenses would seem perfectly appropriate, rather than anomalous, as it appears when one is viewing the juvenile court as a special court for dealing with crimes committed by children. Abuse and neglect would be seen as some of the most powerful and unambiguous signs of breakdown in the nexus of care for children, and they would thus trigger a serious review of conditions. The court would intervene to protect the rights and interests of children, promoting society's well-being not only by vindicating the rights of children but also by avoiding the disastrous, long-run consequences of allowing children to be abused.

In this framework, the court's jurisdiction would also include so-called status offenses, such as truancy and incorrigibility. These offenses would be seen not as special kinds of crimes committed only by children but rather as violations of special obligations that children have en route to becoming resourceful citizens and as signs of deficiency in the arrangements that exist for supervising and caring for children.

Second, this vision of the juvenile court would suggest the wisdom of making private and public caretakers, as well as juvenile offenders, parties to the court proceedings, especially in the case of abuse and neglect. But it would also be important in the case of delinquency and status offenses. Making the caretakers parties to the process would not only symbolize the fact that they share in the responsibility for the particular problem; it would also increase the likelihood that they would be involved in the ultimate disposition of the case. As long as caretakers have not been in the courtroom, it has been far too easy for the court to think of the problem in terms of an individual offender and hence to choose the "liquidation" rather than the "restructuring" option. With the caretakers in the court, and with the right to impose duties on them as part of the disposition of the case, the "restructuring" option would seem more plausible.

Third, this vision of the juvenile court would redefine the overall goals of the juvenile court. The court would not be responsible—neither for effective crime control nor for rehabilitation of juvenile offenders. Instead, it would be responsible for helping to establish more just and plausibly effective relationships among those responsible for the tasks of child rearing. In effect, the court would be responsible for creating as fair and strong a nexus of supervision, assistance, and care for children as could be fashioned from the available materials, including whatever nubs of family existed and whatever public re-sources could be made available, all held together with the court's authority to obligate those caretakers to make their particular contributions.

Fourth, of necessity, this vision of the juvenile court would be able to make much more extensive use of private and public caretaking institutions. It would not think only in terms of state institutions on the one hand or no action on the other. It would see the vast social service apparatus as providing resources that could be used to strengthen faltering caretaking arrangements that were faltering. It would think of the welfare department, the schools, and the public health department as instrumentalities that could help bring about justice for children and society and could also contribute to juvenile court dispositions.

Fifth, this vision of the juvenile court would also radically change the func-tion of caseworkers and probation officers, who would both describe the nexus of care and supervision that surrounds particular children and make recom-mendations about how that nexus could be strengthened. They would also have the responsibility for seeing to it that the court's dispositions were hon-ored and its specific obligations complied with. Finally, they would be respon-sible for reporting to the court any changes in conditions that would necessi-tate an adjustment in the court's oversight.

Sixth, this vision of the juvenile court would require the development and routine use of a much wider variety of dispositions than are currently used. Family mediation, integrated family services, case management in detention centers, community restitution, community-based halfway houses, and youth employment programs would all be used much more intensively as parts of juvenile court dispositions.

This may all seem quite far-fetched. What is interesting, however, is that the theoretical and operational basis for each part of the enterprise already exists. In effect, the various necessary bits and pieces are gradually assem-bling themselves without anyone's having to make it happen. The most seri-ous obstacle to accepting this conception may simply be the tendency to rely too much on the analogy with the adult criminal court rather than accept two obvious points: namely, that child rearing is a public responsibility, and that the institutions that perform the task—both private and public—are publicly accountable for a minimal level of performance.

The "Family Bankruptcy Court": Worries and Cautions

After reading this vision of the juvenile court as one that superintends break-downs in social arrangements for caring for and supervising children, one can step back and ask why this vision of the court is preferable to any of the visions of the juvenile court as a criminal court for dealing with crimes committed by or against children. In addressing this question, I acknowledge that it is entirely possible that this vision of the court is not better than any of the others. At this stage, I am not insisting on its superiority. I am rather proposing it as a provocative alternative to see if it might be helpful in extricating us from what seem to me to be increasingly sterile debates about juvenile justice. Having acknowledged this key point, I may proceed to note several attractive features of this vision.

First, it seems to me to be consistent with the country's political values as they have been enacted over time in public policy rather than expressed in political speeches. Despite all the criticism of the juvenile court, it seems clear that society will not do away with it entirely. The proposals to make it more like an adult court have scored some rhetorical successes but, so far, few legislative successes. Moreover, I think it is significant that just as the society is calling for more emphasis on juvenile crime, it is also becoming increasingly alarmed about runaways, truants, and abused children. Society can escape neither from its continuing concerns about the conditions under which children are being raised nor from its desire to use the law—civil rather than criminal—to regulate conduct in this domain.

Second, the concept seems consistent with developing legal doctrines that view the juvenile as "semi-autonomous" (Zimring, 1982). That status insulates the child from full exposure to criminal accountability as it would be experienced in the adult court. But it also implicates the child's caretakers in the child's difficulties, and exposes the child to some special responsibilities associated with making the transition from "semi-autonomous" to "fully autonomous" personhood. In effect, while juveniles have some special privileges in the form of special excuses and claims on public resources, they also have some special responsibilities.

Third, the concept addresses itself to some problems that are growing increasingly important in our society. In particular, it treats abuse and neglect of children as at least as important a part of the jurisdiction of the juvenile court as the crimes committed by juveniles. In addition, it encourages the court to begin thinking in terms of a nexus of care wrapped around children—responsibilities that are met not only by the family proper but also by publicly created families and constellations of publicly provided services. This imagery seems appropriate in a world in which traditional families are fast becoming the exception rather than the rule and poor families often need extensive and integrated services to remain functional.

Fourth, the concept encourages the continuing development of some of the most interesting and exciting programs being created in the world of juvenile justice. These include family mediation, integrated family services, case work, and the development of dispositions more varied than either institutionalization or pro-forma probation.

Fifth, it challenges legislatures and courts to explore the potential of an instrument that has not yet been widely used but is fundamental to the juvenile court: the use of legal authority to help create a coherent nexus of care for children from otherwise disjointed private and public homes.

These are the principal reasons to be interested in this concept. The principal reasons to be doubtful or hostile include the following:

First, it might turn out that the authority of the court is not helpful in organizing a nexus of care around children. It may turn out that it introduces issues of guilt and blame that destroy rather than help foster proper relationships. Or it may turn out that the court and its "special masters" are simply not skilled enough in using this resource to make it valuable. They may even be guided by the wrong principles and values.

Second, it could also turn out that the juvenile court can not rid itself of race and class biases in diagnosing child care relationships and proposing interventions. As a result, the system could deepen rather than ameliorate the disadvantages of the children and families who come before it.

Given the history of the juvenile court, it would not be unreasonable to be concerned about both of these problems. But to conclude that the juvenile court has no role to play in responding to the enormous problems now faced by the nation's poor families, as well as the weaknesses of the social service systems now in place to serve them, might equally be an error. The question remains how society might use laws and courts and dispositions to help shore up the sagging mechanisms through which society seeks to produce reasonable opportunities for children to become resourceful citizens. That is what children deserve and what society ought to be interested in providing.

References

Bremner, Robert H., John Barnard, Tamara K. Hareven, and Robert M. Mennel, eds. (1974). *Children and Youth in America.* Cambridge: Harvard University Press.

Feld, Barry C. (1984). "Criminalizing Juvenile Justice: Rules of Procedure for the Juvenile Court." *Minnesota Law Review* 69 (2):141–276.

—— (1987). "The Juvenile Court Meets the Principle of the Offense: Legislative Changes in Juvenile Waiver Statutes." *Journal of Criminal Law and Criminology* 78 (3):471–533.

Golden, Olivia (1992). *Poor Children and Welfare Reform.* Westport, Conn.: Auburn House.

Moore, Mark H., et al. (1987). *From Children to Citizens.* Vol. 2, *The Mandate for Juvenile Justice.* New York: Springer-Verlag.

Moore, Mark H., Susan R. Estrich, Daniel McGillis, and William Spelman (1984). *Dangerous Offenders: The Elusive Target of Justice*. Cambridge: Harvard University Press.

Platt, Anthony M. (1969). *The Child Savers: The Invention of Delinquency*. Chicago: University of Chicago Press.

Silberman, Charles E. (1978). *Criminal Violence, Criminal Justice*. New York: Random House.

Springer, Charles E. (April 1986). *Justice for Juveniles*. Washington, D.C.: U.S. Department of Justice, Office of Juvenile Justice and Delinquency Prevention.

Vera Institute of Justice (1981). *Felony Arrests: Their Prosecution and Disposition in New York City's Courts*. Rev. ed. New York: Longman.

Zimring, Franklin E. (1982). *The Changing Legal World of Adolescence*. New York: Free Press.

4

Cell Out
Renting Out the Responsibility
for the Criminally Confined

Jess Maghan

Accountability in the Privatization
of Corrections

In a society in which organizations compete either for economic resources or for the loyalty and support of group members, the prison has
a unique position. It is noncompetitive in the sense that no other organization challenges it directly. The prison therefore need not, as ultima
ratio of its existence, maintain competitive standards, adapt itself rapidly to technological progress, or respond to fluctuations of market conditions; nor is it immediately dependent on the good will, benevolence,
or loyalty of a group of sponsors or followers, as are many other nonprofit organizations. (Grosser, 1969)

Grosser's characterization of the prison as a noncompetitive institution
clearly demonstrates the dramatic reappearance of private prisons. Private-
for-profit incarceration companies now maintain an aggressive market enterprise in the United States and globally. This market parallels in scale the
military defense industry of recent times. Concurrently, it is also strongly
influenced by privatization in law enforcement, public safety, security, and
social welfare services, as well as the vast new markets in the cybernetics and
communication technology fields (Bernstein, 1996; Crenshaw, 1995; Hobsbawm, 1994; Lilly and Knepper, 1992; Maghan, 1995; Stolz, 1997). Private-
for-profit incarceration portends much of the emerging character of correctional custody in the twenty-first century.

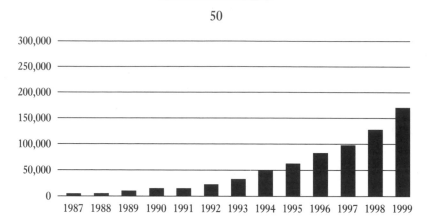

Fig. 4-1. The growth of private prisons. Shown are the number of secure adult prison beds operated by private management companies since 1987 (with estimates for the years 1997–1999). *Source:* Center for Studies in Criminology and Law, University of Florida.

Feasibility of the Privatization of Correctional Services

The private prison business has become one of the fastest-growing industries in the nation. It is here to stay for the foreseeable future. Private-for-profit incarceration is now past the point where a single scandal will kill the movement. Until it becomes clear that private correctional facilities are neither cheaper nor better than public facilities, the growth of private correctional facilities will continue. The number of inmates in privately managed or owned prisons is expected to exceed 80,000 in 1996, up from 3,122 in 1987, with projected annual growth of 35 percent over the next few years. Figure 4-1 profiles this growth.

The Standard-Bearers of Correctional Privatization

The Correction Corporation of America and Wackenhut Security are now substantially larger than many public-sector departments of correction and certainly larger than most jail systems. The Corrections Corporation of America (CCA) is now one of the fastest-growing companies traded on the New York Stock Exchange. In 1995, CCA shares soared from eight to thirty-seven dollars a share, an increase of 385 percent. As of October 1997, the value of CCA shares had reached approximately $3.5 billion. Wackenhut Corporation follows as a close contender in these growth stock trends of privatized prison and security systems. These figures clearly reflect an exponential growth of private-for-profit incarceration and demonstrate a viable market. On the industrial-product side, these two giants of private-for-profit incarceration appeal to politicians as an immediate cost-savings alternative to public prisons. The boundaries are yet to be defined.

Organizational Theory

The political nature of the public sector correctional system, reporting to the executive branch of government at the local, state, and federal level, leaves it vulnerable to a host of external forces, particularly regarding budget and operational philosophy. The public correction system is a residual agency. Positioned downstream from all other components of the criminal justice system, it has always been prey to the ideology of the political majority (Maghan, 1997). This situation is described as a matter of territorial concern, a level of concern that is increasingly manifested in "strategic political issues" relating to community perceptions of crime and crime control policies (Mullen, Chaotar, and Cartow, 1985:74).

In 1992, a survey of perceptions of privatization among public sector prison wardens (Kinkade and Leone, 1992) found that privatization, as established on the fringes of public jails and prisons (such as minimum security alcohol/substance abuse centers and immigration detention centers), represented no threat to public prison wardens. These private correctional facilities were actually perceived as providing additional alternative sentencing options. The current spin of privatization into medium and maximum security prisons, however, is engendering propriety concerns among both public sector prison wardens and prison watchdog groups. Organizations maintain their domains by differentiating themselves from competitors and by maintaining autonomous control over their respective areas (Aldrich, 1979). The external competition from the private sector is raising new concerns of encroachment by the private sector on a domain long held by public sector officials.

The Past Is a Prologue

The cause and effect issues of contemporary correctional privatization are markedly similar to those of the privatization movement of the 1860s—increasing prisoner populations and a declining economy in the larger society. Likewise, past problems intrinsic to contractual arrangements, such as failure to meet contract stipulations, costs associated with contracts, and quality of contractors' services, are also reappearing (Durham, 1989, 1993; Lewis, 1965; McConville, 1987; McKelvey, 1977).

Smith (1993) cites the convergence of three trends in the mid-1980s as

instrumental to the current correctional privatization movement: (a) the ideological imperatives of the free market; (b) the huge increase in the number of
prisoners; and (c) the concomitant increase in imprisonment costs.

Economic Politics

The connection between economics and the intolerance of crime is a major
platform issue in the politics of the 1990s. The Republican majority that cap-
tured Congress in the 1994 elections has had a direct impact on state and
local correctional agencies. The demand for tougher criminal laws, longer
prison sentences, mandatory life sentences for repeat offenders, more execu-
tions with fewer delays, and harsher forms of incarceration is manifest in the
public mind. Currently, a conservatively bound definition of modern confinement precludes much of the public debate on the purpose of incarceration, its
costs, and the alternatives. "The current conservative penology is a new fantasy of control, as dubious in its assumptions, yet as historically significant as
Bentham's panoptic vision. In blunt terms, it is markedly less concerned with
responsibility, fault, moral sensibility, diagnosis, or intervention and treatment of the individual offender. Rather, it centers on techniques to identify,
classify and manage inmates in groupings sorted by dangerousness. The task
is managerial, not transformative" (Feely and Simon, 1992:452).

Views about private imprisonment services are closely linked to deeper political values, making it difficult to resolve the public policy debate about contracting. Knowing more about the actual experiences and consequences of
contracting will go a long way toward identifying the desirable combinations
of public and private responsibilities and interests.

The Florida Corrections Commission (FCC) has developed a detailed
oversight map for identifying and monitoring costs and quality of services
relating to privatization. This process represents a promulgation of processes
and procedures in evaluating privatization decision making. The chapter appendix outlines these oversight factors.

Accountability in the Privatization
of Correctional Services

That private prisons have not been declared unconstitutional does not resolve
the question of whether contractual delegation of administrative authority
over imprisonment is proper or desirable. In a legalistic sense, the inmate has
injured the interest of the state and not an individual. Since it is the state that
has been injured, it is the state's duty to punish the transgressor. There have
been no lawsuits to challenge the fundamental idea of contracting out correc-

tional services. The existing lawsuits regarding private correctional contractors are essentially the same as those concerning public agencies—claims of poor medical care, excessive use of force—that is, operational issues. A particular jurisdiction may need statutory authorization to contract, but this is not a definitive situation.

The June 23, 1997, ruling by the U.S. Supreme Court (*Richardson v. McKnight*), however, denied entitlement of qualified immunity to private prison staff. This is the first formal legal precept regarding the legal responsibilities of private prisons. It further narrows both the operational liability and cost disparities between private and public correctional facilities. The question remains: Can state or local government delegate its power to punish (Collins, 1987; DiIulio, 1990; Logan, 1990; Maghan, 1991; McDonald, 1990a; Robbins, 1988)?

> The real danger of privatization is not some innate inhumanity on the part of its practitioners but rather the added financial incentives that reward inhumanity. The same economic logic that motivates companies to run prisons more efficiently also encourages them to cut corners at the expense of workers, prisoners, and the public. Private prisons essentially mirror the cost-cutting practices of health maintenance organizations: Companies receive a guaranteed fee for each prisoner, regardless of the actual costs. Every dime they don't spend on food or medical care or training for guards is a dime they can pocket. (Bates, 1997:7)

The Social Impact of Privatization

The internal logic of privatization consists of mutually reinforcing a set of beliefs that are inherently expansionistic (Gilbert, 1996a). In that view, there is literally no limit to either the amount or type of social control functioning that could be privatized. Presumably, even capital punishment could again be privatized, and, through privatization, as many people as possible could be confined (Gilbert, 1996b). Consequently, the social impact of private-for-profit incarceration presents the potential for an ever-widening capacity for imprisoning more inmates. The possibility that a private prison industry lobby could affect important decisions, such as whether to develop alternatives to imprisonment, seems credible (Maghan, 1991; Morris and Rothman, 1995). The current trend toward privatization of corrections, which is forcing criminal justice into the business world, may escalate the need for increased attention to ethical issues in criminal justice (Silvester, 1990).

In this context, cost should not be the single motivating factor in prisons, but rather the issue of who is to punish those who refuse to abide by the rules of the state. However, the goal of cost efficiency requires a correctional manager to prioritize, for example, where and how incoming funds are to be spent. Doing this appropriately requires that the manager have not only a solid grasp of the demands of the marketplace but also an understanding of the ethical ramifications of decisions that are made. For example, labor costs in a service-delivery business are usually one of the major expenses, and consequently they constitute an area in which reduced expenditure can directly affect net income. Cost-cutting in this area has implications for the quality of service delivered. Individual states have a tremendous responsibility for the custody of inmates that cannot be delegated to the private sector without strict surveillance of contractor performance.

Accountability for the private entrepreneur is always the profit margin as the baseline of cost-effectiveness (Gandy and Hurl, 1987; Harrison and Gosse, 1985; Walker, 1994). As Silvester (1990) notes: "When settings are created in which the pragmatic concerns of the business world interact with the ethical dilemmas produced by the conflicting ideologies intrinsic to the justice system, individuals unseasoned in the principles of ethical decision-making are faced with an increasing array of problems. What appear to be simple decisions of policy, such as which staff to hire and how to train them or which clients to accept and when to refer, begin to take on new meaning when money and careers are directly impacted" (68).

The assumption by many privatization advocates that private markets and self-interest economics are inherently self-regulating cannot be supported. The invisible hand of free market forces has clearly not prevented market failures or abuses of public interest. As epitomized with the 1980s collapse of American Savings and Loan, private economic interests have exploited public interests as opportunity targets in a deregulated marketplace (Denhardt, 1988; Fasenfest, 1986; Luttwak, 1996; Starr, 1987; Wolfe, 1989).

Differing Definitions of Accountability

Spurred by a tax revolt that spread across the United States in the late 1970s and early 1980s, citizens were voting down bonding proposals, even though they were at the same time demanding that more criminals be imprisoned in the hope of making their communities safer. Public officials saw the lease-purchase arrangements as a convenient way out of this dilemma—a rent payment can be paid out of government operating budgets (McDonald, 1994). A recurring controversy cited in government and academic studies of privately run correctional facilities is the practice of lease/purchase financing as a method of circumventing the debt ceilings and referenda requirements of general-obligation bonds. Because no voter approval is required, lease/purchase agreements undeniably reduce citizen participation in corrections policy (Johnson, 1985).

In the traditional business arena, the knowledge that when service is poor the paying customers eventually stop coming serves as a safeguard. Privatized correctional services, however, serve "clients" who have been ordered there by the courts, who have little political influence, and who, therefore, have minimal immediate impact on or control over the finances of the business.

Private prison corporations answer criticism by insisting that their prisons run efficiently without scrimping on essentials or impinging on prisoners' rights. The Corrections Corporation of America notes in its 1994 annual report that the stock options it offers to employees foster a sense of ownership and makes them more receptive to complaints from prisoners.

Privatization in Texas: A National Model

The reemergence of the private sector's involvement with the Texas prison system signaled a new era in Texas corrections, an era distinguished by progressive methods for aiding the thousands of Texas inmates. The most important aspect of this privatization experiment pertains to the type of facility that is operated by the private companies. By using small (five-hundred-man) facilities that offer prerelease programs, lawmakers are taking major steps toward preparing inmates for life outside prison walls.

The operation and management of small, specialized facilities that house low-risk inmates has been championed as a possible role for the private sector in the nation's correctional system (Folz and Scheb, 1989; Johnson and Ross, 1990). Other states might follow the example of Texas. According to Logan (1990), this already may be a trend: Most of the privately operated state prison units in the United States house fewer than five hundred low-risk inmates.

A second feature of the Texas privatization experiment is the financing scheme contrived to pay for the construction and operation of prerelease centers. Lawmakers devised a bonding mechanism that did not need voter approval. By using lease revenue bonds, the state does not technically create a debt. Although the use of such bonds proved successful in Texas, the issuance of bonds that do not need voter approval to pay for prison construction has been criticized because the government can expand prison construction without public input (Leonard, 1990; McDonald, 1989).

A third aspect of the Texas privatization experience pertains to the contract negotiations between the state and private companies. On the basis of the original contracts, the contract monitors' reports, and the companies' responses to the reports, it appears that some portions of the contracts were ambiguous (for example, educational programs, vocational programs, and prerelease programs). As a result, the companies and the Texas Department of Corrections spent a great amount of time and money in reaching agreements on how to carry out the contracts properly (Ethridge and Marquart, 1993).

The Dilemma of Cost-Benefit Analysis

Krulwich (1981:12) refers to the series of costs related to inappropriate or inadequate regulation as "secondary effects that are rarely considered in the rush and newness of privatization." For example, regulation at times causes delay, which, in turn, imposes its own set of costs. Failing to take into account effects that accumulate over time has been suggested as one cause of some of these problems. More often, costs (and benefits) that economists cannot measure are ignored or merely cited as possibilities the agency also considered without attempting to quantify.

In a profile analysis entitled *Privately Managed Prisons—At What Cost?* the Prison Reform Trust of the United Kingdom provides an analysis of cost factors. This analysis concludes that privately managed prisons are not the benchmark on which to base publicly managed prison budgets. A detailed account of the consternation of attempts at comparative cost analysis and the concomitant political and bureaucratic foray involved in the public use of private prisons continues to raise concerns. For example:

• Comparisons between public and private prisons are complex, as it is difficult to establish true "like with like" conditions. For example, in addition to the stated overall contract price for a private prison, as compared with the annual budget for a publicly run prison (even if they were the same kind of prison, of the same age, with the same design, number, and category of prisoners from the same locality with exactly the same needs and services provided—all of which must be unlikely), there are a myriad of hidden costs to be taken into account. These would include prison service headquarters costs; the resources of outside agencies, such as police, fire department, local authorities, national health services, health and safety agencies, and other central government departments and voluntary groups that provide services to prisons; the public provision of local infrastructure to prisons; and not least, the cost to taxpayers of the entire privatization itself.

• Taxpayers also foot the bill for costs that are exclusive to the private sector and that are included as an element of the contract price, such as the need to make profits, create returns on capital investment and dividends for shareholders or payments to parent companies for technical know-how, expertise, or management/administrative fees. There is also the loss in corporation tax revenue if the company makes a loss.

• Despite the claim that privately managed prisons are cheaper to run, the Prison Service has been unable to publish meaningful cost comparisons. It is arguable that this exercise might not even be possible. (Nor has the issue been resolved in the United States or Australia, both of which have had longer experience of privately managed prisons than has the U.K.)

• The claim that privately managed prisons automatically provide better value for the money is also, at best, unproven, as the performance of three of the existing privately managed prisons in the U.K. testifies. The fourth, Buckley Hall, has not yet been independently evaluated (Penal Lexicon Home Page: United Kingdom, September 15, 1996).

Accountability:
Private Versus Public Prisons

Privatization advocates discount concerns over the erosion of governmental sovereignty. They argue that sovereignty is retained through the contract and enforced by the government's power to terminate the contract. This view fails to recognize the fact that progressive privatization of correctional production (that is, the creation and delivery of correctional services) gradually transfers public policy making functions to the private sector (Dahl and Glassman, 1991; Gilbert, 1996a; Keating, 1990; Kolderie, 1986; Leonard, 1990; McDonald, 1990b; USGAO, 1991).

A vivid test of the sovereignty of governmental oversight occurred in the June 18, 1995, riot at the 350-bed Immigration and Naturalization Service (INS) Detention Center in Elizabeth City, New Jersey, contracted at $54 million to Esmore Correctional Services, Inc., a private correctional management firm (J. Sullivan, 1995).

The INS, a federal agency with little experience (and few options) for operating a custodial detention center for illegal immigrants, had sought private contractors out of the sheer expediency of creating detention facilities quickly. These minimum security centers, located in unobtrusive locations, provoked little controversy or even notice. The convenience of contracted detention services pre-empted INS concern for contracted detention centers. This matter continues to play out with protracted litigation on behalf of the immigrant detainees. In this tragedy it has become painfully obvious that accountability is not always a clear-cut matter in this mix of private and public prisons.

As Mullen et al. (1985) speculated it would, the correctional privatization movement appears to be shifting from initial declarations of cost savings to more neutral issues of "flexibility and the provision of special services" (7). Essentially, there is little evidence of anything imaginative or exciting coming out of the new private prison facilities. To date, the development, design, operation, and management of private prisons has turned out to be much like those of their traditional counterparts. The administrative ranks of the private prisons continue to grow with managers and supervisors that have been mostly recruited (or are retired) from public sector correctional agencies.

Privatized Correctional Services
Have a New Cell Mate

Private welfare management and training companies are lining up for a market that expanded overnight when President Clinton, in September 1996, signed the new law to replace the sixty-year-old guarantee of federal aid to poor children with lump grants to the states. Privatization is now being championed as an enhancement for the new welfare law. For the first time, the law allows states to buy not only welfare services but also gatekeepers to determine eligibility and benefits. The privatization of social-welfare functions has become a dominant theme for twenty-first-century human resource functions, including education, health and medical services (HMOs), and a growing range of social infrastructure maintenance services. Because of a mutuality of the clients served, linkages with these newly privatized human service agencies will engender collaborative services with and among public and private correctional programs.

The tough job ahead for both public and private penal experts is to continue to create constitutionally protected justice environments geared to both economic and social improvements. The past decade of aggressive privatization in correctional services is clarifying fundamental demarcations of privatization claims. Consider what privatization might and might not do: (a) It cannot ease the credit crunch caused by budget deficits; (b) it cannot relieve government of its social responsibilities; (c) it isn't likely to make monopolies more efficient; and (d) it may even temper political demands for inefficient operations. The real hope for innovative change lies in a middle ground.

Possibility Thinking and the Privatization
of Correctional Services

The racial demographics of our prison population mirror deeper social problems, problems that prisons are increasingly being asked to solve. The American prison system already functions as a surrogate national public health system, a national job training and literacy program, and, unfortunately, as a second-rate mental hospital. Tapping into the emerging public-private partnerships evolving out of the past decade of privatization may help solve this crisis.

Potential Partnerships

It is time to redefine the purpose of the prison, to peel away all of these social engineering tasks the prisons are assuming. Let the prisons truly become a penal system for long-term and dangerous inmates and turn remaining custodial control into a restructured system of correctional programs leading to positive behavior, such as community service and boot camp programs. Such centers (public and private), concentrating on programs of self-esteem and personal development skills for inmates, can put our correctional system back into balance with other criminal justice and social service agencies. This could well be the beginning of a correctional version of the popular and successful community policing programs throughout the United States. In this context, accountability for both public and private prisons can be linked to creativity and community partnership. How can this process be achieved?

While the United States represents a pioneer market in the incarceration-for-profit industry, it can also serve as a laboratory for the development of a new "social contract" with private correctional entrepreneurs. The utility of these partnerships will emerge as government seeks new modes for custodial care of geriatric prisoners, prisoners with alcohol- and drug-related problems, and prisoners with emotional and mental problems (Cullen, 1986; Matthews, 1989). One of the most significant outcomes of the privatization debate is that a fundamental rethinking of every facet of the existing system is widely recognized as not only desirable but very necessary (Matthews, 1989). These partnerships are stimulating new forms of oversight responsibility by both government and private agencies (Crants, 1991; Cullen, 1986; Matthews, 1989, 1990).

The privatization movement has now matured enough to bring some reasoning to the usual reactive stance of both advocates and adversaries. There is an emerging community of interests that recognizes a mutuality of mission in meeting the ever-growing correctional custodial needs of the nation. It can be hoped that this community of interests will lobby for increasing legislation to create privatized minimum security centers for drug addicts, alcoholics, and special-need offenders.

It is not science fiction to speculate that the prisons (private and public) of the twenty-first century will constitute even more gigantic correctional complexes, providing a full range of institutionalized geriatric and public health services. The mix of public and private correctional systems is inevitable. The maintenance of the social accountability and integrity of these new partnerships must be inculcated in the institutions of both sectors. This necessitates a return to the teaching of vocational and economic civics: public and private partnerships.

Subjective Social Costs of Prison Privatization

As a prelude, the current intoxication with the return of private-for-profit incarceration is the most recent indicator of an emergent fourth wave of correctional reform at the cusp of the twenty-first century. The reappearance of prisons-for-profit as a fourth wave reform movement is opening old wounds and creating new dilemmas of social engineering and the possibilities for positive change. The net-widening capabilities of privatized incarceration are ominous. In this context, privatization manifestly represents *less eligibility reborn*. Sparks (1996) offers a resounding cautionary tone: "The prospect that penal services might be provided by a private sector not 'incentivized' toward relentless improvement but instead constrained by a rhetoric of austerity exposes a range of impending troubles for the legitimacy of the private corrections industry which have until now been largely suppressed" (89).

This is a keenly insightful point shadowing the current reprogramming of private-for-profit incarceration. Prison privatization confronts us with subjective social costs that are not so readily quantifiable. There is a concern for the consequences of commercialization in influencing current criminal justice policy. International human rights experts are joining in voicing concerns that privatization of prisons is not in accordance with international human rights law (Beyens and Snacken, 1996). The embodiment of new public and private correctional partnerships may be the end product of this aggressive correctional privatization. The mix of public and private correctional systems is inevitable. Reforms that will define and ensure the social accountability and integrity of these new partnerships will constitute the dominant interplay in the institutions of both sectors. The importance of prisoner rights advocacy in both private and public prisons must now shift to an expanded corporate model. The dilemma continues.

Appendix
Florida Corrections Commission

PROJECT: Identify Costs and Quality of Service Factors Relating to Privatization of State Prisons

1. ISSUE: Identify factors to consider for evaluating costs and quality of services for use in comparing private versus state prisons.

2. BACKGROUND/HISTORY: The increase in privatization of correctional facilities in the late 1980s and first half of the 1990s was part of a philosophical shift toward privatization of many government services. The advantages of privatization are said to be its cost efficiency, similar or better quality services, and its ability to bring facilities on-line quickly. Opponents believe that one of the core functions of government is punishment and that private companies profit motives have no place in the administration of justice, where it may create a conflict of interest between the public safety and private profit.

Private involvement with adult correctional institutions has three major models:

(1) private financing and construction of prisons;
(2) private industry involvement in prisons through vocational, academic, work and support programs; and,
(3) the management and operation of an entire correctional facility by a private contractor.

There is general agreement that privatization is a management tool that, when used, requires government to make a series of decisions. These decisions are policy decisions to determine:

- the level of privatization;
- which services may be considered for privatization;
- cost/benefit decisions to determine whether the public or private sector could produce those services most effectively and efficiently;
- evaluation decisions whether output or outcome evaluation should be utilized to determine if privatization decisions made are meeting intended goals.

Many state corrections agencies believe that privatization in corrections has sufficient merit to justify further study. Some advocates of privatization believe that cost savings can be realized from increased flexibility in competitively shopping for prices. Most private companies involved in corrections do not offer traditional pension plans to its employees, but rather offer vested employees opportunities in profit-sharing plans. Advocates state that one feature of private involvement in corrections is the capacity of the private sector to expand criminal sanctions, through new forms of intermediate level control and new surveillance and control technologies.

SECTION 944.105(1)—FLORIDA STATUTES, authorizes the Department of Corrections to enter into contracts with private vendors for the provision of the operation and maintenance of correctional facilities and supervision of inmates. It requires that prior to entering into or renewing a contract for a privatized prison, the DOC must determine that the contract offers substantial savings and that the contract provides for the same quality of services as that offered by the department.

3. CHAPTER 957: The Auditor General is charged with certifying to the Correctional Privatization Commission actual costs associated with the construction and operation of similar facilities or services; and developing and implementing an evaluation of the costs and benefits of each contract entered under this Chapter.

The evaluation must include a comparison of the costs and benefits of constructing and operating prisons by the state versus by private contractors. The Auditor General (again, by agreement, OPPAGA [Office of Program Policy Analysis and Government Accountability] will conduct these reviews) is further charged with evaluating the performance of the private vendor at the end of the term of each management agreement and making recommendations to the Legislature as to continue the contract.

By contract, the private vendor must provide a full-time contract monitor, who is appointed and supervised by the Correctional Privatization Commission.

DESCRIPTION/SCOPE OF WORK: This FCC issue would require the cooperation and support of the Correctional Privatization Commission, the Department of Corrections, and individual private correctional contractors (Wackenhut Corporation, U.S. Corrections Corporation, Esmor Correctional Services, and the Corrections Corporation of America). FCC activities would include, but not necessarily be limited to, contacting other states with multiple privatized prisons to determine:

- The model(s) of privatization utilized;
- The profile of offender populations (adult, pre-release, jail, juvenile) at the contracted facilities;
- The statutory authorization for contracting correctional facilities;
- The statutory authorized entity for contracting correctional facilities;
- The cost and quality of services contractually required for the continued operation and renewal of contract;

- The cost and service quality criteria reviewed to determine contractual compliance;
- The entity which reviews and evaluates the cost and service quality criteria of private prisons;
  The availability of evaluations comparing the cost and service quality criteria of private v. public prisons.

Review existing research literature to identify methods and criteria utilized in measuring and evaluating costs and quality of services in private versus public prisons.

Review all Florida contracts for privatized prisons for language pertaining to cost savings and the provision/quality of services—including academic, vocational training, and substance abuse program services.

Identify innovative facility design or program operations of privatization facilities.

Develop cost and service quality factors for statutory authorized entities to consider for evaluating and comparing private versus public prison operations in Florida.

4. BENEFIT OF PROJECT: The primary benefit of FCC conducting an analysis to identify cost and service quality factors would be to policy and decision makers involved in privatization of correctional facilities. Sections 944.105 and 944.710-719, Florida Statutes, and Chapter 957, Oversight via Florida Statutes, each prescribe varying responsibilities for cost savings, audits and monitoring contract compliance. Although cost comparison will be an essential part of the Auditor General's review, that review will not occur until completion of the second year of operation, in preparation for the decision of renewing the contract. (Florida Corrections Commission, 1996)

References

Aldrich, H. E. (1979). *Organizations and Environments*. Englewood Cliffs, N.J.: Prentice-Hall.

Bates, Eric (1997). "Private Prisons." *Nation* 8 (1):11–38.

Bernstein, Nina (1996). "Giant Companies Entering Race to Run State Welfare Programs." *New York Times*, September 11, 14.

Beyens, Kristel, and Sonja Snacken (1997). "Prison Privatization: An International Perspective." Pp. 240–65 in *Prison 2000: An International Perspective on the Cur-

rent State and Future of Imprisonment, Roger Matthews and Peter Francis, eds. New York: St. Martin's.

Collins, William C. (1987). "Privations: Some Legal Considerations from a Neutral Perspective." *American Jails* 1:28–34.

Crants, Doctor R. (1991). "Private Prison Management: A Study in Economic Efficiency." *Journal of Contemporary Criminal Justice* 7 (1):49–59.

Crenshaw, Martha (1995). *Terrorism in Context.* University Park, Penn.: Pennsylvania State University Press.

Cullen, F. (1986). "The Privatization of Treatment: Prison Reform in the 1980s." *Federal Probation* 50:8–16.

Dahl, J. G., and A. M. Glassman (1991). "Public Sector Contracting: The Next Growth Industry for Organizational Development." *Public Administration Quarterly* 14 (winter):483–97.

Denhardt, K. G. (1988). *The Ethics of Public Service.* New York: Associated Faculty Press.

DiIulio, John J. (1990). "The Duty to Govern: A Critical Perspective on the Private Management of Prisons and Jails." Pp. 116–28 in *Private Prisons and the Public Interest,* D. C. McDonald, ed. New Brunswick, N.J.: Rutgers University Press.

Durham, Alexis M., III (1989). "Origins of Interest in the Privatization of Punishment: The Nineteenth and Twentieth Century American Experience." *Criminology* 27:107–39.

―――― (1993). "The Future of Correctional Privatization: Lessons from the Past." Pp. 33–49 in *Privatizing Correctional Institutions,* G. W. Bowman, S. Hakim, and P. Seidenstat, eds. New Brunswick, Conn.: Transaction.

Ethridge, Philip A., and James W. Marquart (1993). "Private Prisons in Texas: The New Penology for Profit." *Justice Quarterly* 10 (1):30–48.

Fasenfest, D. (1986). "Using Produce Incentives to Achieve Social Objectives: An Assessment of the Marketplace and Public Policies." *Policy Studies Review* 5 (February):634–42.

Feeley, S., and J. Simon (1992). "The New Penology: Notes on the Emerging Strategy of Corrections and Its Implications." *Criminology* 30 (4):449–74.

Florida Corrections Commission (1996). *Project: Identify Costs and Quality of Service Factors Relating to Privatization of State Prisons.* Tallahassee, Fla.: OPPAGA.

Folz, David H., and John M. Scheb, II (1989). "Prisons, Profits and Politics: The Tennessee Privatization Experiment." *Judicature* 73 (2):98–102.

Gandy, J., and L. Hurl (1987). "Private Sector Involvement in Prison Industries: Options and Issues." *Canadian Journal of Criminology* 29:185–204.

Gilbert, Michael J. (1996a). "Private Confinement and the Role of Government in a Civil Society." Pp. 13–20 in *Privatization and the Provision of Correctional Services: Context and Consequences,* G. Larry Mays and Tara Gray, eds. Cincinnati: Academy of Criminal Justice Sciences (ACJS) and Anderson Publishing.

―――― (1996b). "Making Privatization Decisions Without Getting Burned: A Guide for Understanding the Risks." Pp. 61–73 in *Privatization and the Provision of Correctional Services: Context and Consequences,* G. Larry Mays and Tara Gray, eds. Cincinnati: Academy of Criminal Justice Sciences (ACJS) and Anderson Publishing.

Grosser, George H. (1969). "External Setting and Internal Relations of the Prison." P. 11 in *Prison within Society*, L. Hazelrigg, ed. Garden City, N.Y.: Anchor Books.

Harrison, E., and M. Gosse (1985). *Privatization: A Restraint Initiative. Policy Report.* Victoria: British Columbia Ministry of Correction.

Hobsbawm, Eric (1994). *The Age of Extremes: A History of the World, 1914–1991.* New York: Pantheon Books.

Johnson, Byron R., and Paul P. Ross (1990). "The Privatization of Correctional Management: A Review." *Journal of Criminal Justice* 18:351–58.

Johnson, Judith (1985). "Should Adult Correctional Facilities Be Privately Managed?" *National Sheriff* 38 (2):18–21.

Keating, J. M. (1990). "Public over Private: Monitoring the Performance of Privately Operated Prisons and Jails." Pp. 87–94 in *Private Prisons and the Public Interest*, D. C. McDonald, ed. New Brunswick, N.J.: Rutgers University Press.

Kinkade, Patrick T., and Matthew C. Leone (1992). "The Privatization of Prisons: The Wardens' Views." *Federal Probation* 56 (4):58–65.

Koldrie, T. (1986). "The Two Different Concepts of Privatization." *Public Administration Review* 46 (July–August):285–91.

Krulwich, Andrew S. (1981). "Cost-Benefit Evolves under Regulators, Legislators." *Legal Times of Washington*, June 8, pp. 12–13.

Lampkin, Linda M. (1991). "Does Crime Pay? AFSCME Reviews the Record on the Privatization of Prisons." *Journal of Contemporary Criminal Justice* 7 (1):41–48.

Leonard, H. B. (1990). "Private Time: The Political Economy of Private Prison Finance." Pp. 48–60 in *Private Prisons and the Public Interest*, D. C. McDonald, ed. New Brunswick, N.J.: Rutgers University Press.

Lewis, W. D. (1965). *From Newgate to Dannemora*. Ithaca, N.Y.: Columbia University Press.

Lilly, J. Robert, and Paul Knepper (1992). "An International Perspective on the Privatization of Corrections." *Howard Journal* 31 (3):174–91.

Logan, Charles H. (1990). *Private Prisons Cons and Pros*. New York: Oxford University Press, 1990.

Luttwak, Edward (1996). "The Middle Class Backlash: Turbo-Charged Capitalism and Its Consequences." *Harper's Magazine*, May, pp. 48–60.

Maghan, Jess (1991). "Privatization of Corrections: Anticipating the Unanticipated." Pp. 135–49 in *Perspectives on Deviance: Dominance, Degradation and Denigration*, Robert J. Kelly and Donald E. J. MacNamara, eds. Cincinnati: Anderson Publishing.

——— (1995). "Terrorist Mentality." Unpublished keynote presentation, Fifth European Conference of Law and Psychology, Budapest, Hungary, September 2.

——— (1997). "Training Cannot Do What Management Cannot Do: The Evolvement of Centralized Training in Modern Correctional Services." *Corrections Management Quarterly* 1 (1): 40–48.

Matthews, Roger (1989). *Privatizing Criminal Justice*. Thousand Oaks, Calif.: Sage Publishers.

——— (1990). "New Directions in the Privatization Debate?" *Probation Journal* 37 (2):50–59.

McConville, Sean (1987). "Aid from Industry? Private Corrections and Prison

Crowding." In *America's Correctional Crisis: Prison Populations and Public Policy*, S. Gottfredson and S. McConville, eds. Westport, Conn.: Greenwood Press.

McDonald, Douglas C. (1989). "The Cost of Corrections: In Search of the Bottom Line." *Research in Corrections* 2:1–6.

—— (1990a). "When Government Fails: Going Private as a Last Resort." Pp. 179–99 in *Private Prisons and the Public Interest*, D. McDonald, ed. New Brunswick, N.J.: Rutgers University Press.

—— (1990b). "The Costs of Operating Public and Private Correctional Facilities." Pp. 28–37 in *Private Prisons and the Public Interest*, D. C. McDonald, ed. New Brunswick, N.J.: Rutgers University Press.

—— (1994). "Public Imprisonment by Private Means: The Reemergence of Private Prisons and Jails in the United States, the United Kingdom, and Australia." *British Journal of Criminology* 34:29–48. (Special issue)

McKelvey, B. (1977). *American Prisons: A History of Good Intentions*. Montclair, N.J.: Patterson Smith.

Morris, Norval, and David J. Rothman, eds. (1995). *The Oxford History of the Prison: The Practice of Punishment in Western Society*. New York: Oxford University Press.

Mullen J., K. Chaotar, and D. Cartow (1985). *The Privatization of Corrections*. Washington, D.C.: National Institute of Justice.

Prison Reform Trust (1996). *The Penal Lexicon Home Page*. United Kingdom, September 15:12–14.

Robbins, Ira (1988). *The Legal Dimensions of Incarceration*. Washington, D.C.: American Bar Association.

Silvester, Deanna Buckley (1990). "Ethics and Privatization in Criminal Justice: Does Education Have a Role to Play?" *Journal of Criminal Justice* 18:65–70.

Smith, Phil (1993). "Private Prisons: Profits of Crime." *Convert Action Quarterly* 18 (2):26–46.

Sparks, Richard (1996). "Penal 'Austerity': The Doctrine of Less Eligibility Reborn?" Pp. 74–93 in *Prison 2000: An International Perspective on the Current State and Future of Imprisonment*, R. Matthews and P. Francis, eds. New York: St. Martin's.

Starr, Paul (1987). "The Limits of Privatization." In *Prospects for Privatization*, vol. 36, no. 3, S. H. Hanks, ed. New York: Proceedings of the Academy of Political Science.

Stolz, Barbara Ann (1997). "Privatizing Corrections: Changing the Corrections Policy-Making Subgovernment." *Prison Journal* 77 (1):92–111.

Sullivan, Harold J. (1989). "Privatization of Corrections and the Constitutional Rights of Prisons." *Federal Probation* 53 (2):36–42.

—— (1993). "Privatization of Corrections: A Threat to Prisoners' Rights." Pp. 139–55 in *Privatizing Correctional Institutions*, G. W. Bowman, S. Hakim, and P. Seidenstat, eds. New Brunswick, N.J.: Transaction Publishers.

Sullivan, John (1995). "Six Guards in New Jersey Charged with Beating Jailed Immigrants." *New York Times*, October 14: A12.

United States General Accounting Office (1991). *Private Prisons: Cost Savings and BOP's Statutory Authority Need to Be Resolved*, GAO/GGD-91-21.

Walker, Donald B. (1994). "Privatization in Corrections." Pp. 570–85 in *Correctional*

Counseling and Treatment, P. C. Krateoski, ed. Prospect Heights, Ill.: Waveland Press.

Wolfe, A. (1989). *Whose Keeper? Social Science and Moral Obligation.* Los Angeles: University of California Press.

Case Cited

Richardson v. McKnight, No. 96–318, U.S. Supreme Court (1997).

5

Managing to Prevent Prison Suicide

Are Staff at Risk Too?

Alison Liebling

Possibly if they had more consideration for the prison officer, they would get more value back from them. We do a very hard job. I'm not saying I don't like it, I do. I enjoy dealing with people. It's the best job I've ever had. But I do wish that people outside were more concerned about us. We're only a member of the public doing our job. We seem to be isolated from the public, and if anything happens, they think it's us that's done it.

—prison officer

Prisons are closed and total institutions. Their populations do not constitute a credible interest group. . . . In the last analysis, the control exercised over them is bluntly coercive; and considerations of control and security . . . dictate a great degree of secrecy in their operation. Mundane aspects of life, such as access to lawyers or relatives, communication in general, and a whole range of issues from sanitation to sexual activity, are subject to detailed regulation by prison staff. . . . All these features of prison life indicate that extensive discretion is exercised over every aspect of inmates' existence. The volume of such decisions, their detailed nature and the extent to which they are taken in camera, indicates a need for a correspondingly far-reaching and detailed system of accountability.

—Maguire, Vagg, and Morgan, 1985

Introduction

Nowhere are issues of accountability more urgent than in the case of deaths in custody. Prisons represent a most extreme form of state power. It is a basic requirement of democracy and justice that staff and management be answerable to the public as to the exercise of such power. Achieving effective accountability in prison is a highly complex and poorly understood process (see Morgan, 1993; also Maguire, Vagg, and Morgan, 1985). In the case of any death in custody in the U.K., a full and public inquest must be held (Jervis, 1993) in front of a jury, in order to establish certain facts: the identity of the deceased, the cause of death, and the circumstances surrounding the death. In *Regina v. South London Coroner*, ex parte Thompson (1982), Lord Lane argued: "The function of an inquest is to seek out and record as many of the facts concerning the death as the public interest requires" (see also Broderick, 1971; Jervis, 1993:6). It is "not the purpose of a coroner's inquest to provide a forum for attempts to gather evidence for pending or future criminal or civil proceedings" (Jervis, 1993:7; *R. v. Poplar Coroner's Court*). Verdicts cannot be "framed in such a way as to appear to determine any question of criminal liability *on the part of a named person* or civil liability" (Owen, 1991).

Criticisms of this inquisitorial process include the use of uncontrolled discretion by coroners, including the choice of witnesses, the questions asked, and the order in which witnesses are called; the lack of access for families to primary evidence and official inquiry reports; the undemocratic appointment of coroners; the inadequate training of coroners; the denial of legal aid to families wishing to be represented; and the close relationship between coroners and their officers and the state representatives being investigated (see Coles and Ward, 1994; Hogan et al., 1988; Owen, 1991; Scraton and Chadwick, 1987).

Despite the validity of the arguments raised above, a major omission in debates about accountability in relation to prison suicide, particularly concerning the arena of the inquest and its role in securing such accountability, has been the lack of any attempt to gain an understanding of the perspective of the prison staff who appear at such inquests—those at the sharp end of events, policies, procedures, and often—of public and academic criticism. Their accounts have been missing from a debate that has been polarized between, on the one hand, critics (see Benn and Walpole, 1986; Coles and Ward, 1994; Hogan et al., 1988; Institute of Race Relations, 1991; Scraton and Chadwick, 1987) and on the other, albeit silently, the state.

In the U.K. since 1987, prison suicide inquests have become more complex and in many respects more significant in their impact upon policy and practice in relation to suicide prevention in prison. Prison staff have an increasingly complex and detailed set of procedures to follow in order to identify and manage prisoners who may appear to be at risk of suicide (see Home Office, 1987; Prison Service, 1994a, 1994b). These procedures may fail to achieve their aims—prisoners at risk are notoriously difficult to identify (see Liebling, 1992). Staff do not feel especially confident that the identification of suicide risk is a skill they possess or can easily acquire (see Liebling, 1992; Liebling and Krarup, 1993). Once—and if—identified, communication of this information, observation of the prisoner, and the provision of various forms of support may not exclude the possibility of suicide. If a suicide does occur, staff may be affected by feelings of guilt, shock, anxiety, and depression both at the time of the death and surrounding the inquest proceedings, at which searching questions are asked, emotional scenes may occur, and different participants may come with agendas the inquest is not intended to satisfy (see Prison Service, 1994a). Inquests may take place several months after the death, thus exposing all those concerned—families and staff—to lengthy periods of uncertainty and anxiety.

This chapter considers prison suicide inquests from the perspective of prison staff. This is not to say that the experiences of families are insignificant or that the calls for more accountability for coroners are unjustified. On the contrary, the urgent case for fairer treatment for families at inquests has been put and requires little further elaboration here. Campaigns aimed at challenging aspects of policy, procedure, and practice have succeeded in bringing about major changes in the way families are treated, information is released, and in the way in which inquests are conducted (Coles and Ward, 1994; Prison Service, 1994a, 1994b). The case for reform of inquest proceedings in relation to the autonomy of coroners is equally pertinent (see Scraton and Chadwick, 1987). More complex, and consistently overlooked in the prison suicide literature, are the ways in which inquest proceedings may expose prison officers to feelings of individual accountability in a way that is potentially damaging and that may in fact secure compliance to a set of instructions in a way that is not always in the best interests of the "at risk" prisoner. Just as in any assessment of the effects of imprisonment on prisoners, fear of violence may be as significant as actual violence (see Hay and Sparks, 1992); in any proper evaluation of the concept of accountability, fear of being held accountable may be as significant in determining staff behavior as formal mechanisms and procedures, however heavily weighted these formal procedures may actually be in favor of the state. This recognition of staff feelings of vulnerability does not detract from the case for improvements in methods of accountability in prison. On the contrary, it illustrates the need for formal and detailed procedures that are clearly understood not just by those outside the prison system (prisoners' families, the general public, commentators, and so forth) but also by those working within it (staff and managers, policy makers) or alongside it (coroners, the probation and social services, police, and lawyers).

The Problem of Prison Suicide

In England and Wales there were 387 self-inflicted deaths by prisoners being held in prison department establishments between 1988 and 1995 inclusive (Liebling and Krarup, 1993; Prison Service, 1992). These deaths were distributed as shown in table 5-1.

The suicide rate in prisons in England and Wales is between 40 and 80 per

Table 5-1. Self-Inflicted Deaths in Prison in England and Wales, 1988–1995

	Adult Male	Under 21 Male	Female	TOTAL
1988	28	9	0	37
1989	35	11	2	48
1990	39	10	1	50
1991	37	5	0	42
1992	33	6	2	41
1993	43	3	1	47
1994	51	10	1	62
1995	49	9	2	60

Sources: Prison Service, 1992; Liebling and Krarup, 1993.

100,000 prisoners, or about four times that of the general population (Dooley, 1990a; HMCIP, 1990; Liebling, 1992, 1994). When equivalent populations are compared, it is found that the prison suicide rate is still higher than would be expected among equivalent groups in the community (Liebling, 1992; O'Mahony, 1994; Winfree, 1985). Factors relating to the prison environment (including peer pressures, isolation, loneliness, lack of contact with outside, lack of activity, and breakdown in relationships) have been found to be related to a high proportion of these suicides (Backett, 1987; Dooley, 1990a; Liebling, 1992; Liebling and Krarup, 1993; Lloyd, 1990; Wool and Dooley, 1987). It is likely that most officers will be directly involved in a prison suicide during their career and that many will be directly involved in several.

Prison staff interviewed during the course of two long-term research projects investigating the causes of suicides and suicide attempts in prison (see Liebling, 1992; Liebling and Krarup, 1993) were eager to describe their experiences, often commenting that this was their first opportunity to admit such feelings:

I'm sure you never feel comfortable, especially when you come across a suicide. My first set of nights here, I cut down six attempts and found about four or five slashings in one seven night period. There was about six in the first four nights, actually. That was when there were twelve hundred prisoners here. One or two of them were very serious. When we were getting so many, it was possible that there were only four staff and myself on duty, and we'd all be attending to one, then somebody else does it at the same time—you can't attend everywhere. We were lucky to get there in time. They can be very upsetting, actually. (principal officer)

During this period of research, 210 prison staff were interviewed formally, several prison suicide inquests were attended (some lasting several days), and informal, lengthy discussions were carried out with staff at all levels. The main focus of the research was on prisoners. These results have been published elsewhere (Liebling, 1992, 1994; Liebling and Krarup, 1993).

Fifty-six percent of staff interviewed during the second phase of the research had experienced a prisoner suicide, and a further 29 percent had been involved in a serious suicide attempt during their career to date:

Well, yes, one or two come to mind. One was at [prison X]. The prisoner had been locked away at lunch time and we were on patrol. Somebody rang the bell of another cell, he was on his own. We went round there and he'd gouged his neck out with a small stub of pencil and taken the jugular out and there was blood everywhere, the whole ceiling. He'd actually got to the stage . . . he'd committed suicide. He'd lost blood at such a rate that he'd attempted to get to his cell bell and he couldn't reach it on the wall. You saw that vision of his hands trying to reach and coming down the wall. It was not a nice sight. Death leaves that feeling. . . . Another one was a cell fire, this was again over a lunch time lock up. This was at [prison Y]. He was up on the top landing, he'd rang the bell, and there was not many staff there to deal with things so he hadn't had his bell answered straight away. He'd barricaded up and sealed the door and window, with sellotape. (principal officer)

Almost half of the staff reported feeling shocked and upset at the time: "It was shock, just absolute shock. I just couldn't believe it" (principal officer). "I don't know. It was in my formative years as a prison officer. It made me want to pack the job in" (prison officer). "I felt terrible, actually" (senior officer). It was common for prison officers to cope with these feelings using a mixture of denial, humor, increased solidarity with colleagues, and diversion/avoidance (drinking, socializing, smoking, and so forth).

Staff expressed considerable anxiety about the inquest procedures, which put them "in the dock" and expected them to defend each activity, movement, and decision taken during the hours (and sometimes days) leading up to the death. Such a defense took place in unfamiliar, formal territory that resembled the trials of those they confined. Their knowledge and understanding of procedures relating to suicide prevention would be tested, the quality of their judgments considered, and the extent of their communication with the prisoner addressed. Any failure to adhere to instructions, communicate effectively with other staff, or to notice and follow up possible indications of suicide risk would become the focus of intense concern from the coroner. This intense questioning may occur in the context of inadequate training, lack of confidence among officers about their skills in relation to suicide prevention, staff shortages, overcrowding, inadequate medical support, and sometimes quite serious efforts made by the officer concerned to enlist help for the prisoner during the days before his death.

The reality of such an "ordeal" (as it was sometimes described) from the officer's point of view is in stark contrast with accounts presented by critical appraisals of the inquest system, which aim their criticisms (often wholly justifiable) at a structural level while failing to address adequately the experiential level, where both staff and families are in reality located. Both the structural and experiential levels should be fully addressed in order to properly evaluate issues of accountability. In practice, it is staff perceptions of the potential risk of criticism or liability in the inquest that is most likely to determine their behavior regarding at-risk prisoners. Their sense of exposure in this regard may actually inhibit officers from taking risks, from keeping prisoners on a wing where they are in contact with others, or from otherwise becoming actively engaged in the prisoners' management. The instinct to refer the problem to a specialist (health care) service, where little practical or therapeutic help is guaranteed, is felt strongly by staff.

In fact, prison suicide inquests may be very effective in bringing to light areas where policy and practice should be improved. From the point of view of individual officers, it is unlikely that they will fail to follow procedures to the letter or to take sufficient precautions once through the public screening procedure that inquests can provide. The threat of "lack of care" verdicts and of public criticism has been instrumental in spurring several significant changes to policy since 1987. In fact, it is arguable that many of the improvements introduced since 1987 have their history in cases such as the lack of care verdict brought by the jury in the highly publicized case of Jim Heather-Hayes, who was found hanged in his cell at Ashford Remand Centre in 1982 (Home Office, 1984; Scraton and Chadwick, 1987). The jury's verdict may make a significant difference to the outcome of liability claims made by families following such a death, despite the legal direction outlined earlier (Jervis, 1993).

Obviously, from the family's point of view, the inquest may be a far more unsatisfactory form of accountability in retrospect, as they too have to wrestle with formality, direction by the coroner, lack of information, and the exposure to the outcome of a series of investigations that they have no power to influence. It is during inquest proceedings that shortcomings in policy or staff training as to the requirements of this policy may become exposed (Coles and Ward, 1994). Families often find this process traumatic and frustrating. Yet it is officers who feel the impact of their distress.

74

The Experience of Prison Suicide Inquests

On January 18, 1994, an inquest was held into the death of a prisoner found hanged in his cell at 1:30 A.M. on October 17, 1993. The prisoner had been on remand; he was aged thirty-three and had been in the prison only three days at the time of his death. The City Chamber was booked for three days. In the event, only one full day was required. Staff at all levels had had to find and arrange replacements for their posts, prepare to be away for several days, and warn those they worked with that they would be absent. Twenty-five witnesses were called. Staff from the prison, including a doctor, a governor, a senior officer, and two basic grade officers came together in a prison van. All were dressed out of uniform, in their best suits. A senior medical officer and other senior staff attended the inquest for moral support. The City Chamber was filled with family members, police, court officials, legal representatives, a jury of eleven, and members of the public. The parents of the deceased prisoner asked questions of many of the witnesses and were visibly distressed throughout the proceedings. The coroner's questions to the witnesses focused on the questions of, first, how the death came about, and then, secondly and explicitly, whether the death had been potentially avoidable. In the case of self-inflicted deaths both in and out of prison, these questions are complex and problematic (Maltsberger, 1986; Morgan, 1990; Pallis et al., 1988; Sainsbury, 1988). Questions relating to signs of risk, communications with the prisoner, actions taken, notes taken, and information passed on to other staff were asked of officers and specialists at all levels.

This inquest was a relatively straightforward affair. Despite high levels of preparation and support and the knowledge that procedures had been followed professionally and that every effort had been made to revive the prisoner, each officer emerged from his exposure to the witness box looking exhausted, relieved, and under considerable strain. Severe criticism was made of the police handling of the prisoner, as previous knowledge regarding a suicide attempt made eight months earlier had not been passed on to the prison staff. An officer had failed to record this information; it was felt by the coroner that such information, had it been received by the prison reception staff, might have affected the decisions subsequently made about the appropriate location and observation of the prisoner during his first few days in custody. A verdict of "suicide" was brought by the jury. The family intended to bring civil action against the police in the light of the information that emerged during the inquest. Prison officers left feeling that "it could have been them," so difficult is it in the life of a busy remand center to adhere to all instructions, to respond appropriately to what may seem like contradictory information, to make the right decisions, and to take the appropriate steps. This is expected of them in the exercise of the "duty of care" they have for prisoners (see

Livingstone and Owen, 1993; *Knight and Others v. the Home Office and Governor of HMP Brixton*; *R. v. Birmingham and Solihull Coroner*; *R. v. Southwark Coroner* on "duty of care"). Their reality suggests that such a duty may be difficult to define and carry out in all its various aspects without highly professional training—a training officers have often lacked (HMCIP, 1990; Liebling, 1992; Liebling and Krarup, 1993).

At least four identifiable factors act to inhibit staff confidence and professionalism in the performance of their duty of care to prisoners, particularly in relation to the suicidal. Each of these factors contributes to a feeling expressed by staff that they are exposed unfairly at inquests (whatever the structural reality): first, the operational conditions under which they work (overcrowding, high turnover, staff shortages, and so forth); second, the conflict that many prison staff perceive between their security and "welfare" responsibilities; third, and relatedly, the problem of lack of training. Staff knowledge about suicide risk in prison may be perfunctory and inadequate. Only very recently in the U.K. has a clear training strategy based on research findings in the prison context been launched in reponse to growing criticism of procedures and of training and as a result of several highly publicized inquest cases. Finally, and most neglected in previous studies, the damaging sense that staff problems are of no concern to others: "We're the ones who have to put up with this shit. No one gives a damn about us!" (Carroll, 1975). This sense may contribute to denial and avoidance of prisoner problems, or the expression of frustration and other negative attitudes toward prisoners in distress (see Liebling and Krarup, 1993:128-39).

Operational Conditions

What are the operational constraints under which staff perform their "duty of care"? Since 1987, persistent problems of overcrowding have plagued local and remand centers in the U.K., where the highest number of "at risk" prisoners are found (Dooley, 1990a; Liebling, 1992). After a brief respite between 1992 and 1993, a steep rise in the size of the prison population, with no corresponding increase in the number of prison places available, is forecast for the near future (see Cavadino and Dignan, 1992; Home Office, 1993, and Christie, 1993 [in the U.K.]; Zimring and Hawkins, 1994 [elsewhere]). A series of riots and disturbances on an unprecedented scale have left staff shaken and demanding better conditions, increased numbers, and better training (HMCIP, 1990; Stern, 1993; Woolf, 1991). Calls for more constructive and positive regimes from within the new prison service agency and a wide-ranging external review of the many problems of the prison service have signaled welcome improvements to conditions, programs, and training (HMCIP, 1990; Prison Service, 1993, 1994a; Stern, 1993; Woolf, 1991), which will have direct implications for suicide prevention (Liebling, 1994). Market testing and privatization have been introduced on a large scale in order to ensure improvements in "performance" and value for money from existing and new establishments (Fulton, 1989; Sparks, 1994). In this context of population pressures, rapid organizational change, increased monitoring of performance, and constant critical review, prison staff are themselves feeling rather vulnerable (Liebling, 1992). Their feeling is that instructions in one area of their work (prison suicide) have to be seen and interpreted in the light of a number of significant constraints: limited time, conflicting demands, cell shortages, decreasing resources, and lack of access to specialist support. Inquests do not address these contextual issues in sufficient detail, nor with the required expertise: "[They operate] . . . totally out of context in the daily life of an institution—they don't take account of the context, of the busy life of a wing, our other Circulars—on security and control" (senior officer). "Well, it's very difficult really, because sometimes they say that they don't consider them to be a medical problem, they're more of a discipline problem. They say to us, 'Oh, it's personality disorder, we can't do anything about it, because they're not medically ill, they're not mentally ill!' But if people are cutting themselves up and doing all sorts of weird and wonderful things, I mean we sometimes feel completely out of our depth, don't we? Completely" (senior officer).

Conflict Between Custody and Care

A second area of concern is the question of whom staff see as the primary agents of care in relation to prison suicide. This has been confused by the over-medicalization of prison suicide research, training, and procedure in the past (Liebling, 1992; Liebling and Krarup, 1993; Prison Service, 1994a) but is in any case a major problem for prison staff in their approach to all aspects of care. Many officers still see their security and discipline functions in conflict with their "welfare" responsibilities, particularly in relation to the time they have available—this despite increased awareness of the centrality of good relationships between staff and prisoners to security and disciplinary concerns (Dunbar, 1985; Hay and Sparks, 1991; Liebling and Krarup 1993):

> Trouble is, there are so many constraints on time, you tend to put their problems on hold. It's particularly difficult here. Some things, you forget to go back, because something more important crops up: The prison's got to run. You can say, for example, that it'll take half an hour for me and a colleague to slop out a landing, but during that time, if you get a couple of major welfare problems, you can't really do anything about it,

because you've got the landing to slop out. You can't stop what you're doing. (prison officer)

Hay and Sparks argue in their well-received paper in the *Prison Service Journal* (1991) that the particular difficulties and complexities inherent in the role of being a prison officer have been neglected in both theoretical and policy debates (2). Staff feel that their expertise is in security matters; these are the kinds of tasks in which their professionalism and skills tend to be located and judged (see also King and McDermott, 1990). It is partly in this context, of confusion over role, that suicide "prevention" is viewed. Many officers felt that "suicide risk" is an area of specialist responsibility with little scope for their opinion or input: "I don't think we should have to deal with it. We do have to deal with it because they're unpredictable facts of life, but no . . . it should not be our problem. It should be people trained to deal with the depressed and the mentally ill. We're not mental nurses" (prison officer).

Over a quarter of the staff in the two research projects referred to here reported feeling unable to deal with the problems of suicide and suicide attempts; two-thirds argued that they had insufficient training, and a third of those who had received some training felt it did not go far enough (Liebling, 1992; Liebling and Krarup, 1993): "[I've had] . . . National training only at my initial training course, but it was just basically telling you what forms to fill in and what the procedure is" (senior officer). "I thought it was useful. I thought it raised very good discussion points but I don't think we had enough time to give it the attention it needs, because we had one session and that was it. There's been no follow up. It was given by a training officer who went away on a course, so it's what I term second-hand. I think it ought to be given by people who have been involved in that kind of field for a longer period of time" (prison officer).

Prison staff's tendency to locate the causes of suicide almost exclusively in the individual rather than in pressures generated by the environment led to the underestimation of the power they had to effect change for prisoners who were at risk as a result of such pressures (Liebling and Krarup, 1993:130–32; Liebling, 1992: ch. 8). This is a matter of raising awareness of the roles and the responsibilities of all staff. Recent training and policy guidance is aimed at improving this aspect of practice in the U.K. (Prison Service, 1994a and 1994b).

Staff need to be encouraged to see the centrality of their own role in the support, observation, identification, and care of prisoners at risk (see Liebling and Krarup, 1993; Rowan, 1994). They should be trained to value their own contributions and to appreciate the nonpsychiatric aspects of suicide risk in the prison setting (see Liebling, 1992). Some of the staff we spoke to recognized this need: "I don't think you can treat suicide prevention as a bolt-on extra. I don't think it's like a go-faster stripe you put down your car. It's got to be an intrinsic part of the care and routine of the establishment. . . . You've got to have an atmosphere where they can talk to people about their problems; you've got to have good access to people outside, including uncensored mail, telephone calls, visits" (prison governor).

It was clear from our research, however, that insufficient attention had been paid to the relationship between staff responsibilities for security, care, and justice (cf. Woolf, 1991). The difficulties encountered in achieving the right balance between these tasks were made even more complex by competing signals, instructions, and training needs emerging from different parts of the prison service, from the news media, and from official reports.

Staff Problems and Suicides

A growing interest in stress among occupational groups has been matched by a growing awareness of the sometimes excessive levels of stress and anxiety suffered by prison officers, particularly in the event of riots and disturbances (Staples, 1990; Woolf, 1991), hostage-taking incidents (Bowden, 1991; Stern, 1993), and threats, but also during the course of their general work (for example, Bagshaw and Baxter, 1987; Cheek and Miller, 1983; Duffee, 1974; Gerstein et al., 1987; Launay and Fielding, 1989; Long et al., 1986; OPCS, 1985; Poole and Regoli, 1980; Stern, 1993; Thomas, 1972; and Thomas and Pooley, 1981). It is more recently that the impact of suicide attempts and suicides have been considered (Liebling, 1992; Liebling and Krarup, 1993). Support and counseling is now offered to staff discovering a body, failing to revive a prisoner, or otherwise directly affected by a suicide (see Prison Service, 1994a and 1994b). Sickness levels have been a major concern to management charged with providing efficient and effective services to prisoners (Home Office, 1992). Whatever the original motivation, staff "welfare" issues are at last on the reform agenda.

Perhaps of most interest here is the question of prison staff suicide, itself a clear indication of the need for greater emphasis to be placed on staff perceptions of their role both in general and in the particular case of prison suicides. Prison staff in both research projects reported high levels of stress, depression, poor physical health, and sense of isolation. Ninety-five percent of the staff interviewed reported that in their view, prison staff suffered from unreasonable levels of stress in the job:

They do. I've one off at the moment. A good lad, must have about fifteen years' service in; he's seen it all, done it all. A fortnight ago he was good as gold on the landings, yet he's suddenly gone off with anxiety. He's been in touch with the Governor; he just can't face coming in at the moment, the pressures have got to him. So you do get it. Different people might go home and start drinking; there's all sorts of ways. (principal officer)

Almost two-thirds of the staff thought that the main cause of staff stress was "the nature of the job." Feeling individually accountable was one of the significant stressors:

Oh of course they do. . . . The ones who deny it are the ones who are under the biggest strain. . . . It's perhaps a feeling of isolation. Every time something goes wrong there's an inquiry and then a form comes down and the staff think at the end of the day, is that all my personal worth is—a form? There's not enough problem-solving on a personal basis, you can't talk to anybody. . . . So at the end of the day you probably take everything home, which is one of the reasons why there are so many divorces. Or I know a lot of staff who turn to drink, and there's a lot of sickness. (prison officer)

Some of the staff identified some of the operational problems identified above as being central to the levels of stress they experienced "just trying to get the job done." "My job? Well, it depends what job you're on . . . dealing with a thousand and one requests: private cash, visits, legal aid and all that. Between food and water, there are all these things to do" (prison officer). These reflections and frustrations were important in understanding some of the apparently "hardened attitudes" of staff toward suicide and suicide attempts reported by prisoners:

I think it's the nature of the job. You're dealing quite long hours with other people's problems. You go home, and especially when the kids are young, you're too tired to look after your own family. So you're doing it under stress, and you're probably dealing with your family harsher than you would inmates. You get no time to recover—you're doing exactly the same job when you get home. Twenty-four hours a day, you're dealing with other people's problems. You have to learn to accommodate certain pressures—to deflect the ones that, in your opinion, don't matter, and you deal with or absorb the ones that do. . . . When you're younger, it's a case of absorbing the lot. Staff get used to self-injury. I remember my first self-injury, I just panicked. I would be like a normal outsider, I didn't know what to do. Now, I don't. . . . You learn to accommodate the situation. The SS got used to murdering the Jews, didn't they? In the end, it didn't mean anything. (prison officer)

Such extreme analogies are important in understanding how "lack of care" in the handling of prisoners may come about in an important sociological sense untouched by questions from coroners (Toch and Klofas, 1982). How far can individual officers be held accountable for holding such views? Bauman shows dramatically in his *Modernity and the Holocaust* (1989) how modern institutions with their managerial and bureaucratic ethos distance individuals in a way that makes brutality possible or even inevitable. Aspects of prison life (the use of a "Body Book" to sign for handing over prisoners; the use of seclusion in stripped conditions for suicidal prisoners) occasionally make Bauman's thesis seem credible. Who is accountable for the emergence of such a context, in which care and concern for the prisoner become so difficult to secure?

Almost half of the staff we interviewed knew officers who had committed suicide. A further 10 percent knew officers who had attempted suicide (Liebling and Krarup, 1993). Others knew officers who had contemplated suicide, and one or two talked with us at length about their own (in one case, current) thoughts of suicide. Two staff members told us they had made suicide attempts:

> I know two that's actually done it, and three or four what's either been unsuccessful or who've contemplated it. One, young lad, was domestic. One was partly work related. You never know, had they been in a manual job they may have been able to cope with their difficulties better than being in a stress job. I realized that after being off for two months myself. When I got rid of it all and thought, you can see why people get fed up. You don't realize it until you've been away from it for a long time. (prison officer)

Staff talked about feeling isolated and unsupported at these times and about how unable they had been to find anyone to listen to them. Unsupported staff will leave prisoners unsupported. In a coroner's court, staff are never asked about the difficulties they face in their work, or about the suicides they have prevented.

Conclusions

Most of our accounts of the role of staff in cases of custodial deaths are written from a critical perspective (Benn and Walpole, 1986; Coles and Ward, 1994; Hogan et al., 1988; Institute of Race Relations, 1991; Scraton and Chadwick, 1987). They have often been concerned with the general category of controversial deaths in police and prison custody, which include suicides and apparent suicides, but which also raise slightly different and more complex issues. Such accounts have been significant in bringing injustices to light, in alerting the public to an issue of considerable concern, and in steering prison, police, and other authorities toward improvements in practice.

They have focused on structural and organizational aspects of inquest procedures (Scraton and Chadwick, 1987), on suicide prevention procedures, and on unprofessional behavior by staff, arguing convincingly that issues of discretion and power are uneven and that ineffective accountability is the inevitable result of such an imbalance. While not wishing to take issue with this basic point and while acknowledging the deplorable exposure of prisoners' families to the idiosyncratic style of individual coroners, there has been a missing dimension to the debate about prison suicide inquests. Staff perceptions of their own accountability in inquest situations can leave them feeling defensive, resentful, and exposed. Officers have long memories, and perceived injustices or instances of unfair criticism in a public arena may reduce their behavior to an obsession with procedures. The question of whether all or even most prison suicides are in fact potentially avoidable is a crucial and as yet largely unresolved issue, with or without suicide prevention procedures.

In fact, prison suicide procedures have until very recently (and in many jurisdictions) been largely ineffective and arguably inhumane in their application to prisoners at risk of suicide. They have consisted largely of intermittent observation, isolation in stripped conditions, and the removal of all possessions from cells. Families more informed about the limitations of such forms of "care" may not have wished staff to stick rigidly to such procedures in the best interests of their imprisoned relative. This call for strict adherence to what may be ineffective procedures is often all that families have. Their only method for expressing their distress, their sense of powerlessness, and their anger is to search for disparity between actions and instructions. So inquest proceedings are dominated by the effort to demonstrate using all the available evidence whether or not procedures have been followed to the core. Whether such procedures operationalize officers' "duty of care" has never been at issue in the arena of the coroner's court. For staff trying to prevent suicides, minimize risk, maintain contact with the prisoner, and continue with their normal duties, this disparity may be all too obvious.

There is an overwhelming case, already argued elsewhere, for effective accountability in the event of a prison death:

Beyond the basic human concern that attends the death of any fellow human being, the issue is a serious public concern for two major . . . reasons. State agencies are charged with particular public responsibilities and equipped with considerable public resources, and what are often extensive powers, to manage and coerce the lives of others in their care or custody. The vesting of such powers and responsibilities must be coupled with appropriate mechanisms of public accountability. A death is the most serious consequence that may result from state activity or omission in relation to those in its charge. It must always be an occasion for inquiring into the circumstances surrounding the death, . . . for identifying the diverse factors contributing to such deaths in the hope of being able to rectify . . . at least some of them.

A second reason for examining such deaths with particular care is that death is . . . the most serious outcome of brutality, neglect or excessive zeal; it is not the only one. The incidence and nature of deaths at the hands of the state may tell us a great deal about the general quality of state institutions and practices. . . . A closer examination of such deaths may suggest what needs to be done to enhance the quality of these institutions and practices, or in many cases radically reform them. (Hogan et al., 1988:6)

There are dangers, however, in too rigid a system of procedures in this highly complex and sensitive area of human life and state power. Staff may actually perform their "duty of care" more professionally when they have the confidence, the training, the support, and the permission to apply discretion, to take informed risks, and to tailor their response to an individual's situation. At present, "not following the rules" is too great a risk for staff to take in the light of their experiences of inquests. The rules are at last being rewritten in order to facilitate a certain amount of discretion, joint decision making, and nonspecialist opinion in the new prison service strategy on suicide awareness. These changes are likely to bring about problems of their own. The unearthed problem in relation to accountability in the case of prison suicide prevention is how to structure the use of such discretion in order to secure compliance with a real and meaningful "duty of care" and then how to measure and evaluate its use.

Note

I would like to thank Helen Krarup, formerly a research associate at the Institute of Criminology, Cambridge, and David Neal of the Directorate of Inmate Activities, Prison Service, for their help throughout the research and in preparing the ideas included in this essay.

References

Backett, S. (1987). "Suicides in Scottish Prisons." *British Journal of Psychiatry* 151:218–21.

——— (1988). "Suicide and Stress in Prison." Pp. 70–84 in *Imprisonment Today*, S. Backett, J. McNeil, and A. Yellowless, eds. London: Macmillan.

Bagshaw, M. (1988). "Suicide Prevention Training: Lessons from the Corrections Service of Canada." *Prison Service Journal* 70:5–6.

Bagshaw, M., and K. Baxter (1987). "Interactive Skills Training for Prison Officers." Pp. 167–80 in *Applying Psychology to Imprisonment*, B. J. McGurk, D. M. Thornton, and M. Williams, eds. London: HMSO.

Bauman, Z. (1989). *Modernity and the Holocaust*. London: Polity Press.

Benn, M., and K. Walpole (1986). *Death in the City*. London: Canary Press.

Bowden, P. (1991). "Drinking at Work." *Prison Service Journal* 83:37–39.

Broderick Report (1971). *Death and Certification of Coroners*. London: Cmnd. 4810 HMSO.

Carroll, L. (1975). *Hacks, Blacks and Cons: Race Relations in a Maximum Security Prison*. Lexington, Mass.: Heath.

Cavadino, M., and J. Dignan (1992). *The Penal System: An Introduction*. London: Sage.

Cheek, F., and M. D. S. Miller (1983). "The Experience of Stress for Prison Officers: A Double-Bind Theory of Correctional Stress." *Journal of Criminal Justice* 11:105–20.

Christie, N. (1993). *Crime Control as Industry*. London: Routledge.

Coles, D., and T. Ward (1994). "Failure Stories: Prison Suicide and How Not to Prevent Them." Pp. 127–42 in *Deaths in Custody: International Perspectives*, A. Liebling and T. Ward, eds. London: Whiting and Birch.

Dexter, P. (1993). *Suicide Attempts at Highpoint Prison*. Unpublished master's thesis, Birbeck College.

Dooley, E. (1990a). "Prison Suicide in England and Wales 1972–1987." *British Journal of Psychiatry* 156:40–45.

——— (1990b). "Non-natural Deaths in Prison." *British Journal of Criminology* 30 (2):229–34.

Duffee, D. (1974). "The Correctional Officer and Organisational Change." *Journal of Research in Crime and Delinquency* 11 (2):155–79.

Dunbar, I. (1985). *A Sense of Direction*. London: Prison Department Report, Home Office.

Fulton, R. (1989). "Private Sector Involvement in the Remand System." Pp. 1–11 in *Punishment for Profit?*, M. Farrell, ed. London: ISTD.

Gerstein, L., C. Topp, and G. Correll (1987). "The Role of the Environment and Person When Predicting Burnout among Correctional Personnel." *Criminal Justice and Behaviour* 14 (3):352–69.

Hay, W., and J. R. Sparks (1991). "What Is a Prison Officer?" *Prison Service Journal* 83:2–7.

——— (1992). "Vulnerable Prisoners: Risk in Long-Term Prisons." Pp. 301–25 in *Criminal Justice: Theory and Practice*, A. K. Bottomley et al., eds. London: British Society of Criminology.

Hayes, L. (1994). "Jail Suicide Prevention in the USA: Yesterday, Today and Tomorrow." Pp. 196–203 in *Deaths in Custody: International Perspcetives*, A. Liebling and T. Ward, eds. London: Whiting and Birch.

HMCIP (1990). *Report on a Review by Her Majesty's Chief Inspector of Prisons For*

England and Wales of Suicide and Self-Harm in Prison Service Establishments in England and Wales. London: HMSO.

Hogan, M., D. Brown, and R. Hogg (1988). *Death in the Hands of the State.* New South Wales: Redfern Legal Centre Publishing.

Home Office (1984). *Suicides in Prison.* Report by HM Chief Inspector of Prisons. London: HMSO.

—— (1987). *Suicide Prevention.* Circular Instruction 3/1987. London: HMSO.

—— (1992). *Managing Sick Absence.* London: HMSO.

—— (1993). *Criminal Justice Digest.* London: HMSO.

Institute of Race Relations (1991). *Deadly Silence: Black Deaths in Custody.* London: Institute of Race Relations.

Jervis, J. (1993). *On Coroners.* London: Sweet and Maxwell.

King, R. D., and K. McDermott (1990). "My Geranium is Subversive: Some Notes on the Management of Trouble in Prisons." *British Journal of Sociology* 41 (4):445–71.

Langlay, G. E., and N. M. Bayatti (1984). "Suicide in Exe Vale Hospital, 1972–1981." *British Journal of Psychiatry* 145:463–67.

Launay, G., and P. Fielding (1989). "Stress among Prison Officers: Some Empirical Evidence Based on Self-Report." *Howard Journal* 28(2):138–48.

Liebling, A. (1992). *Suicides in Prison.* London: Routledge.

—— (1994). "Suicides Amongst Women Prisoners." *Howard Journal* 33 (1):1–9.

Liebling, A., and H. Krarup (1993). *Suicide Attempts in Male Prisons.* London: Home Office.

Livingstone, S., and T. Owen (1993). *Prison Law: Text and Materials.* Oxford: Clarendon Press.

Lloyd, C. (1990). *Suicide in Prison: A Literature Review.* Home Office Research Study 115. London: HORPU.

Long, N., G. Shouksmith, K. Vogues, and S. Roache (1986). "Stress in Prison Staff: An Occupational Study." *Criminology* 24 (2):331–45.

Maguire, M., J. Vagg, and R. Morgan (1985). *Accountability and Prisons.* London: Tavistock.

Maltsberger, J. T. (1986). *Suicide Risk: The Termination of Clinical Judgement.* New York: New York University Press.

Morgan, G. (1990). *Persons at Risk of Suicide: Guidelines on Good Clinical Practice.* Nottingham: Boots PLC.

Morgan, R. (1993). "Prisons Accountability Revisited." *Public Law* (summer): 314–32.

Office of Population Census and Surveys. (1985). *Staff Attitudes in the Prison Service.* London: OPCS.

O'Mahony, P. (1994). "Prison Suicide Rates: What Do They Mean?" Pp. 45–57 in *Deaths in Custody: International Perspectives,* A. Liebling and T. Ward, eds. London: Whiting and Birch.

Owen, T., and L. Haines (1991). "Surviving Inquests." *Solicitors Journal* 135: 1168–69.

Pallis, D. J. (1988). "Open Forum Discussion." In *The Clinical Management of Suicide*

Risk, G. Morgan, ed. Proceedings of a Conference held at the Royal Society of Medicine, London.

Poole, E. D., and R. M. Regoli (1980). "An Analysis of the Determinants of Juvenile Court Dispositions." *Juvenile and Family Court Journal* 31 (3):23–32.

Power, K. G., and A. P. Spencer (1987). "Parasuicidal Behaviour of Detained Scottish Young Offenders." *International Journal of Offender Therapy and Comparative Criminology* 31 (3):227–35.

Prison Service (1992). *The Way Forward: Caring for Prisoners at Risk of Suicide and Self-Injury*. An Information Paper. London: Home Office.

—— (1993). *Doing Time or Using Time*. London: HMSO.

—— (1994a). *Caring for the Suicidal in Custody: A Training Pack*. London: Home Office.

—— (1994b). *Caring for the Suicidal in Custody: A Resource Pack*. London: Home Office.

Rowan, J. (1994). "The Prevention of Suicide in Custody." Pp. 166–74 in *Deaths in Custody: International Perspectives*, A. Liebling and T. Ward, eds. London: Whiting and Birch.

Sainsbury, P. (1988). "Suicide Prevention—An Overview." Pp. 3–6 in *The Clinical Management of Suicide Risk*, G. Morgan, ed. Proceedings of a conference held at the Royal Society of Medicine, London.

Scraton, P., and K. Chadwick (1987). *In the Arms of the Law*. London: Pluto Press.

Sparks, J. R. (1994a). "Suicides in Prison by Alison Liebling." A review in *British Journal of Criminology* 34 (1):61–62.

—— (1994b). "Can Prisons Be Legitimate? Penal Politics, Privatization and the Timeliness of an Old Idea." *British Journal of Criminology* 34:14–28.

Sperbeck, D. J., and R. R. Parlour (1986). "Screening and Managing Suicidal Prisoners." *Corrective and Social Psychiatry* 32 (3):95–98.

Staples, J. (1990). "Editorial." *Prison Service Journal* 79:1.

Stern, V. (1993). *Bricks of Shame: Britain's Prisons*. 2d ed., rev. London: Penguin.

Thomas, J. E. (1972). *The English Prison Officer since 1850*. London: Routledge and Kegan Paul.

Thomas, J. E., and R. Pooley (1981). *The Exploding Prison: Prison Riots and the Case of Hull*. London: Junction.

Thornton, D. (1990). "Depression, Self-Injury and Attempted Suicide Amongst the YOI Population." Pp. 47–55 in *Proceedings of the Prison Psychologists' Conference*, N. L. Fludger and I. P. Simmons, eds. DPS Report Series 1(34). London: HMSO.

Toch, H. (1992). *Mosaic of Despair: Human Breakdowns in Prisons*. Rev. ed. Washington, D.C.: American Psychological Association.

Toch, H., K. Adams, and D. Grant (1989). *Coping: Maladaptation in Prisons*. New Brunswick: Transaction.

Toch, H., and J. Klofas (1982). "Alienation and Desire for Job Enrichment among Correctional Officers." *Federal Probation* 46 (1):35–47.

Winfree, L. T. (1985). *American Jail Death Rates: A Comparison of the 1978 and 1983 Jail Census Data*. Paper presented at the annual meeting of the American Society of Criminology, San Diego, California.

Wool, R., and E. Dooley (1987). "A Study of Attempted Suicides in Prisons." *Medicine, Science and the Law* 27 (4):297–301.

Woolf, Lord Justice (1991). *Report of an Inquiry into the Prison Disturbances*. London: HMSO.

Zimring, F. E., and G. Hawkins (1994). "The Growth of Imprisonment in California." *British Journal of Criminology* 34:83–96.

Cases Cited

Knight and Others v. the Home Office and Governor of HMP Brixton (1990) 3 All ER 237.

Regina v. Birmingham and Solihull Coroner, ex. parte Secretary of State for the Home Department 155 JP 107.

R. v. Poplar Coroner's Court, ex. parte. Thomas (1993) 3 W. L. R. 485 and 547.

R. v. South London Coroner, ex. parte. Thompson (1982).

R. v. Southwark Coroner, ex. parte. Hicks 2 All ER 140 (1987); 1 W. L. R. 1624.

6

"It's Not Your Fault!"

A Message to Offenders from
Criminal Justice and Corrections

William C. Collins

On a rainy December afternoon in Seattle (is there any other kind?), a lawyer indulges in some self-pity about "ungrateful clients, misanthropic opposing counsel," and other woes attendant to the practice of law (Reisler, 1993). In a mood as gray as the Puget Sound sky, the lawyer ponders the worth of his career. Perhaps because of the season, he lapses into a Dickensian reverie, suddenly finding himself in the presence of a heavenly guardian lawyer.

In convincing the depressed barrister of the value of his legal career, Clarence, the guardian lawyer, takes his earthly client to the state prison, where they see a "young, tattooed felon . . . carving the passage of time into the wall." The lawyer recognizes the man as a former client whom the lawyer successfully represented on a shoplifting charge in a juvenile court proceeding, getting him off scot-free, even though "he was guilty as sin." The lawyer cannot understand why the former client now languishes in the Big House.

Clarence explains. Because in his dream the lawyer chose a career other than law, another attorney represented the young man on the shoplifting charge and lost the case. The result was that the young man was incarcerated, where he learned how to be a criminal and went on to a life of crime. When our hero represented the young man, he was "scared straight" by his brush with the juvenile court and went on to lead an exemplary life.

One lawyer's fantasy. Permit me another, perhaps closer to reality and that reflects the point of this paper.

The juvenile, dodging the bullet of responsibility because of our hero's skillful work in the shoplifting case, leaves the courtroom with a reinforced belief that the criminal justice system cannot and does not hold people accountable for their actions and that a good lawyer's role in life is to help un-

87

convicted criminals stay that way so they can continue to pursue their felonious little plans. The "they can't—or won't—hold me responsible" message from juvenile court was even more impressive to the young man than the similar message he had gotten from the schools, where his athletic prowess more than compensated for his inability to read beyond a fifth grade level.

Buoyed in his belief of criminal invulnerability, the young man moves from shoplifting to more lucrative criminal endeavors, which culminate in his shooting a convenience store clerk with a stolen 9 mm pistol. Good lawyers notwithstanding, he is caught, convicted, and sentenced to death. Since the conviction was only two years ago, he can look forward to perhaps another decade of life in prison as other lawyers pursue appeals and habeas corpus petitions challenging the conviction and the death penalty. During his trial, he heard—and began to believe—his lawyer blaming the schools, abusive parents, poverty, racism, and a drug habit, among other things, for the robbery-murder. In addition of all of these reasons why he wasn't guilty, the youth became further convinced of the injustice of the criminal proceeding because of the various procedural issues his lawyer raised at trial and on appeal, issues that the lawyer said demanded dismissal of the case. The young man didn't understand his lawyer's arguments about broken chains of custody or fruit from poisonous trees, but he certainly understood the lawyer's demand that these mistakes required dismissal of all charges.

As he now languishes on death row, the youth's bitterness toward the criminal justice system and the prison, which have so obviously wronged him, grows. Knowing he is a victim of the criminal justice system, he feels justified in threatening correctional officers, throwing urine on them when they don't comply with his demands and schedule, and suing them over real or imagined slights.

The criminal justice system in general and its corrections component in particular are supposed to hold people responsible for their actions and to encourage them to accept personal responsibility for their actions. But are these goals being accomplished? Is the message the defendant/inmate receives one of responsibility, or that "it's not my fault"?

The person a criminal defendant is closest to in a criminal action is his lawyer. From the time a lawyer first begins to represent a client, through trial, sentencing, and incarceration, the client hears the lawyer offering reasons why the client should not be held accountable, even though the client may have in fact committed the act that is the basis of the government's concern. The reasons for exoneration may be either substantive or procedural. In early 1994, a lawyer in Seattle was trying to push the limits of the battered victim defense to include his client, a man in his twenties charged with shooting a former schoolteacher from across a parking lot. The client was justified in killing the teacher, the argument went, because the teacher allegedly had sexually abused him in years past. There was no current abuse nor current threat of harm. (The argument ultimately failed, and the man was convicted.) In addition to the defendant-as-victim defense in the criminal trial, the defendant also filed a civil suit seeking damages from the school district and others, based on the alleged abuse. The Bobbit and Menendez cases, emblazoned into the American consciousness through extensive news media coverage, are other examples of past victimization being used to "justify" behavior far removed from at least traditional notions of self-defense. A defense based on something called "urban survival syndrome" apparently led to a mistrial in a Texas murder case but was rejected by a jury in a second trial. Despite this setback, the defense will be heard from again.

How much time is consumed in criminal proceedings arguing over alleged procedural mistakes? The search was bad. A confession was improperly obtained. A time limit was exceeded. What the defendant hears in such situations is that because the government made some error (which may or may not have any relevance to guilt), the case should be dismissed and the defendant allowed to go free.

Where the procedural claim is successful and the case is dismissed, does the defendant breathe a sigh of relief at this good fortune and vow never to sin again? Not likely. Even when the claim fails and the defendant is convicted, there is now a reason for the defendant to refuse to accept responsibility.

These sorts of concerns do not end with the criminal trial or appeal, in which the defendant hears and accepts the defense lawyer's claims as to why the defendant should be held blameless. The lessons learned about nonaccountability continue through the rest of any punishment imposed. The prison inmate charged with a disciplinary infraction tries to evade responsibility for his or her behavior—but rarely succeeds—by complaining about procedural errors in the disciplinary process. A classification decision moving an inmate from one institution to another, more secure one is challenged because the decision was not accompanied with enough procedural steps, not because it was incorrect. A mistake by institution staff voids the inmate's responsibility for his or her own behavior.

It is rare for a court to hold a correctional administrator liable for *not* trying to hold an inmate accountable for his or her behavior. It is not rare for a court to hold the same administrator accountable—perhaps for damages—for trying to hold the inmate accountable but making a procedural mistake in the attempt (such as not giving an acceptable reason for refusing to call a witness requested by the inmate in a disciplinary hearing). In such a case, the court is unlikely to ask if the inmate was guilty of the rule violation. Except where a claim of harmless error forces a reviewing court to consider the substantive evidence of guilt, the question of guilt is irrelevant. Where an error is found, the administrator-defendant may be permitted to correct it by holding a new hearing but also may be punished through damages and an order requiring expungement of the record.

While prison administrators must give due process its due, sometimes doing so results in much ado about not very much. Review of a disciplinary hearing decision imposing a sanction of thirty to sixty days in segregation can take years, beginning with a dismissal of the inmate's lawsuit at the trial court level, reversal of that dismissal on appeal, a new trial at the district court, and perhaps yet another appeal. A case in point is *Sandin v. Conner.* This case involved an inmate's protest over thirty days in disciplinary segregation, imposed by Hawaii prison officials in 1987. The inmate claimed that officials had improperly denied his request for witnesses. Although the Supreme Court upheld the decision of the officials, four justices dissented. Had they persuaded one more justice to their position, the case would have been remanded to lower courts for further review of the reasons for denying the witness request.

The criminal justice system of course is not alone in the contradictory ways it deals with—or avoids—imposing responsibility. Members of society as a whole demand accountability of other people or groups of people but struggle mightily to avoid accepting responsibility for their own actions. When "accountability" is measured in six- or seven-figure damage claims and astronomical attorneys' fees, it is easy to see why few people, companies, or agencies (especially those with deep pockets) want to utter the fatal words "I'm sorry; it's my fault." A common way to sidestep responsibility is to argue that other forces or factors contribute to the problem and "until they are addressed, I shouldn't be made a scapegoat."

A variation of the perpetrator-as-victim defense has the accused attacking the accuser. Politicians tell us that the only reason they use negative ads in their campaigns is that they work. How long until this philosophy, bolstered by carefully prepared expert psychological opinion, becomes part of every lawyer's trial arsenal? "Justice" becomes replaced by marketing. While this has always been true to some extent, it is now being scientifically refined, improved, and raised to the level of art.

The perpetrator-as-victim defense (in its increasing number of permutations) may be intellectually understandable to some lawyers, judges, and mental health experts, but it threatens to make the criminal justice system a laughingstock in the eyes of the general public. In addition to eroding the credibility of the system, it sends the public an ever-stronger message that it is easy to avoid responsibility. Even where a perpetrator-as-victim defense fails, it may "succeed" in convincing the perpetrator that "it wasn't my fault." Even if a defense fails in one case, the publicity that attends it helps create a perception that the defense might succeed. Unless such defenses are rejected by courts as a matter of law, defense counsel certainly will continue to offer them, furthering the perception that the key to the criminal justice system is simply a clever lawyer or, as the O. J. Simpson case suggests, having an unlimited supply of money.

Even a defense counsel and civil libertarian with the credentials of Alan Dershowitz expresses concern over what he calls the "abuse excuse," arguing that "we must stop making excuses and start taking responsibility. What is at stake is far more than the punishment of criminals and the deterrence of crime. It is the very nature of our experiment with democracy" (Dershowitz, 1994:13A).

The phenomenon may be an inevitable product of at least the American judicial system, which is always open to taking incremental steps into the trees without realizing, as it does so, that it increasingly loses sight of the forest. Our system, with its reliance on the emotion of juries, experts (of all stripes and ethics), and the courtroom performance skills of lawyers, invites manipulation, form over substance. Why else would a trial lawyers' group schedule a continuing legal-education workshop entitled "Trial as Theater" (Washington Trial Lawyers Association, 1994) and tout it as helping attendees "achieve power in advocacy . . . give a compelling performance . . . maximize jury impact . . . raise the odds of success?"

In the correctional context, the courts' love affair with procedural issues constantly threatens to override the substantive aspects of a given type of decision. The results may be pleasing in the courtroom but also may threaten to paralyze decision making in the institution. Until *Sandin v. Conner* adopted a new test, the "state created liberty interest" test the Supreme Court followed to determine if certain decisions of prison officials were protected by the Due Process Clause produced litigation that focused exclusively on arcane issues about the wording of policies and procedures, *Howard v. Grinage*. Under the state created liberty interest approach, the nature or consequences of a particular type of decision did not determine whether some form of due process protection must accompany the decision. Instead, the question was whether the rules or policies under which the decision is made contain sufficient mandatory terms limiting the criteria upon which a decision may be based, and, perhaps, whether a particular result is mandated if any of those criteria are found, *Kentucky v. Thompson*. In Sandin, the Court recognized that it had created the unhealthy dilemma for officials that saw them increasing their exposure to litigation and liability as a result of trying to write detailed policies and procedures. The new test adopted by the Court for determining if the state has created a liberty interest around a particular action or decision, which can only be made consistent with some level of procedural due process, the so-called "atypical and significant deprivation" test, at least returns the focus to what is being taken away, rather than studying the language of agency rules.

Defense counsel who convince the jury to acquit an otherwise guilty defendant because of what the victim may have done to the defendant years before, or who succeed in obfuscating the facts so that one juror cannot find guilt beyond a reasonable doubt, or who succeed in having a confession suppressed are only doing their job and doing it well by contemporary legal measures. It is someone else's responsibility if the freed defendant goes on to commit more crimes.

The court that requires that a notice and hearing and written record accompany a type of decision a prison may make hundreds or even thousands of times a year is pleased because that decision will, in theory, be made more fairly. The cost, in terms of increased paperwork, administrative appeals, and litigation that accompanies that enhanced fairness, is of no consequence. And the actual increase in fairness may be marginal, at best.

Certainly decisions made throughout the criminal justice system, including corrections, should be made fairly and for adequate reason. But goals of fairness through procedure should not overshadow the substantive decision. As important as is how decisions are made, the *process* should not become more important than the *substance*.

Similarly, it is fair that compelling circumstances that contribute to a criminal act be considered, but should they exonerate the defendant entirely, or should they be considered in sentencing? The goal of imposing responsibility can be lost, or at least frustrated, if the defendant can avoid responsibility by attacking the system or the victim.

Society tries to supplant personal vendettas as a response to criminal behavior by promising the victim that government will impose criminal liability on a perpetrator. Men and women working in corrections are told not to discipline an inmate personally because "the system" will respond to misbehavior. Yet if the various governmental systems that are intended to replace personal vendettas become unable to respond because of the excuses they accept for behavior or because they become so bogged down in procedure, technicality, and delay that they seem unable to reach a decision (consider how many years are consumed in reviewing death penalties), those systems break their fundamental covenant with the people. That the cost of the ticket to ride the court system is beyond the reach of most people only adds to the dissatisfaction and frustration. As the fractures in the covenant grow, the systems lose their ability to serve the people whom they were created to serve. Gradually the people may turn to other systems to meet their needs for public order and accountability. The growth of alternative dispute resolution methods, while commendable, is in part a recognition that courts have become incapable of effectively responding to many legal disputes, particularly when the parties cannot afford to invest tens of thousands of dollars to resolve a thousand-dollar issue.

One may argue that I exaggerate the severity of the issues I describe. I probably do. After all, the urban defense syndrome argument failed. The Menendez brothers were finally convicted. The sexual abuse victim who shot his former assailant from across the parking lot was convicted and may lose his civil suit as well. But even if he does lose both his claims, money, time, and effort will have gone into rebutting them. In the civil case, an insurance carrier will weigh the dollar costs of settlement against the costs of defense and may decide to settle the case because settlement is cheaper than defense. Courts overturn but a microscopic fraction of the hundreds of thousands of prison and jail disciplinary decisions made every year, but, to a large degree, the perception is as important as the reality. More and more people believe that the justice systems, both criminal and civil, are becoming increasingly ineffective at adjudicating cases and dispensing justice that is both fair to the parties and to society at large and holds the right persons accountable for their behavior.

References

Dershowitz, Alan (1994). "Getting Off the Hook." *USA Today,* December 13, p. 13A.

Reisler, Steven A. (1993). "It's a Wonderful Life. And It's Legal Too." *Washington Journal,* December 13, p. 15.

Washington Trial Lawyers Association (1994). "Trial as Theater." Workshop, Seattle, December 9.

Cases Cited

Howard v. Grinage, 6 F.3rd 410 (6th Cir., 1993).

Kentucky v. Thompson, 109 S.Ct. 1904, 1910 (1989).

Sandin v. Conner, 115 S.Ct. 2293 (1995).

7

Responsibility—A Key Word in the Danish Prison System

William Rentzmann

Give a man a fish and you will feed him for one day. Teach him
to fish and you will feed him for the rest of his life.
—Chinese proverb

Introduction

Responsibility is something that all decent people felt in the old days—toward
their closest family, toward their employees, toward the weak. A sense of responsibility was one of the characteristics of a good citizen and was probably
to a high degree a social necessity if the society of that time was to survive.

The Danish author Karen Blixen (*Out of Africa*) was a person of the old
school. Her favorite motto was *"Je responderay"*—I am responsible—I will
give everyone his due. To Karen Blixen, mottoes were of great importance.
She thought that a person influences his or her motto, but more interestingly,
that a motto influences its person. Her whole life, not least the period in Africa, showed that this motto was in her blood.[1] It was a fundamental idea with
her that one had to take responsibility for one's own fate, but at the same
time, as an employer and mistress of a large household, she felt great responsibility toward the many people on the farm who depended on her. One could
argue that her exercise of this responsibility corresponded well with what the
Danish philosopher K. E. Løgstrup called "the ethical demand."

This demand originates from the fact that one always—although to varying degrees—holds a neighbor's life in one's hand. Everybody has power over
one's neighbor. The gist of the demand is that one should seek to achieve the
best for one's neighbor and not try to exploit him for one's own purposes. But,
says Løgstrup (1971), "The responsibility for another can never consist in
taking over his own responsibility."

The entry of the welfare society—which had far-reaching consequences, especially in the Scandinavian countries—may have made the concept sink somewhat into oblivion. The government—the public authorities—took over the responsibility to a major or minor extent. Nor was it so common to feel responsibility for others—and as time passed, not even for oneself. If problems arose, there was always another person who could (and had to) solve them. Responsibility became professionalized, perhaps to an excessive degree. In any case, today's West European, especially Scandinavian, societies are exhibiting a general tendency toward returning to the old virtues.

Other countries in the world may not have gone through a similar development. The reason may be that they never left the old virtues—or that they never possessed them. The latter is most likely the case, especially in distinctly individualistic societies where one has to look after oneself, and where any sense of responsibility primarily covers oneself and, at best, one's very closest family. I shall not pretend to know anything about such countries but merely consider the situation in my own part of the world.

In Denmark, undoubtedly, the concept of responsibility is of increasing importance. This applies in many fields of society. In the care of the elderly, nursing home occupants have lately been given the right to dispose of their own money, and in return they then have to pay for the services they receive. The homeless and mentally disordered can live more independently in the institutions where they are placed, and they have got more influence on and greater responsibility for their everyday lives. Mutual contracts are increasingly being used with addicts as the basis for a course of therapy. This renders the addicts responsible to the therapy plan. Addicts help to plan the therapy themselves and assume (in writing) part of the responsibility for concluding the therapy as agreed. Something similar applies when youngsters are at the beginning of the slippery slope of crime. In this case the youngster, the youngster's parents, the social authorities, and the legal system can conclude a so-called youth contract in which the youngster undertakes to undergo therapy, pay damages, commence an education, or the like.

In general, basic social work shows an increasing tendency to involve clients in marginalized groups in their own futures—for example, in the form of action plans that the clients themselves help to draft and for whose performance they are thus expected to be (co-)responsible.

The Danish minister for social affairs, Karen Jespersen, who is a member of the Danish Social-Democratic Party, has introduced a bill to change the basic social legislation so that the social clientele will face more demands. The fundamental idea is to demand activation of those receiving social assistance, cash benefits, or the like and thus remove them from the passive role of recipients. According to Jespersen, the aim of the whole change in the social legislation is to create a greater sense of responsibility. This, she says, is completely in line with the fundamental values of the Danish welfare society: "responsibility for the community, but also the awareness that this makes heavy demands on the individual's sense of responsibility."

So if the Danish Correctional Service has focused strongly on the concept of responsibility in recent years, this is not an isolated phenomenon but a general trend in society, where the Correctional Service has merely been in the lead.

Responsibility of Staff

When the Danish Correctional Service refers to responsibility as a principle, most people will think of the concept in relation to the inmates and the other clientele. As will be explained, this is because responsibility is one of the main principles in the Mission Statement of the Correctional Service.

But we must not be blind to the fact that handing over responsibility to the inmates presupposes that the staff has extensive powers and influence on their daily lives. A system cannot function in which inmates have extensive influence on their own situation while at the same time the staff is organized in a very hierarchical and patriarchal structure. So if we aim at rendering the inmates responsible for their daily lives and treatment—in the last instance, for their own lives—we must start by giving staff members responsibility for their own daily lives. In other words, to a very large extent we must decentralize and delegate powers from the central authorities to the local ones, and from local management to the individual staff members.

This philosophy is the background for the structural change undergone by the Danish Correctional Service over the past ten years. The structure builds on a common European strategy in which the basic staff is placed in a far more central role than one of conventional security—the man who locks the inmate up and out, the screw. The strategy was most clearly formulated at an East-West-European prison governors' meeting in Sicily in 1989.

Not all countries have shown equal zeal in following the strategy. The Scandinavian countries—and perhaps especially Denmark—have come far, but several other countries have also implemented parts of the strategy.

In one way, these thoughts may look like a showdown with the experts of the prison system, the pedagogues, the welfare officers, the lawyers, and so forth. But that is not what it is. The idea is that the basic staff has to be able to carry out the basic daily functions in most areas of prison life. They have to process cases—that is, prepare and to some extent decide on issues concerning leaves, visits, work assignments, educational planning, releases, and so on. And they have to plan and perform leisure activities with the inmates. They have to participate in workshop tasks and in the operation and maintenance of the institution. And then, naturally, they also have to see to security.

This structure does not render pedagogues, welfare officers, or the like superfluous, but it changes their roles. They now have to guide and supervise the basic staff, as well as take care of more complex problems in their subject areas. As a whole the treatment effort should preferably be substantially strengthened in that the whole staff takes part in it.

Some people might ask whether the security in this model will not be substantially downgraded when the officers are occupied with all sorts of other things for the major part of their working time. This, however, was never the intention. Of course, security in a prison is many things. There is the technical security inherent in surveillance equipment, bars, fences, and walls; then there is the control function performed by the staff; and finally, the dynamic security—that is, the security inherent in the fact that the staff knows the inmates and knows what is going on in the prison. Also there is the security inherent in the fact that the inmates know the staff. One of the great advantages of the structure is that staff and inmates get an opportunity to see each other as whole individuals and not only as one-dimensional figures who either have to watch or be watched.

The structure means that the individual staff member has a very great responsibility for treatment of the inmates—especially those two or three inmates to whom he is personal officer. He has to make decisions of far-reaching importance for the individual inmates. For this to be sound, a relatively explicit system of rules and, not least, a mission statement are necessary. The latter reflects the philosophy and the attitudes on which staff behavior is to be based. And then such a decentralized system requires staff training and personal qualifications to correspond to the demands made. This is why very careful recruitment is necessary, emphasizing especially attitudes and approach to other people. And another must is training that incorporates numerous relevant subjects, such as social case processing, psychology, communications, conflict resolution, and computer processing, as well as the more traditional prison subjects.

Therefore, if you visit a Danish prison you should not be surprised quite often to find the officers in front of their computers preparing a case relating to an inmate—or in a meeting with colleagues and experts discussing the situation of individual inmates or more general prison conditions.

The structural change has had two clear, direct consequences: The officers have received a major salary increase owing to their expanded duties, and the tone between staff and inmates has improved (further). Not least of all, this latter aspect is one that foreign visitors usually note as a vital difference between Danish prisons and more traditional prisons.

I do not want to pretend that this process, consisting in giving the staff new tasks, has not caused any problems. Nor will I pretend that the system presents no problems in daily operation. Many staff members have found it difficult to assume completely new roles and functions and—despite various forms of supplementary training—many do not feel able to perform their new tasks in a satisfactory manner. Others perhaps find that this is not the sort of work they had in mind when they applied for the Correctional Service in the first place. And finally, we must not underestimate the inertness and conservatism that will always be present in a system like a prison service, characterized as it is by tradition, hierarchy, and rigidity.

In addition to the inmate-related tasks, the delegation of tasks has also greatly influenced the planning of daily staff service, such as the planning of the staff's working hours, time off, and holidays. In certain institutions, staff on the individual wards (in cooperation with the inmates) has had a certain budget competence delegated to it regarding maintenance of the ward, including the vandalism account and the account for purchase of articles such as televisions, microwave ovens, and the like. This part of the decentralization has been far more easy to implement.

The mission statement mentioned above concerns not only the conditions of the inmates but also a number of viewpoints of principle concerning staff. These include the establishment of good staff facilities and proper working conditions, an obligation to adapt the staff structure so as to enable close contact with the inmates, and an obligation for management to delegate responsibility and competence to the greatest extent possible and to encourage staff to demonstrate independent initiative and creativity. Finally, the management of the prison service is enjoined to create a staff policy program that promotes staff members' ability to perform the jobs given to them, increases their job satisfaction, and ensures good and up-to-date staff administration. At present we are attempting to fulfill this obligation by means of a committee in which management and staff organizations cooperate to create a so-called Staff Policy Program of Principles.

Responsibility of Inmates

As mentioned, some years ago the Danish prison service prepared an ethical program for its activities.[2] The program of principles was prepared at the initiative of the central directorate but with the cooperation in principle of the whole Correctional Service staff (and to a certain, limited extent, of the inmates—that is, to the extent that the individual prisons followed the directorate's recommendation of letting the inmates' viewpoints be included in the comments to the directorate's proposal). The draft issued by the directorate was discussed for three quarters of a year at all service stations and was then adapted on the basis of the comments. It was further discussed with the various managerial groups of the Correctional Service and with the staff organizations. Finally, it was politically approved by the minister of justice and the Legal Committee of the Danish Parliament, the *Folketing*. It thus expresses some fundamental viewpoints endorsed by a wide circle of interested parties.

In the way of such ethical statements, the program of principles is formulated quite widely to be able to accommodate both the prison system and the probation and aftercare service, just as both pretrial institutions and prisons for short-term inmates and for mentally deviant long-term inmates have to be covered by the wording. This means that the principles must necessarily be rather general and not very tangible—and may therefore feel noncommittal and remote to the person working "at ground level."

But to ensure that the principles have an impact on daily activities, each service station has been asked, on the basis of the overall program of principles, to prepare its own local program of principles relating the general principles to local conditions and to the specific tasks to be performed by the service station in question. This means that each service station under the Correctional Service now has its own program of principles and will be held responsible for its fulfillment—for example, in connection with internal and external inspections of the institution.

The absolutely overall principle for the activities of the Danish Correctional Service is the so-called normalization principle. This means that every time rules have to be established for some area, or every time a concrete decision has to be made, the first thought must be: "How would this have been done in the ordinary community?" The next thought then ought to be: "Are there any special reasons for doing it differently in the prison system?" and if so, those reasons must be specified in detail. By arranging conditions to deviate as little as possible from daily life outside the prisons, the negative sides traditionally associated with a prison sojourn are reduced.

In my eyes, the principle of responsibility—which is the subject of this article—is part of, or perhaps rather a consequence of, the normalization principle. The nature of prisons as total institutions has traditionally had some side effects, hardly intended, in provoking aggressions and being incapacitating, dispiriting, and socially crippling. Normalizing the conditions and to the extent possible equalizing them to conditions in the outside community reduce the inexpedient side effects, and at the same time a more fertile soil is created for treatment during the imprisonment. The principle of responsibility is an amplification and specification of a central aspect of the normalization principle, which means that the Correctional Service has to plan its activities so that the inmates have an opportunity to develop responsibility, self-respect, and self-confidence and are motivated to work toward a life free of crime.

One of the reasons for this principle is that the so-called hotel and service functions, traditionally an integral part of a prison sojourn, in actual fact reduce the inmates' ability to administer an ordinary daily life after their release. The main content of the principle is that the inmates should themselves be responsible for their lives, and the treatment given by staff should therefore above all consist in motivation, counseling, and guidance. Obviously this activity must be combined with ordinary human care and support in cases in which the inmate requires it.

Saying that the inmates must be motivated to assume responsibility for their own lives does not mean, of course, that they will be allowed to do as they please. It appears from the context that the inmates have to administer this responsibility within the regime defined by the actual purpose of the activity—to wit, a reduction of crime.

The focusing on responsibility as an important element in the treatment of criminals is no Danish invention. Thus, the U.N. Standard Minimum Rules for the Treatment of Prisoners (United Nations, 1977) states that "the regime of the institution should seek to minimise any differences between prison life and life at liberty which tend to lessen the responsibility of the prisoners" (Article 60). This clearly shows the correlation between the normalization principle and the principle of responsibility. The instrument later states that "the treatment shall be such as will encourage their self-respect and develop their sense of responsibility" (Article 65).

This idea has been emphasized as "a basic principle" in the European Prison Rules (Council of Europe, 1987), where it is established already at the beginning that "the purpose of the treatment of persons in custody shall be such as to sustain . . . their self-respect and . . . to develop their sense of responsibility" (Article 3).

This is elaborated in Article 69, which states:

Within the regimes, prisoners shall be given the opportunity to participate in activities in the institutions likely to develop their sense of responsibility, self-reliance and to stimulate interest in their own treatment.

Efforts should be made to develop methods of encouraging co-operation with and the participation of prisoners in their treatment. To this end prisoners shall be encouraged to assume . . . responsibilities in certain sectors of the institution's activity.

If read according to their wording, the rules are a strong breach with the traditional paternalistic understanding of what is best for the inmates and may well come into conflict with other good intentions regarding daily life in the prisons. The reason for the former distinct "room service" in the prisons—such as morning calling, serving breakfast in the cells, laundry and mending of clothes, and dispensing of soap, toothpaste, and other articles of personal hygiene—was not, of course, to pamper the inmates. These arrangements were considered necessary for order and discipline or to achieve an unexceptionable hygienic standard.

When we demand now that inmates themselves have to get up in the morning, do their own cooking, and launder and mend their clothing themselves, we must be prepared to accept that this will mean that some get up too late, some do not have breakfast every day, the food they get does not live up to the recommendations of the health and food authorities concerning calories, vitamins, fat content, and so on, and that they may not change their underwear every day.

However, as long as inmates administration of daily life lies within what one could call the normal area and their eating habits and hygiene do not cause direct discomfort to others, deviations from the ideal condition must be accepted. This may, however, be difficult for prison staff brought up with the good old virtues. That it has also been difficult for the authors of the international rules to implement the idea of responsibility fully comes out in other parts, for instance, of the European Prison Rules. Thus they prescribe that "prisoners . . . shall be provided with such toilet articles as are necessary for health and cleanliness" (rule 20) and that "the administration shall provide the prisoners at the normal time with food which is suitably prepared and presented, and which satisfies in quality and quantity the standards of dietetics and modern hygiene" (rule 25).

Danish prisons have established grocers' shops run by outside grocers where the inmates can buy what is needed for cooking and for personal hygiene, laundry and the maintenance of clothing, and so forth. And an amount is paid weekly to inmates based on the calculation by an external authority of how much an average male citizen in this country needs for food that satisfies health standards. In addition, as before, they are paid hourly rates for working, corresponding to up to about one-tenth of the hourly wage for unskilled workers on the ordinary labor market. It is presupposed that this money is spent on other necessities. In addition, kitchens and washing machines have been provided in each ward.

When we introduced this form of self-administration, the scheme encountered quite a lot of resistance both among inmates, who suddenly saw the service level drop, and among staff, who thought that the inmates—or at least some of them—had neither the ability nor the will to administer such a scheme. However, the negative expectations have not materialized, and the scheme is now massively backed up by all parties.

Of course, there are some inmates who cannot live up to these demands fo one reason or other, for example because they have incurred debt for drugs or gambling and therefore have no money for food. Others simply may not have the required skills in cooking and therefore cannot immediately look after themselves. Such problems—and other similar ones—will naturally occur, but they are hardly so tough that they cannot be solved. The problem of lacking skills in cooking can be overcome either by the inmates forming food groups, which is very normal, and helping each other, or by holding courses in "ordinary daily life training," where inmates are simply taught to cook everyday foods.

If an inmate spends all his money on cigarettes, candy, and fast food, a talk given by the staff, including the health staff, on the consequences of poor nutrition may perhaps be in order, and likewise poor hygiene can be countered a good part of the way by means of information and guidance. Concerning problems of indebtedness and the like, such problems may be solved, for example, by replacing cash with plastic cards intended only for purchases in the shop. Danish prisons are at present experimenting with such schemes.

In addition to giving inmates greater responsibility for their everyday life in the prisons, it is also possible in other ways to appeal to or build up responsibility in the individual criminal. One of the reasons why we in Denmark commit the majority of prisoners to open prisons with no physical barriers against leaving is that we believe that most of them will be able—or can be enabled—to understand the advantage of living up to the confidence shown them. The motivation lies in the fact that anybody leaving the prison without permission will be transferred to a closed prison. The overall majority of those committed to open prisons live up to the responsibility; that includes recidivists and also inmates with relatively long sentences of up to five or six years for relatively serious crimes.

Similar forms of responsibility are a precondition for the very extended leave schemes from Danish prisons. At some time or other during their sojourn, practically all inmates are allowed to leave the prison every third weekend and are expected to return voluntarily on Sunday evening. Almost all of them do so. A few arrive a little late or are under the influence of alcohol or drugs when they arrive, and that of course affects their future leave opportunities and may also mean transfer to a closed institution. But the great majority are able to withstand the temptation not to return.

A reason why we in Denmark can also use alternatives to imprisonment to the very considerable extent we do—about 50 percent of all sentences are made conditional—is also our confidence that the convicts can and will fulfill the conditions—for example, to show up at their supervisor at the times fixed, to observe a long-term treatment for alcoholism, or to perform community service.

As mentioned above, there is an increasing tendency to base treatment of criminals on action plans. This is now obligatory in the probation and aftercare service and will soon become so in connection with persons serving prison sentences. Such action plans, which determine what the time in prison and after the release is to be used for, must be drafted in cooperation with the criminal to the greatest extent possible. Several good reasons exist for this, but one of the best is that the criminal will then feel more obliged to keep to the plan. In certain cases, especially when quite young people or addicts are concerned, the action plan is in the form of an actual contract that specifies in detail the rights and duties of the authorities and of the criminal during the course of therapy. This to an even greater extent appeals to the criminal's coresponsibility for not falling back into addiction or crime.

Our experience so far seems to indicate that such methods present considerable advantages over the traditional paternalistic methods of treatment—provided, and this is important to stress, that the reactions have the requisite consistency if the criminal does not live up to his (co-)responsibility. There is no sense in talking about responsibility if no reactions are associated with not living up to it.

Before concluding this summary overview of how the concept of responsibility is used in the Danish Correctional Service, I would like to point to one meaning of the concept of responsibility that I have not mentioned—and that some might miss. Probably some would ask whether the most important form of responsibility is not the one by which the criminal assumes responsibility for the crime. Or, in other words, that the criminal above all "as a man" assume the blame for what he has done rather than blame society, parents, or bad company.

I suppose that in most cases the reasons why a person commits a crime are to be found both within the person and in more general factors. But on this occasion, I will leave that debate to others. On the other hand, I am prepared to admit that although this part of the concept of responsibility lies outside the issues that I have chosen to discuss in this article, there is naturally a correlation between this form of responsibility and the one that we try to build (on) in connection with the enforcement of punishment. It is thus difficult to imagine that a person who refuses any form of personal responsibility for a criminal act will be able to mobilize the form of responsibility upon which the initiatives discussed here are based.

There are still some questions that I feel some might miss. After becoming acquainted with the American experiments of boot camps and tent prisons in the desert of Arizona and the like, I will more probably be asked this question in the United States than in my part of the world. The question is: Why? Why, for heaven's sake, should we enter upon all these exercises of making expectations and demanding responsibility? Well, if the purpose of punishment is seen only as a backward infliction of suffering for what the criminal has committed, then it is naturally a waste of time and money. But if the purpose—in accordance with the international agreements on treatment of criminals, including the U.N. Standard Minimum Rules—is to attempt to make criminals function in society again in a socially acceptable manner, then one has to be more than normally naive if one believes that this can be obtained by denying them all responsibility and all human dignity. Then there is no other way than the long and tough one, and it is built on principles such as normalization and responsibility.

Conclusion

I am very eager to reemphasize that the fact that people are given greater responsibility for their own lives does not mean that they can behave as they please. It will still be legitimate for a community—and especially a prison community—to set out certain limits within which behavior may vary and also certain rules for what is acceptable behavior. K. E. Løgstrup recognizes these modifications to the main principle that "the responsibility for another can never consist in taking over his own responsibility." It is thus reasonable, he says, that the minions of the law have been endowed with a certain law-defined power over others to protect third persons against abuse by those others.

It is just as important to emphasize that the fact that to a greater extent people are given responsibility for their own lives does not mean that they are left to fend for themselves. Those who cannot administer the responsibility must have the necessary support, care, and guidance. In that phase it will be wise to mind the words of another Danish philosopher, Søren Kierkegaard: "That when in truth one is to succeed in leading a person to a certain place, one must above all take care to find him where he is and start there. This is the secret of all aid." But this is actually also the secret if we are to succeed in giving inmates responsibility for their own lives. Here as well, the important thing is to meet the inmate at the level where he is and start there.

Deep down, the reasoning is based on a belief that inmates (and staff) react to stimuli like all other people. As a general statement, I believe that this has never been disproved. The idea is that when you give people responsibility—for themselves or for others—they end up feeling responsible. They grow with the job, if necessary. Naturally, there will be exceptions; some people will abuse the confidence shown. This is merely a sign that inmates—and prison officers—are just as diverse as other people. But if we let such exceptions from the rule determine what course we choose, we will end up with a prison system that closes around itself, a rigid and inhumane system that in the last analysis worsens the problem it set out to solve.

Appendix
Excerpts from the Danish Prison and Probation Service's Program of Principles for Prison and Probation Work in Denmark (1994)

Foreword

Prison and probation work has a *main purpose.*

Society lays down certain *requirements* for the fulfillment of this main purpose upon which prison and probation work must build. These requirements should therefore be accepted by all employees of the Danish Prison and Probation Service.

The requirements for the fulfillment of the main purpose enable a *primary task* to be formulated.

The requirements also provide the frames of reference for carrying out the primary task and achieving the main purpose. They can be seen as *principles* for accomplishing the primary task.

Each of the principles can have as *outcome* a number of practical precepts and directives—, i.e., the principles become operationalised.

Outcomes in terms of precepts and directives can be formulated for the *Prison and Probation Service as a whole,* for its *various service stations (prisons, probation offices, etc),* for *particular units within service stations,* and, finally, in relation to the daily conduct of *individual staff members*—i.e., outcomes can relate to different levels of the organisation.

The present programme of principles concludes with outcomes for the whole prison and probation system. Outcomes in relation to service stations, constituent units, and individual staff members can be formulated at the appropriate organisational levels.

Main Purpose

The main purpose of prison and probation work is to contribute to reducing criminality.

Requirements

1. Human Worth
All prison and probation work shall respect the individual person and generally accepted human rights.

2. Non-encroachment

Prison and probation work shall not place more restrictions on offenders than follow from legislation and the implementation of the sanction.

3. Enforcement of Law

When arranging for the implementation of sanctions, prison and probation work shall respect the generally accepted considerations which underlie the sanction.

4. Sense of Justice

The Prison and Probation Service shall take account of the general sense of justice in society and among the victims of crime.

Primary Task

The primary task of the Prison and Probation Service is the implementation of the sanction.

Principles

1. Normalisation

The daily activities of the Prison and Probation Service shall, in general and whenever specific agreements are reached, be related to normal life in the general community.

2. Openness

Prison and probation work shall be organised so that the offender is offered good opportunities to make and maintain contact with the ongoing life of the community. Similarly, contact between the various parts of the Prison and Probation Service and society shall be strengthened to the greatest possible extent.

3. Exercise of Responsibility

Prison and probation work shall be so organised that the offender has the opportunity to develop a sense of responsibility, self-respect, and self-confidence, and become motivated to actively strive for a crime-free life.

4. Security

Prison and probation work shall ensure that the sentence of the court is carried out with due attention paid to the protection of the community from crime as well as protecting the inmate from aggression or damaging influences emanating from other persons.

5. Least Possible Intervention

The Prison and Probation Service shall choose the least intervenient means for dealing with any particular task.

6. Optimum Use of Resources

The Prison and Probation Service will use resources effectively, flexibly, and in relation to perceived needs. It will therefore make all necessary provision to have well-qualified staff who are capable, in terms of both professional training and personal competence, of carrying out their tasks in accordance with the Programme of Principles.

Outcomes

1. NORMALISATION

The outcome precepts from this principle are as follows:

1.1

The Prison and Probation Service will strive to ensure that offenders are given the opportunity to exercise their civil rights and, to the greatest possible extent, are given the same opportunities as other citizens for training and education, work, social help and benefits, medical assistance, culture and leisure activities, etc.

1.2

Inmates will be allocated to prisons that, as far as possible, enable them to maintain contact with their own home environment ("proximity principle"). When there are special reasons for doing so, inmates will be differentiated on grounds of age, gender, criminality, mental or physical health, etc.

1.3

The Prison and Probation Service will strive to ensure that the physical conditions of the prisons (size of institutions, wings, rooms, etc.) conform, to the greatest possible extent, to contemporary standards and to the requirements of the community in general.

1.4

The Prison and Probation Service will work to eliminate a climate of institutionalisation by allowing inmates reasonable opportunities to have personal property in their possession. Staff clothing and ways of behaving and speaking to inmates shall be such as will promote sound social contact between the staff and the inmates.

1.5

The Prison and Probation Service will utilise the helping services of the community to the greatest possible extent, rather than set up parallel services. However, where inmates have no possibility to make use of community services, the Prison and Probation Service will endeavor to provide relevant forms of help and treatment.

2. OPENNESS

The outcome precepts from this principle are as follows:

2.1

The point of departure for the allocation of inmates is that they shall be placed in open prisons where the possibilities of contact with the community are greatest.

2.2

Opportunities for correspondence, visits, and leaves, etc., shall be given, which enable inmates to maintain and develop their contacts with relatives and with life in the community.

2.3

Inmates shall be given opportunities for association to the greatest possible extent.

2.4

The Prison and Probation Service will collaborate both generally and in practical matters with other parts of the criminal justice system and other relevant sections of society. It will strive to provide as full an information as possible on criminal policy and the content of, and conditions for, its work.

2.5

The Prison and Probation Service will give full co-operation to external inspectorial and supervisory bodies and be open for visits by the press and generally accepted humanitarian organisations.

3. EXERCISE OF RESPONSIBILITY

The outcome precepts from this principle are as follows:

3.1

Every effort will be made to ensure congruity in the work of the different sectors of the Prison and Probation Service ("continuity and co-ordination principle"). This shall at all times motivate offenders to take responsibility for their own lives.

3.2

Inmates will be required to the greatest possible extent to take responsibility for daily doings such as the preparation of food and the laundering and repair of clothing (self-management).

3.3

Guidance will be given to offenders so that they may solve their own problems rather than have problems solved for them. They will be allowed to choose between relevant offers of help, rather than have specific arrangements thrust upon them.

3.4

Offenders will be given the opportunity to exercise influence on the planning of measures of help and to carry out the particular parts of such plans.

3.5

Inmates will be given flexible opportunities to exercise influence and share responsibility for conditions in the prisons.

Notes

1. Her perception of the importance of mottoes was first expressed in the United States in 1959 at a dinner meeting address upon the anniversary of the National Institute of Arts and Letters.
2. Extracts of the program are printed as an appendix to this article; it can be ordered in its entirety from the Ministry of Justice, Correctional Service, 1, Klareboderne, DK-1115 Copenhagen K, Denmark.

References

Council of Europe (1987). *European Prison Rules.* Strasbourg: Council of Europe.

Danish Prison and Probation Service (1994). *A Programme of Principles for Prison and Probation Work in Denmark.* Copenhagen: Danish Prison and Probation Service.

Løgstrup, K. E. (1971). *The Ethical Demand.* Philadelphia: Fortress Press.

United Nations (1977). *Standard Minimum Rules for the Treatment of Prisoners.* New York: United Nations.

PART III

OFFENDERS AND RESPONSIBILITY

8

Moral Disengagement and the Role of Ideology in the Displacement and Diffusion of Responsibility among Terrorists

Robert J. Kelly

This chapter explores the intellectual artifacts and mechanisms that enable terrorists to do what they do—to kill indiscriminately in the name of political, social, or cultural causes. In order to understand how individuals can be mobilized into violent extremist groups, it helps to know something about the contexts and the psychological and main social underpinnings that provide the instrumental bases of terrorist actions.

The term "terrorism" evokes images of assassination, hijacking, kidnapping, and bombing. However it is defined or described, and the definitions are numerous and hotly disputed, it is a political sundae of diverse causes ranging from preposterous, long-forgotten ethnic rivalries to grim nationalist struggles, relentless religious grievances, and romantic class struggles of one sort or another.

Reactions to terrorism have matched its varied manifestations, with demands for extermination of the brutes to soft-hearted sympathy for the devil. And whether these organizations consist of disaffected intellectuals or fanatical clerics, the surest way to unintentionally abet them has been to deny their authenticity and determination.

Terrorism is a dangerous occupation. This observation is obvious but also dumbfounding. One must wonder why, given the high rate of casualties and failures that terrorist groups experience, individuals continue to embrace it as a means for change, and, in many cases, a way of life. Although it is illegal, to describe terrorism simply as criminal is misleading and erroneous; mere criminals rarely purport to act on behalf of an entire nation, class, religion, or ethnic group, nor do they ordinarily accept martyrdom. And although it is political behavior, it is not really warfare either, since the combatants are few and their relationships to larger political insurgent organizations are questionable. Terrorism is quasi-crime that aspires to become warfare. One of its goals, beside spreading general fear, is to link the political agendas and values of a small vanguard of militants to the oppressed masses whom they wish to lead and represent; to do this they must awaken these oppressed sleepers and lead them to power.

The Causes of Terrorism

Efforts to explain the character and mental makeup of terrorists present many problems. In the 1870s, for example, as terrorism was gaining strength not only in Russia but also in Italy, Cesare Lombroso, who believed that criminality in general was a congenital condition, attributed terrorist behavior, and in particular bomb-throwing, to pellagra and other vitamin deficiencies. A century later, persistent attempts to explain terrorist violence in terms of biology remain strong. Some have suggested that there may be a link between inner-ear vestibular function and terrorism (Hubbard, 1983:188–97). Others think that brain chemistry, specifically the inhibitory effects of gamma-amino-butyric acid and serotonin, may have something to do with it, and that through an extrapolation of biochemical research findings on rats that the Ayatollah Khomeini could have benefited from drug treatment (Brown and Goodwin, 1986; Bunney, 1982:287–307). If this is so, not only would the Ayatollah have been helped but so would a host of others in Iraq, Kuwait, and throughout the whole Persian Gulf, including the thousands of terrorists reportedly blown up while detonating their way to Paradise or Utopia.

While it is widely recognized that there are no neat explanations for terrorism, that has not deterred research that seeks to discover underlying causes in the makeup of the terrorist personality.

Other types of explanation are more common and seek to attribute terrorist behavior to mental illness. But such analyses are similarly reductionistic. By examining terrorist behavior and finding one or another psycho-neurological cause, some writers conclude that deep down terrorists are psychopaths (Corrado, 1981; Heskin, 1980). The attractiveness of these perspectives, whatever their intrinsic merit, is not difficult to understand. By the nature of their professed goals and methods, terrorists tend to inhabit the political fringes of society; terrorism thus is likely to appeal to individuals with various mental disorders, so that the proportion of a terrorist group's membership that is composed of mentally ill persons, deviants, and criminals may be higher than the percentage in the general population. Specific research on this very issue concerning the prevalence of mental illness among terrorists found (at least among Italians) that psychopathic tendencies and delusions do not appear to be the primary source of terrorist motivation or activity (Ferracuti and Bruno, 1983; Kelly, 1991).[1] Certainly not all psychological theories choose to concentrate on clusters of pathology in the activist.

Motivations of Terrorists

Without presuming too much, it is fair to say that a psychologist begins with an individual whose characteristic way of behaving is formed out of a complex interaction between emotional and neurological materials and social experiences. If sociologists or political scientists are to explain the power and limits of the law, they must understand why people sometimes obey it and sometimes do not. If psychologists are to explain how those characteristic ways of behaving develop, they must understand individual differences in both the extent to which people internalize certain legal and moral commands and the degree to which they anticipate and act on the likely future consequences of their own actions.

Over the past decade, many social scientists have begun to explore economic theories of rational choice in an attempt to explain criminal and deviant activity, just as these theories have been used to explain the actions of consumers, investors, and voters (Moore, 1987). Psychologists and sociologists have been taking note of differences in orientation, intelligence, and temperament, as well as differences in social circumstances, between those who do and those who do not frequently break the law. Perhaps these economic perspectives can help illuminate terrorist behavior and supplement many sociopsychological approaches that rely almost entirely on references to social environmental factors.

Economists see individuals allocating scarce resources among competing alternatives in order to satisfy their preferences, but economists rarely have much to say about the source or content of those preferences. Psychologists have a great deal to say about how preferences are formed but not much to say about how institutions frame the available alternatives and only relatively little to say about how the sense of justice influences the way individuals evaluate those alternatives.

These different approaches can indeed enrich each other. While it is essential to examine the social contexts of terrorism, it is also crucial to explore the emotional and mental makeup of those who decide—and how they decide and maintain their commitment—to pursue a course of violence-prone action.

In his comprehensive review of terrorism, Laqueur (1987) notes that the analyses of motivations are as numerous and diverse as are the definitions and myriad forms of the phenomenon. Laqueur is probably correct in arguing that explanations accounting for all forms of terrorism's manifestations are bound to be unsatisfactory because they must be too general and vague if they are to be historically comprehensive.

Examinations of the social origins of terrorism show that in most cases, but not all, the unrelieved pain of groups victimized by severe social, political, and economic abuse creates a groundswell of sentiment favorable to the use of precipitate violence against the putative causes of the problem—especially if attempts at nonviolent reforms have failed. In a standard sociological scenario, idealistic young people soured by failed reforms opt for terrorist solutions; they choose to resort to indiscriminate violence, or violence against innocent persons in the service of a revolutionary cause.[2] But not all young, idealistically minded persons embrace terrorist methods. Is there perhaps a terrorist personality that is disposed to random violence? In this connection, Freedman observes: "A psychological profile of a model terrorist cannot be drawn. The personalities are disparate. The contexts and circumstances within which terrorism, both political and ecclesiastical, has been carried out are diverse in chronology, geography and motive" (1979:390).

People declaring war on the state may be quite sane, or criminal, or psychopathic. They may or may not be expressing repressed hatred of parents; they may harbor suicidal impulses; they may be overwhelmed by feelings of guilt and feel compelled to restructure society for the cause they believe in (Rieber and Kelly, 1991).

It would be far-fetched to think that the person next door, given the right circumstances, could be a terrorist. What little is known about those who define themselves as terrorists and declare by their actions that they are revolutionaries, those who do not shrink from assassination and bomb-throwing, suggests that they tend to be alienated young adults, primarily male (but include, interestingly, many females) with a crusading sense of mission. They come from middle-class or upwardly mobile, respectable, working-class families that may be religiously dedicated (Gurr, 1990).

There is also information from the terrorists themselves—though much of it must be read as self-serving. Memoirs and autobiographies of careers, ambitions, hopes, and fears dot the polemical landscape (MacStiofain, 1975). These accounts, coupled with scholarly studies, make it possible to describe not a terrorist personality as such but rather a terrorist sensibility—a modality of interrelated feelings and beliefs common to diverse personalities. What figures most prominently in this psychological orientation is what Trotsky thought was a haunting sense of vengeance and despair. The psychology of the vendetta may play a role in any violent struggle, but most modern forms of terrorism are more like warfare than mafia feuds.

Many terrorists, according to their own accounts, begin their careers not as gunmen and bomb-throwers but as idealists full of hope, with some respect for the conventional institutional processes of change. Many believed that they could make a difference by reform through nonviolent means. But when disenchantment and disillusion take hold, some retreat into apathy; others become aggressive and find the "philosophy of the deed" more fulfilling and gratifying (Collin, 1989). They reject the victim role and paradoxically eschew the polemics and rhetoric of confrontation and seek action.

The recognition that they were deceived by clever manipulators and the realization that public apathy is the preponderant collective reaction to radical proposals for reform can produce identity-shattering blows to the ego. It must strongly suggest to some that in a world of hypocrisy and equivocation only violence is unambiguous and trustworthy, and, as Fanon put it, personally vindicating, purifying, and liberating (1963).

But far more is involved than mere disenchantment and personal frustration: the impotence of the victims, the perceived implacable callousness of the conventional political system, contrasted with an ideology that depicts violence as the only viable means to foster action. Paradoxically, most terrorists remain steadfastly committed to a faith that affirms the power and value of ideas and words—that these can transform society without a shot being fired.

One might think of the terrorist as politically naive and as a morally ambitious intellectual twice seduced: first by ruling elites, and then by apathetic masses. Unable to lead the oppressed and unwilling to join the oppressors, only action and violence as a last-ditch effort is capable of penetrating the web of illusion and mystification that envelop the masses. Turning society into a battlefield may help some terrorists regain or achieve the roles they deeply crave: that of the violent social savior capable of mending the wounds that polarize and enervate society. But are the circumstances sufficiently desperate to focus the energies of the morally outraged? Great disparities in wealth and a despair widespread throughout society have been identified as making up the social bases that launch terrorism.

Are these enough to envelop one emotionally in violent confrontations? Perhaps. Doubtlessly, there are individual psychological benefits derived from participation in terrorism. Crenshaw (1986) points out that analysts have examined a range of possible incentives from the thrills of high risk and excitement to the intoxicating sense of power that the individual participant experiences. There are also the socially induced needs of identity, belonging, and approval that a close-knit, conspiratorial organization promotes, which may play a vital role in luring some into terrorist groups.

Many issues surround the question of individual motivation. Different terrorist groups operate from different political agendas, and while the emotional needs of, say, Palestinian fighters may be similar to those of IRA activists despite different social contexts and historical circumstances, does the individual makeup of radicals come together through a peculiar politicization and socialization of the imagination that enables them, but not others, to cross a mental Rubicon into terror? How do social and political circumstances in societies riven by divisive religious, class, racial, and ethnic conditions differ from those in more integrated and cohesive societies in creating the kinds of psychological rewards that terrorism offers? Does one become a terrorist gradually, or is it a sudden conversion? How does one manage a split identity as both an agent and representative of humane values and also a bomb-thrower? And what of state terrorists, government "death squads" rounding up people, torturing, plundering, and murdering? Are they emotionally insulated enough to protect themselves against the pain and suffering they administer? It may be scientifically dangerous to try to understand a complex phenomenon exclusively in psychological terms, especially when it is so confounded by historical, political, and cultural forces and no less by disputes as to its very definition. Any reductionist scheme, though laudable in intent, seems bound to breach prudential explanation and valid limits. And though it may seem evasive, some integration of psychological and rational choice may yield the conceptual mix that provides a more comprehensive account of terrorist motives and behaviors.

We now turn to techniques of emotional concealment that enable the violent to rid themselves of the terrorist taint. Veiling actions, engaging in systematic self-deception by both revolutionaries and government officials, possess some cognitive symmetries. For the government functionary doing his "job," the relationship to violence may be purely instrumental: It is another expedient "tool" in the repertoire of control and containment tactics. For revolutionaries, the objectives and purposes of the movement itself provide exculpation from guilt or self-doubt about violence. Still, even with these rationalizations it is important to ask how practitioners of violence disguise their terror as nonterror or as justifiable violence—no matter how grisly, indiscriminate, or potentially stigmatizing.

Prelude to Terror: The Psychosocial Dynamics of Moral Disengagement

To engage openly in indiscriminate violence, the individual must "morally disengage." Whereas hatred and violence are usually impulsive, when deliberately planned they seem to be far more dangerous and destructive, especially when they are principled. In the instance of terrorist violence, individuals may be subject to psychological devices that relax moral inhibitions and socialize them into personal codes that foster cruelty, hatred, and violence against particular targets.

Terrorist organizations and their ideological machinery may be seen as self-exonerations needed to erase prohibitions against violent behavior and ha-

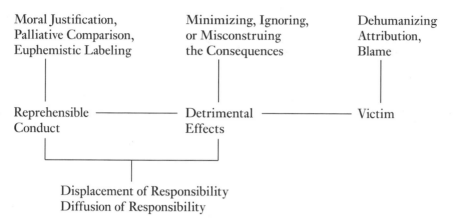

Fig. 8-1. Psychological mechanisms of moral disengagement. Based on A. Bandura, "Mechanisms of Moral Disengagement," p. 162 in *Origins of Terrorism: Psychologies, Ideologies, Theologies, States of Mind*, W. Reich, ed. New York: Cambridge University Press, 1990. Used with permission of the publisher.

tred. Bandura's sociopsychological model is useful for understanding this process (see figure 8-1).

The model sketches a dynamic through which moral self-sanctions are relaxed so that the internalized guides and deterrents to conduct socially defined as unacceptable may be disengaged. Regulatory psychological mechanisms can be neutralized in several interconnected ways by blotting out personal agency in harmful activities, by acquiring attitudes that disregard or misrepresent the detrimental consequences of one's actions, by blaming or dehumanizing the victims, and by reconstruing one's behavior as serving morally desirable purposes. In this process, destructive conduct is made personally and socially acceptable for its members by portraying such behavior as in the service of socially desirable goals.

Intensive exposure to terrorist ideological literature has effects on attitudes and behavior: In group settings, individual behavior and judgment are strongly influenced by the powerful forces of group dynamics. Pressures are magnified so that for the participant the group may become the only authentic and trustworthy source of information—and, in the face of external hostility and threat, the only source of security. Consequently, those who may otherwise deplore violence can be transformed rapidly into individuals filled with the intense emotions of hatred and gain, even a sense of pride in their violent behavior.

The "conversion process" of the socialized into dedicated revolutionaries is not achieved only by altering their personality structures, aggressive drives, or even moral standards. By cognitively restructuring the moral value of crimes committed against specific groups so that the crimes can be done free from censuring doubt, the task of making violence morally defensible is facilitated. What further augments the process is the political isolation of fringe groups. And since nonviolent options have appeared not to work effectively, militant action comes to be regarded as the only recourse for redressing grievances.

Violent conduct may be justified by the rhetorical discourse of terrorist groups where they redescribe social reality and the nature of the cause, its problematics and solutions. By changing the language that defines the political conflict, it is possible to mask reprehensible activities, and this process may be enhanced further when descriptions of the opposition forces are couched in melodramatic, colorful metaphors that demonize and criminalize the objects of terrorist activity. Thus, terrorists issue communiqués detailing the "crimes against the people" committed by the government and its agents and describe their violence in terms that denude their own acts of moral repugnancy. Sanitized vocabularies whose convoluted euphemisms mislead actually serve to transform "assassinations" into "terminations," "bombings" into "surgical strikes," and "mass slaughter" into "collateral damage" (Kelly and Rieber, 1992). They typically minimize their slayings as the only defensive weapon at their disposal for curbing the widespread cruelties inflicted on their people. And in the eyes of terrorist partisans and sympathizers, blood-drenched attacks are always directed at the apparatus of oppression (not innocents) such that rather than being perceived as heinous crimes these are acts of selflessness and martyrdom. In Northern Ireland, Bernadette Devlin McAliskey said recently:

> Nobody can say what the balance sheet of suffering is. Certainly the greatest weight of war has been carried within the republican community. Those of us who have been part of the struggle for twenty-five years have children. The children have grown up in a totally military society. The most alarming thing about the situation is that this is normal life for our children. This is the kind of society, the kind of life, the kind of structure, that has provided the normal basis of their growing up. Peace is abnormal to anybody in this country under the age of twenty-five. (quoted in Ridgeway and Farrelly, 1994:36)

Similarly, in the Middle East, Shi'ite clerics have gone to great lengths to justify terroristic acts that would seem to go against Islamic law by citing situational imperatives and tyrannical circumstances that drive oppressed people to unconventional means to fight against aggressors who wield massive destructive power. In what must appear to other Islamic theologians as idiosyncratic logic, dying in a suicidal bombing is interpreted as no different than losing one's life to the enemy on a conventional battlefield (Kramer, 1990).

Purely linguistic solutions deftly defy credibility where personal moral responsibility is interpreted as being dictated by the enemy's behavior.[3]

Hostage-taking nicely illustrates the displacement of responsibility. Terrorists warn officials that if retaliatory action is taken, they, not the terrorists, will be held accountable for the lives of the hostages. And should captivity drag on, terrorists will place the blame and suffering they inflict on officials for failing to make what they regard as warranted concessions that will eliminate or right social wrongs.

Here, even the admission of responsibility is tempered: If it were not for the oppression, for the illegitimacy, cruelty, and criminality of the other, the hostage-taking would not have occurred. Thus, the concept of responsibility is seen with extraordinary clarity if the act and the message of the terrorists are divided into two parts: On the one hand, they take responsibility for the commission of the kidnapping but, on the other, deny blame and accountability for the outcomes.

Responsibility can also be diffused such that an emotional division of labor can occur. Terrorist organizations are organized—this means that there is a fractional compartmentalization of tasks. For reasons of security, performance of a particular job tends to be isolated from the overall strategy, and participants may exercise little personal judgment or discretion in carrying out subfunctions that are related to the general plan by remote, often clandestine links. When terror is somewhat "routinized" into programmatic tasks, attention and emotional tension are likely to shift from the monstrous impact of what one is doing to the details of the job (Kelman, 1973).

Moreover, decision making in a hierarchy of authority may easily induce otherwise sensitive individuals to behave inhumanely because no single person need feel responsible for policies arrived at collectively or imposed by distant, unknown others in the organization's leadership cadres. In both cases, responsibility for actions can be displaced and obscured. Beyond its attribution to a collective instrumentality, self-restraints and responsibility can be weakened by operational expedients characteristic of the transformative socialization processes within extremist groups.

Immersion in the group's ideology, specifically in its dehumanization of the enemy, can deaden moral sensibilities. Like boot camp training in military units, inhibitions toward violence are relaxed in milieus of close interpersonal training, learning, and doing where individuals are insulated from mainstream social life—and the latter, the isolation of terrorist groups and their general estrangement from mainstream politics, is a defining characteristic of their normal operational status. In segregated environments where seclusion and secrecy surround one, constant training in the performance of aggressive acts gradually diminishes the discomfort and blunts self-reproof so that even higher levels of ruthlessness can be achieved. Together, the disengagement practices and ideological indoctrination that dehumanize the enemy accelerate the processes of psychological change in which behavior initially regarded as abhorrent and depraved can be carried out callously.

It is ideological indoctrination that functions as an intellectual engine that trips the disengagement process into action. A body of ideas that define, interpret, analyze, criticize, and redescribe social-political reality in simplified, dramatic language can be catalytic in radicalizing a movement or mobilizing a small but determined group of activists (Kelly and Schatzberg, 1992). One example will suffice to illustrate the point. Nazi ideology, like most others, organized common perceptions around certain widely shared images.

What was distinctive about Nazi ideology was that it prescribed the biological perfection of the people as the prerequisite for social transformation and national glory. That the "Aryan" race, as such, did not exist—it was no more than a fallacy thrown up by the still unscientific disciplines of philology and anthropology—was no real obstacle. Nor was the fact that the biological perfection of any race—eugenics—was and remains substantially beyond the capacities of science. Nazism generated a new national enemy, one that could be used as a rallying cry—the inferior races.

By portraying the "inferior" races and most especially the Jews as a "disease" upon the nation, the Nazis succeeded in making them appear what they were in fact not—dangerous and implacable. No objective evidence could be adduced for these propositions, nor was there any possibility of confirming it in everyday reality. But the iconography of the Nazi propaganda machinery made it appear otherwise: The Jew was everywhere depicted as physically repugnant, as sexually ravenous and hideous, as obese or unaesthetically thin and frail. The images were always extreme and the physical and moral baseness they suggested made the disease metaphor seem like a reality readily confirmed by perception. Indeed, so thoroughly did image substitute for reality that in the wake of Kristalnacht it was the Jews themselves who were made to pay for the damage—the diseased paying for their own cure.

It was, of course, the classic case of pathological enmification. A defenseless minority was turned into a public "enemy" as a means of suffusing a sense of vitality into a policy that was rationally and morally bankrupt and as a means of uniting and mobilizing a disorganized and disheartened populace. Dehumanizing this "enemy" went beyond the extreme of what Erikson (1969:431) has termed "pseudo-speciation," for Nazi ideology ultimately depicted the Jews as something even lower than animals. In the process, the psychological needs of a highly disturbed leadership were assuaged as they projected onto others the evil within themselves. In retrospect, Nazi beliefs are astoundingly incredible, but at the time and in the feverish climate of economic and social disintegration, they offered a hope—however far-fetched and delusional—of national survival and rejuvenation.

The mesmerizing power of an ideology is not limited to politically desperate and naive individuals ready to cling to any set of ideas that promise relief from despair. Even professionals succumbed in Nazi Germany. Lifton (1986) relies on the concept of "doubling," a Jekyll and Hyde notion that describes a psychic cleavage, to explain the emotional ambivalence of Nazi physicians serving in concentration camps. The process is a self-willed splitting of the personality—a case of the right hand not knowing what the left hand is doing—that allows one part of the self to participate in unspeakable acts while the other appears to retain its compassion and humanity. Neither self, if the doubling is successful, is permitted to migrate into the psychic territory of the other. The psychological partitions allow for seemingly everyday persons to shed their normalcy and become utterly monstrous, without the guilt-ridden residues of memory seeping into the interior life of the individual. Such persons, if their compartmentalization is complete and they are capable of generating this profound dissociative activity, do not seem to suffer from leading a double life.

The essence of doubling is its validation of the suspension of ethical inhibitions that enable the individual to avoid accountability for behavior or guilt for harm done to the innocent. Every terrorist in the deepest recesses of the ego might just strike such a Faustian bargain wherein he or she gains peace of mind and release from the consequence of depredations—however "noble" their cause.

Once dehumanized, potential victims are no longer seen as persons with feelings, hopes, and desires but as subhuman objects. The preceding discussion has been mainly concerned with the mechanisms of disengagement—how moral impediments to terrorist violence and dehumanization are attenuated psychologically. Intrinsic to the psychological dynamics of disengagement is the role of ideology and its influence on the political formation of the terrorist sensibility.

Ideology

Unlike more group-restricted or privatized paradigms, ideologies are a rhetoric of public discourse producing what may be called "dramaturgic accentuation" (Gouldner, 1976: ch. 10). The epistemological ingredients that produce an intellectual shock or, more likely, a rather prosaic but nonetheless fresh look on the social world are mobilized into counterdiscourses consisting of a tacit set of psychological strategies for action and, on another plane, a rhetoric that functions as both a critique of existing sociopolitical orders and a new world view.

Ideologically inspired political programs drive contemporary movements that are labeled "terrorist." Their doctrines, principles, concepts, and ideas

serve psychological functions in much the same way that religious ideas organize believers socially and culturally, by affording emotional relief and grati-
fications. Deprived of these influences and guiding principles, activist and
disciples could go off the rails. A movement's idea system constitutes the basis
for appropriate definition and reaction to social events.

Ideologies would appear to be basic foundational elements in cultivating
the motivational structure and "mind-set" of the believer/adherent. Through
immersion in the ideational system, the individual goes through an epistemological transformation and a cognitive reordering of the worldview. Thus, an
ideology is a "world making" apparatus that lays out the parameters of reality.
Central to their dynamics are two psychological assumptions: first, that the
mind is infinitely malleable, capable of being reformed and transformed, and
second, that the will is all powerful, even to the extent that, in Mao's words,
"the Subjective creates the Objective" (Mao Zhe-Tung, 1957).

The importance of a socially inspired belief system resides in its power to
communicate ideals, evaluations, and goals among group members. Believers
are able to appraise their political condition and its prospects for the future
and thereby facilitate the mobilization and direction of energies and resources
for common political undertakings. Psychologically one might say that the
significance of ideology in mobilization is not that it causes one to do anything or provokes one into a particular course of action but that it gives one
cause for doing so. It provides grounds or warrants for the political activity
engaged in. However, to limit explanation to its mobilizing aspects in terms
of its capacity to release passion tends to ignore a vast and important aspect
of how radical political actors understand and orient their activities.

A major feature of ideological thought is the historical consciousness it
breeds among those who embrace it. Of course, the "history" incorporated
into these accounts of a society usually contains a distinctive focus on change
in which change characteristically means the coming into being of new and
specifically different constellations of conditions favored by the belief system
(Shils, 1958).

Ideologies are thus concerned with things to come. For example, although
there are considerable differences in the theoretical content and conclusions
of liberalism, socialism, and fascism, most versions of all three view politics
as striving in accordance with historical developments and trends that will
lead to improved social arrangements. Hence, there is a need to invent conceptions of the future (Litcheim, 1965). How the future is conceived will be
greatly influenced by how the present and the past are understood. And while
there may be some sense of tradition in historical consciousness, tradition is
no longer accepted as a sufficient guide to human action. In ideological ren-
ditions of reality, the shape of the future, the nature of change, and the limits and possibilities of control over these changes become questions of over-

whelming importance. Ideologically tutored consciousness therefore implies the possibility of qualitatively imagining new arrangements, of emphatically placing oneself in them, and of conceptualizing the extent to which individuals might be causally effective in bringing new social arrangements about.

As a method of interpretation, ideologies must possess some logic—they cannot violate the basic canons of sense. The need to make sense qualifies documents and writing that need not be contemporary but that emphasize or forecast significant social change. Thus the key "sacred" texts of so many terrorist organizations may date from the past. As a result, modern political activists may be involved in the strenuous art of intellectual invention, in which old social blueprints need to be adjusted and refined to suit modern political economic realities. (The one thing perhaps that political radicals share with religious fundamentalists is the manner in which they tenaciously cling to the inseminating authority of the past.) When ideologies are or can be shown to have linkage with culturally defining documents and masterpieces of the past, this confers power by distinguishing them from the ad hoc, piecemeal appeals of propaganda. On the other hand, if they logically cohere and seem integral to the cultural and historical ethos of a social group, they gain in potency to the degree that they are distinguishable from impressionistic and unarticulated public opinion.

As programs of action, terrorist insurgencies are rarely isolated phenomena: They tend to reflect the diffuse sympathies, desires, and aspirations of larger segments of society. And rather than the primary or sole means of political protest, terror emerges when other mechanisms of political conflict utterly fail or do not produce desired institutional reforms. The interesting problems here concern the interrelationships and interactions within the political culture of aggrieved communities that provide a milieu in which terrorism can flourish. As a body of ideas reflecting social aspirations, ideologies would appear to play a pivotal role in the formation of a climate receptive to and supportive of politically motivated violence (Gurr, 1990).

Much, but by no means all, terrorist "world making" consists of taking apart and putting together, often conjointly, elements of the social and political system. Ideology plays a role in sculpting the social universe: It aids by providing names, predicates, gestures, pictures, and interpretations of events. The "recipe knowledge" of ideology rewrites history in the interest of a political agenda and enables the terrorist to restructure social reality in ways that lend themselves to revolutionary interventions. For instance, classical Marxist/Leninist doctrines depict society as principally an arena of class conflict: They identify the protagonists in terms of their wealth and class position, analyze the causes underlying inequity and injustice, and sketch a plan (the conspiratorial revolutionary party) for change.

The notion of "relevance" is useful in describing the conceptual sorting, the ideological surveillance, of a social system. Terrorists live in the same social world as everyone else; it is just that their perspective focuses on elements and entities that they believe to be more pertinent to their projects than others. For example, the Black Liberation Army's propaganda located the major sources of black oppression within the law enforcement system (Kilson, 1969:307). Armed with that knowledge, they acted accordingly and attacked the police. On the other hand, the Weathermen identified the military-industrial complex as the ruling elite and attacked the universities because these were considered more vulnerable and because the intelligentsia in the pay of the corporations constituted, in the Weathermen's reality, the armature and support system keeping the ruling classes in power. The skinheads appear to emphasize other dimensions of the economic and political elite structure in the United States. Right-wing groups capable of violence tend to concur that the universities, Wall Street, the broadcast industry, and key federal bureaucracies make the important decisions but do so against the interests of working-class whites and therefore must be opposed and dealt with violently. Differences between the skinhead's view and that of the Weathermen are of emphasis and accent, not content or facts (Sapp, 1991).

The sociological curse of ideologies is that they may be calcified dogmas. But if they are predictable they ought to be controllable. Much of modern terrorism, however, is not rigid; it is not just another blood sport in the name of some high-minded social scheme but resilient and flexible, energized by its political myths. Also, there is the question of its praxis to contend with. The need to act decisively and effectively does away with the need for either a preexistent economic base for revolution (that was essential for Marx) or the presence of a political infrastructure of party vanguards, which is the essence of Leninist agitation. Rather, all that seems to be needed is the cultivation of revolutionary mysticism, what Horowitz describes as "the vaguely anarchical assumption . . . that the sum total of what one really needs is an action group, same kind of organized group of 'foco,' usually clandestine, to create sufficient chaos or destruction of the state and society in selected periods of the capitalist economy" (Horowitz, 1993:63).

Inciardi's descriptions of "narco-terrorism" provide insight into Horowitz's analysis of elitist, avant-garde, revolutionary movements. As with the Red Brigades in Italy, the earlier Tupamaros in Uruguay, and the Cuban model of revolution, the theory of the foco is a theory of the putsch—the secretive, conspiratorial small group capable of seizing power at the proper moment. In Peru with the Shining Path, in Columbia with the Armed Revolutionary Forces of Columbia and the 19th of April Movement (M-9), we see a compromise with political purity for the sake, it may be supposed, of strategic advantage in the struggle. The insurgencies engaged in typical terroristic acts, but they also became directly involved in illegal drug production and distribution—not merely by offering "protection" to the traffickers but also by overseeing the trafficking in certain regions and in coordinating the growing and refining of coca (Inciardi, 1991).

It has been noted how religious leaders engaging in textual hermeneutics on lithophanic verities, or in logical duplicity, can persuade their followers that certain acts of violence are justifiable despite specific doctrinal prohibitions against such behavior. So it does not require a leap of imagination to see how the binding obligations of a cause can be relaxed through an enabling ideology. Authorized interpreters can foster the suppression and repression of some interests and goals in the struggle, even as they give expression to others. The psychological dynamics of radical extremist discourse as it affects the ideologue's sense of accountability for their actions may be understood as consequences of the pliability and intellectual elasticity of doctrine.

Practitioners are pressured to conceal from themselves as well as others any "base" motives behind their politics; they thus become dulled by piety, coming to believe that unlike others they are uninterested in personal perquisites. Their claim is that when they seek office, power, and income these are not sought as private enjoyments but only because they advance group or societal interests. Where ideology serves, on the one hand, as a warrant for ruthlessness in the name of high values, on the other it permits its practitioners to present themselves as having selfless ambitions that rationalize the unrestrained discharge of power, violence, or personal greed.

Immersed in a highly charged climate of significant truth, individuals come to experience themselves as different; the truth is not indubitable but it is usually embattled and, therefore, precarious, which means that it requires vigilant defense and safeguards. Psychologically, within the nerves of an organization the individual may subliminally experience a rebirth of the self (and, as some do, celebrate by acquiring a new name, a nom de guerre). For with the adoption of an ideology, the whole world has a different feel, a boundary line gets drawn in the periodization of the self into a before-and-after, with dim and lucid regions of the mind plainly obvious to the believer.

To the extent that the organization and its social and political theories become the grounding of identity, the task of the terrorist then is not simply an empirical one of proselytizing; more is involved. By becoming a member, a soldier in the struggle through the embrace of doctrine, the parameters of the individual's role become set. First there is the job of spreading the word; second, one must do what is needed, which often entails defending the group against those who seek to discredit it.[4]

Accountability and the Problem of Punishment

Principled political opposition need not always mean violence and the renunciation of culpability. A comparison of terrorists with those who practice civil disobedience is instructive in this regard. What distinguishes the civilly disobedient is not only their methods for effecting change but also their ideologies in response to the resistance they encounter.

It seems clear that in the consideration of terrorism and disobedience we are dealing with two extremes, the ends of a spectrum. They seem so irreconcilable that there would be, at first glance, no rational reason for linking them, that it would tarnish the name, achievements, and history of the civilly disobedient to compare them in any way with terrorists. The two represent polar opposites on a morality-immorality continuum within the framework of political deviance that constitutes law-breaking. But they have much in common. Terrorism and civil disobedience share a determination to effect political and social change, but they do not share a similar attitude toward violence as the means to bring about such change. What they have in common is a contempt for the morality, and often the legitimacy, of the powers or forces that they challenge. It is not only the methods of the civil disobedients that become crucial in lining up the world on one side or the other but also the assumption of responsibility, with all that that implies about their struggles.

When contrasted with terrorism, the civil disobedience movement works in similar and at the same time in different directions. Both deliberately break the law, but the civil disobedient in so doing abjures violence; the law-breaking is performed as openly as possible. Those involved in this type of political deviance do not challenge the enemy violently. They accept the fundamental legitimacy of both government and community; they act to acquit rather than to challenge their duty as citizens. This they do en masse, making advance proclamations of their intentions. The terrorist, on the other hand, secretes a bomb in such manner that it will both do the most damage and at the same time intimidate the civilian population. The terrorist then detonates it, preferably by remote control. The two have in common their law-breaking and sometimes their denial of the legitimacy of the government that they oppose. Whether the strategies of disobedience involve only symbolic protest or lead social movements, they seek to persuade the political leadership that it must attend to the opposition's proposals so that modifications and changes satisfactory to all parties can be achieved.

Terrorists operate from a different strategic imperative. Their acts of violence and destruction are intended to impress upon a public and its government that to maintain current policies and programs that are opposed by some groups within the population will cost more than to change them. The hope of the terrorists is that the price to be paid in fear and loss of life and property will prove unacceptably high and that concessions will have to be made. Such techniques may backfire, however, and become counterproductive for those who initiate them.

If a group believes that it is treated unjustly, that the political process is unresponsive and offers little realistic hope for reversing or changing laws and policies that are deeply resented and offensive, and finally, that nonviolent acts of civil disobedience do not work to produce the desired results or prospects for change, then, given the strength of the group's convictions and the realistic appraisal of demographic and political considerations, terror could seem to be the ultimate resort to weaken, arouse, and stimulate others to action. Who then can assign responsibility forthrightly for what happens when terror is used in a desperate attempt to change intolerable conditions?

Those who participate in civil disobedience do not have to make a public assumption of responsibility, in the sense that theirs is open action, as open as possible, widely publicized with banners and proclamations declaring with pride that it is their parade, their boycott, their sit-in, their disobedience. They give advance warnings of their intentions, and if they do not invite retaliation, they certainly expect it. Some few deny that these movements are nonviolent, because, it is charged, they provoke violence. Aside from other moral issues, responsibility must be placed upon those who commit an act, not blamed on those who brought them to the position of committing it. Nor is provocation a clear-cut issue, for if it is the civil disobedients who provoke the defenders of the status quo into violence, then it is the police and lawmakers who provoke the protesters into civil disobedience. But the distinction between the violent and the nonviolent becomes clarified when it is realized that the violence is almost invariably against those in the civil disobedience movement, and except for instinctive self-defense, they seldom if ever retaliate (Sagarin and Kelly, 1986).

But what of punishment? The terrorist seeks to escape it, the civilly disobedient almost welcome it. The civilly disobedient accept punishment not because it declares the wrongness of the act but because it focuses on the wrongness of the law and the moral righteousness of the act.

The civil disobedient accept the responsibility of law-breaking but deny the responsibility of blameworthiness. They differ from the terrorist not only in their nonviolence but also in another factor: the road to the goal. The terrorist's goal is to instill fear in a population so as to bring about pressure for submission, or, at the very least, the recognition of the grievances; the civil disobedient's goal is to compel and dramatically focus attention upon the nature of the conflict. So certain are they that in the confrontation of two moral systems theirs will be triumphant that their goal is to bring about such a moral conflict. What could be more responsible than this as a course of action designed to effectuate social change?

Most terrorist campaigns are methods to establish claims for their notion of justice, to seek new societies, or to release frustration that cannot be ameliorated satisfactorily through normal political channels. Thus, solutions to the problem of terrorism seem invariably beyond the narrow frameworks of counterterror. Increased surveillance may not discourage terrorists but actually strengthen their resolve to overcome it. What then? What tools and strategies might be utilized in coming to terms with terrorism? The knowledge structures and ideologies of terrorists appear to be of two broad types. Their judgmental heuristics reduce complex social realities to simple moral rights and wrongs. A price is paid for this mental economy. Ideologies and the motivations they stimulate or reinforce are not infallible guides to the nature of social reality. Some terrorist beliefs, theories, and schemes are relatively poor and inaccurate representations of the world they wish to transform or destroy. Thus, a grasp of these ideological maps and the emotional fire they can generate can provide useful data as guideposts about the weaknesses and inadequacies in the social system. Finally, without an effort to understand the political language and self-understanding of terrorist organizations, policies that can frustrate them or open up nonviolent alternatives to them do not seem possible.

Notes

1. An essay that takes sharp, if not deliberately contentious, exception to this research stream is Jerrold Post (1990). The burden of his controversial argument is that "the cause is not the cause" (35). This is a version of Michel's "Iron Law of Oligarchy," in which maintaining the existence of a terrorist organization itself is more important than the official political goals of the organization. Sociologically, this thesis makes sense. The argument's plausibility is also buttressed by its appreciation of the central role that feelings such as revenge and hatred play in the ethos of some terrorist groups—roles that displace and even make irrelevant nationalist agendas. Recently, for example, some 350 Provisional Irish Republican Army members imprisoned in Long Kesh, Northern Ireland, were asked by the general headquarters staff and Sinn Fein whether they would approve a cease-fire initiative and negotiations to end the fighting. The deal would involve London, Dublin, and Belfast, the principal governments caught up in the struggle, and the peace proposals would offer the real possibility of a general amnesty and a chance to abruptly conclude twenty- to thirty-year sentences for these prisoners. Their answer was no. Sean Lynch, the officer-in-charge of the provo IRA prisoner of war unit, said that not until the British retire from the island of Ireland could they be trusted (Ridgeway and Farrelly, 1994). One could argue that these dramatic events confirm Post's earnestly stated views that emotions overrule cool, rational political judgment. His earlier, more radical claim is that "political terrorists are driven to commit acts of violence as a consequence of psychological forces, and . . . their special psycho-logic is constructed to rationalize acts they are psychologically compelled to commit. Thus . . . individuals are drawn to the path of terrorism in order to commit acts of violence, and their special logic which is grounded in their psychology

and reflected in their rhetoric becomes the justification for their violent acts"
(1990:15).

One cannot fail to notice, in the midst of what appears to be compulsive desperate
behavior, teetering on the psychotic and suicidal, a sense of dignity among the
oppressed. Whether among the Irish, Moluccans, Sikhs, Palestinians, Puerto Ri-
cans, or warring factions in the former Yugoslavia, the common impulse seems to
be an incredibly deep urge to keep faith with the past and with one's specific identity. The practical mode of action in the absence of a fully equipped military apparatus is to make the dominant forces of control share some of the pain of what
the vanquished experience. The recourse to terrorism is surely not only instrumental (and here Post has a point); it is also symbolic and expressive—more than
a means to political ends, it is also a registration of powerfully felt grievances.
Once considered marginal in many revolutionary movements, terrorist groups are
now in many parts of the world the very apotheosis of resistance cultures.

What drives the reductionist orientation (of which Post's essay is a good example)
is the metaphysical striving to get at the real, substantive essence of the phenomenon. What is overlooked are the powerful shaping influences of such contingencies
as history, place, and the multitude of beliefs and desires circulating at any given
time. One can scarcely describe such factors as incidental elements in the makeup
of the terrorist organization or personality.

2. Any definition of terrorism that ignores state-sponsored terrorism is shortsighted
   and distorted. Political violence as an instrument of government policy, whether at
   home or abroad, cannot be denied. Moreover, if the definitions were limited to
   frightening, insensate, or illegitimate violence, national states would be the greatest terrorists of all (Rubinstein, 1987).

   There is much debate still over the definition of terrorism, much like the contro-
   versies over the definition of organized crime. It seems that in both instances there
   is nothing peculiar or unique about the actions or crimes in themselves; it is the
   motives and methods of the actors that matter.

   In the case of terrorism, there is a dimension to these behaviors that is sensitive
   to mass media. The need to communicate is basic to mobilizing support, and in
   many cases terrorists have not hesitated to carry out acts for no other reason than
   that their very outrageousness ensures television coverage (Kelly, 1986).

3. Perhaps the best known example of how our sense of moral and ethical rectitude
   can be ignored is the linguistic gymnastics of the Holocaust. "The Final Solution," a phase that now carries horrendous meanings, when first devised permitted
   the Nazi apparatus of genocide to function smoothly because its policy lacked lurid
   descriptiveness. The term was sufficiently vague so that it did not readily alert German citizens or many Jewish victims; it was a clever subterfuge that allowed a mass
   murder machine to function undisturbed throughout the last two years of the war.

4. To the degree that ideological thought can be reflexive, its inherent limits as a
   totalizing discourse that disguises itself from itself become apparent. Gouldner
   puts the issue brilliantly:

Each ideology . . . takes itself as engaged in the analysis of an out-there objective reality. In point of fact, however, it is always interpreting, not simply mirroring reality, social reality always being an object constituted in *part* by its own interpretation. Each ideology thus represses an understanding of itself as a world-*constituting* (not merely world-*reflecting*) discourse. It is in that externalizing way that ideology becomes engaged not only in discovery but also in *recovery* (note: re-discovery of the socially occluded— i.e. the public good). It is a recovery, in some part, because it seeks to enable men to recover, to become aware of their own active role in constructing social reality. (1976:281, emphasis in original)

What dimensions of the psyche are excited by a commitment to ideological doctrines can only be guessed at; we do know that many believers are quite willing to take that irreversible step into eternity in the name of this or that cause without flinching.

References

Bandura, Albert (1990). "Mechanisms of Moral Disengagement." Pp. 161–91 in *Origins of Terrorism*, W. Reich, ed. New York: Cambridge University Press.

Brown, Gerald L., and Frederick Goodwin (1986). "Humor Aggression—A Biological Perspective." Pp. 36–52 in *Unmasking the Psychopath*, W. H. Reid et al., eds. New York: W. W. Norton.

Bunney, William E. (1982). "Human Aggression and Suicide: Their Relationships to Neuropsychiatric Diagnosis and Serotonin Metabolism." Pp. 287–307 in *Serotonin in Biological Psychiatry*, T. Ho et al., eds. New York: Raven Press.

Collin, Richard O. (1989). "When Reality Came Unglued: Antonio Savasta and the Italian Red Brigades." *Violence, Aggression and Terrorism* 3 (4):269–94.

Corrado, R. R. (1981). "A Critique of the Mental Disorder Perspective of Political Terrorism." *International Journal of Law and Psychiatry* 4:293–310.

Crenshaw, Martha (1986). "The Psychology of Political Terrorism." Pp. 128–56 in *Political Psychology*, Margaret G. Hermann, ed. San Francisco: Jossey-Bass.

Erikson, Erik (1969). *Gandhi's Truth: The Origins of Militant Nonviolence*. New York: W. W. Norton.

Fanon, Frantz (1963). *The Wretched of the Earth*. New York: Grove Press.

Ferracuti, Franco, and F. Bruno (1983). "Italy: A Systems Perspective." Pp. 71–93 in *Aggression in Global Perspective*, A. P. Goldstein and M. H. Segall, eds. New York: Pergaman Press.

Freedman, Laurence Z. (1979). "Why Does Terrorism Terrorize?" *Terrorism: An International Journal* 6 (3):390–400.

Goffman, Erving (1961). *Asylums: Essays on the Social Situation of Mental Patients and Other Inmates*. New York: Anchor Books.

Gouldner, Alvin W. (1976). *The Dialectic of Ideology and Technology*, vol. 1. New York: Oxford University Press.

Gurr, Ted Robert (1990). "Terrorism in Democracies: Its Social and Political Bases." Pp. 86–102 in *Origins of Terrorism*, W. Reich, ed. New York: Cambridge University Press.

Heskin, K. (1980). *Northern Ireland: A Psychological Analysis*. New York: Columbia University Press.

Horowitz, Irving Louis (1993). *The Decomposition of Sociology*. New York: Oxford University Press.

Hubbard, David G. (1983). *The Age of Terrorism*. Boston: Little, Brown.

Inciardi, James A. (1991). "Narcoterrorism: A Perspective and Commentary." Pp. 89–105 in *Perspectives on Deviance: Dominance, Degradation and Denigration*, Robert J. Kelly and Donald E. J. MacNamara, eds. Cincinnati: Anderson Publishing.

Kelly, Robert J. (1986). "Implications of the Concept of Terrorism: Terrorism as a Means of Communication." *Journal of International Law Enforcement Intelligence Analysts* 1 (2):30–48.

—— (1991). "Terrorism and Intrigue." *Italian Journal* 5 (1):21–32.

—— (1994). "Fanatics and Fundamentalists." *Journal of International Law Enforcement Intelligence Analysts* 8 (2):221–42.

Kelly, Robert J., and Robert W. Rieber (1992). "Collateral Damage on the Homefront: The Gulf in America." *Journal of Social Distress* 1 (2):106–22.

Kelly, Robert J., and Rufus Schatzberg (1992). "Galvanizing Indiscriminate Political Violence: Mind-Sets and Some Ideological Constructs in Terrorism." *International Journal of Comparative and Applied Criminal Justice* 16 (1):15–37.

Kelman, H. C. (1973). "Violence Without Moral Restraint: Reflections on the Dehumanization of Victims and Victimizers." *Journal of Social Issues* 29:25–61.

Kilson, Martin C. (1969). "The New Black Intellectuals." *Dissent*, July/August, pp. 32–53.

Kramer, Martin (1990). "The Moral Logic of Hizballah." Pp. 131–57 in *Origins of Terrorism*, W. Reich, ed. New York: Cambridge University Press.

Laqueur, Walter (1987). *The Age of Terrorism*. Boston: Little, Brown.

Lifton, Robert J. (1986). *The Nazi Doctors: Medical Killing and the Psychology of Genocide*. New York: Basic Books.

Litcheim, George (1965). "The Concept of Ideology." *History and Theory* 4:164–70.

MacStiofain, Sean (1975). *Revolutionary in Ireland*. London: Gordon Cremones.

Mao Zhe-Tung (1957). "Let a Hundred Flowers Bloom." *New Leader* 40 (9): sect. 2.

Moore, Mark H. (1987). "Organized Crime as a Business Enterprise." Pp. 51–64 in *Major Issues in Organized Crime Control*, H. Edelhertz, ed. National Institute of Justice. Washington, D.C.: Government Printing Office.

Post, Jerrold M. (1990). "Terrorist Psycho-Logic: Terrorist Behavior as a Product of Psychological Forces." Pp. 25–40 in *Origins of Terrorism: Psychologies, Ideologies, Theologies, States of Mind*, W. Reich, ed. New York: Cambridge University Press.

Ridgeway, James, and Patrick Farrelly (1994). "The Belfast Connection." *Village Voice*, February 8, pp. 29–36.

Rieber, Robert W., and Robert J. Kelly (1991). "Substance and Shadow: Images of the Enemy." Pp. 180–217 in *The Psychology of War and Peace*, Robert W. Rieber, ed. New York: Plenum Books.

Rubinstein, Richard E. (1987). *Alchemists of Revolution: Terrorism in the Modern World*. New York: Basic Books.

Sagarin, Edward, and Robert J. Kelly (1986). "Political Deviance and the Assumption of Responsibility." *Deviant Behavior* 7:217–42.

Sapp, Allen (1991). "White Supremacy Groups and Bias-Motivated Crimes." Pp. 105–31 in *Bias Crimes: The Law Enforcement Response,* G. J. Buckwalter, ed. Chicago: Office of International Criminal Justice, University of Illinois at Chicago.

Shils, Edward (1958). "Ideology and Civility: On the Politics of the Intellectual." *Sewanee Review* 66 (summer):450–80.

9

Responsibility, Anxiety, and Organizational Deviance

The Systemic and Elusive Properties of Responsibility in Organizations and Groups

José E. Sánchez

Organizations, Groups, and Individuals as Open Systems

An organization is a living system of organically interdependent units of varying complexity structured to perform a primary task. These units may be individuals, roles, work-groups, departments, or divisions, as well as the organization as a whole. Each interacts with the others across its boundary, and each is affected by and affects the overall functioning of the organization.

An organization performs its tasks and expresses its moral codes, its goals, its priorities, and its culture through the actions of its constituent units, which organize themselves around an overall primary task. The primary task of an organization is the task that it must perform in order to exist. Roles and other aspects of an institution emerge as functions related to the performance of its primary task, as individuals bring the many aspects of their selves into the roles they take up.

Organizations are not simply groupings of individuals. Once within them, individuals become members, and this status is more than an identifying label. It implies a real relatedness to others with real consequences for how individuals may act as members. And, in addition to expressing themselves through their members, organizations also enact through them institutional contradictions, collectively shared anxieties and feelings, and other irrational aspects of its functioning. As Shapiro and Carr (1991:84) argue:

When we speak of organizations as entities that handle people's feelings, the context inevitably includes feelings of which they are not consciously aware. However confident an organization may appear in its public presentation, uncertainty and ignorance [and, I would add, all forms of irrationality] always exist within it. Individuals and subgroups who work within the organization and therefore find themselves identified with its various complex dynamics become filled with [these feelings]. . . . From this perspective, then, we can speak of an organization's "internal life."

As a living, organic whole, an organization uses its members as vehicles to carry out actions on its behalf or as vessels to contain blame, responsibility, authority, anxiety, shame, or aggression. In their reciprocal relationship with the organization, members find it and its units useful in similar ways.

Human groups and organizations function to one degree or another as open systems. Their internal existence depends on exchanges with their environments. The system's boundary with its environment separates what is within it from what is outside. In addition to functioning to selectively import resources, information, and materials from its environment, this boundary provides (a) a means by which the group or organization establishes an identity for itself and its members; (b) a point of contact between it and the larger system and, thus, a causal nexus; and (c) a container for the internal context within which an organizational culture and social structure are generated. Conceiving of individuals, groups, and organizations in this way highlights their membership in systems of progressively greater complexity. The focus of this perspective, therefore, is on membership: the individual as member of a work-group or department; the department as member of the organization; the organization as member of an industry; the industry as member of an economy; and so on. Otto Kernberg (1980:238) summarized this view: "A systems approach to organizations considers the institution as an overall system dynamically and hierarchically integrating various subsystems (such as the personality of leadership, the nature of group processes, the task systems, and administrative structures or the organization) and conceives of the environment of the organization as suprasystems affecting the institution in dynamically and hierarchically organized ways."

Responsibility as a Symbolic and
Transferable Institutional Resource

Responsibility emerges in social interaction. It involves a social relationship within principles that are greater than the individual. In this sense, the character of responsibility is institutional. It may be used to refer to a small group or a family, a social establishment such as a corporation or governmental agency, or a society. An individual, group, or organization behaves responsibly when it takes into account and acts on the basis of social expectations and obligations. To behave irresponsibly is to disregard them. A major challenge facing any organization is the allocation, distribution, and management of responsibility as it relates to its task. Members are expected to carry out certain task activities. A police department expects its officers to enforce the law and to protect and serve the public. Correctional officers are expected to maintain custody and control over their charges. However, they must carry out their roles within more or less prescribed moral parameters, the violation of which renders them irresponsible even if the instrumental tasks they perform are carried out successfully.

Responsibility is the flip side of authority. Whereas authority gives the individual, group, or organization the right to act or to work, responsibility is a measure of how appropriately any of these entities manage the boundaries of this right. Legitimacy may be considered as the proportional relation between the authority bestowed on members and how responsibly they have exercised it.

Responsibility, like authority and legitimacy, is an organizational resource that is distributed and redistributed, earned and lost, through institutional dynamics that are often beyond the control of members. Standing forcefully and outside of the members' awareness and control, organizations often compel them to conform to demands that contradict values that they may hold deeply in other spheres of their lives.

Organizations and responsibility are social facts. It was Emile Durkheim who defined social facts as "every way of acting, fixed or not, capable of exercising on the individual an external constraint" (Durkheim, 1950:13). Social facts "are endowed with coercive power, by . . . which they impose themselves upon [the individual], independent of his individual will" (2) and are neither reducible to nor are the effect of the actions or motivations of individual members.

This perspective flies in the face of the traditional conceptions of responsibility. This is particularly so as it refers to criminal culpability, which is one important manifestation of this concept. American jurisprudence holds that only the individual can be legally responsible for his actions; the individual must possess *mens rea*. Other standards, such as "strict" and "vicarious" liability, have been used in cases in which individual culpability is difficult to establish. Mostly, however, these principles have been applied within the context of civil proceedings. As a result, the criminal prosecution of corporate and governmental deviance remains a challenging and perplexing problem. Organizations may act like individuals but cannot be punished like them.

The problem lies in the fact that corporate and governmental deviance often cannot be traced to the behavior of any one individual, rather being most frequently the product of complex group and organizational processes. Ermann and Lundman (1987:8) have argued that such behavior may result as much from the direct actions of individuals as from a lack of overall knowledge by any individual or department, or from the serendipitous consequences of the implementation of the seemingly rational and "legal" initiatives and strategies of organizational elites.

I take as my starting point the individual's membership in the group or organization. While in the role of member, an individual's behavior may be understood as an expression of group and organizational dynamics unwittingly entered into and acted out on behalf of these social entities. Therefore, the question I will pose throughout this chapter is this: What group and organizational dynamics are enacted on behalf of these social entities by the irresponsible behavior of individuals while in their member roles?

Individuals, groups, and organizations modulate the level of anxiety by managing their structures of responsibility. When faced with a need to defend against anxiety, responsibility is transferred, distributed, and redistributed by individuals, groups, organizations, and societies. How this is accomplished is a key focus of this chapter.

The Perspective: Illustrations and Analysis

Let us look at the following example[1] to demonstrate what I mean.

Case 1

A staff review committee consisting of high-ranking members of the accounting department of a sales firm has been charged with the task of evaluating staff according to formally established criteria and recommending the best candidates for promotion to decision makers at higher levels of the organization. The department's culture has traditionally been oriented toward maintaining peace and avoiding intragroup conflict, and, as a result, the department has managed to develop a reputation within the organization as being a respectable, collaborative, well-managed, and peaceful unit. Behind closed doors, committee members discuss and deride certain candidates. Some of the candidates are described as objectively unqualified for promotion or as incompetent, and this is openly acknowledged in private conversations between members. During formal meetings of the committee, however, members speak positively about every candidate and unanimously recommended them all for promotion. After the decisions are made, committee members privately rationalize their actions by invoking the fear of ostracism, reprisal, and the potential for conflict that negative votes would generate on intradepartmental cohesion and collegiality.

The actions of the committee, which have been institutionalized in the department, clearly violate ethical and professional (and possibly legal) standards. In the minds of its members, the practice exists for a "good cause," although there may be legal grounds for civil or possibly criminal action by applicants who, by all objective criteria, were highly qualified and who were disadvantaged by the review committee's behavior.

But against whom would the charges be made? Was each individual responsible? Or was each individual unable to behave responsibly for fear of ostracism or retaliation, or for fear that the department would break out into conflict? Does this constitute duress, or some other excuse or justification? If so, does that imply that, rather than blaming any one individual, it is the review committee as a whole that must bear the responsibility for its actions? What sanctions could be applied against the committee as a unit? Would such sanctions also acknowledge the mitigating circumstances surrounding the actions of individual members? Or should the entire accounting department be held responsible for encouraging the proliferation of dishonesty and irresponsibility? Or should the higher authorities, the board of directors, or even the organization as a whole be held responsible for the actions of the committee for condoning its grievance against qualified applicants?

Obviously, no easy answer to these questions exists. The situation constitutes what Smith and Berg (1987) refer to as a paradox of group life. The example shows how the group as a whole imposes itself on its members to enforce and sustain a culture of intradepartmental tranquility. Looking at it from a group-as-a whole perspective, Wells (1990; see also Agazarian, 1988; Agazarian and Peters, 1985) sheds light on the dynamics of the committee: "The unit of analysis is the group as a system. . . . Hence, group members are considered interdependent subsystems co-acting and interacting together via the group's . . . mentality. Group-level analysis assumes that when a co-actor acts, he or she is acting not only on his behalf, but on behalf of the group or parts of the group. . . . Simply stated, the co-actor is seen as a vehicle through which the group expresses its life" (54).

In its function of linking its members together in a tacit collusive agreement, the group mentality[2] serves as the vehicle through which members communicate unconsciously and thereby share fears, hopes, and anxieties, as well as other unconscious mental content. The group mentality is a repository of the split-off and projected parts and feelings of members, and it is where the tension between the aims of individual members and those of the group is manifested.

In projecting upward its responsibility to evaluate colleagues objectively, the staff review committee also rid itself of its collective anxiety. Projection was used as a social defense (Bion, 1961; Hirschhorn, 1990; Jacques, 1953, 1955; Klein, 1946; Menzies, 1959; Wells, 1990) against the anxiety generated by the shared but unconscious fear that the accounting department would be riddled with aggression and that committee members would become responsible for the consequences. In a seminal article, A. Kenneth Rice (1969; see also Trist and Murray, 1990:278) writes: "When he joins a group to perform a group task, [the individual] must, by his very joining, commit himself to take the role assigned to him, and hence to control irrelevant activities and sentience. Mature individuals thus find themselves distressed and guilty when in any attempt to reassert 'management control' over their own individual boundaries they recognize, however vaguely, the number of different hostages they have given to so many conflicting sentient groups."

The potentially disruptive effects of acting responsibly in relation to their task was too much to bear. By projecting its competence and its duty to act responsibly out of the group and onto higher authorities, the review committee relieved itself of the anxiety it experienced in carrying out its primary task in the face of their sentient ties to colleagues in the department and their need to protect themselves. Furthermore, the committee made it possible to credit itself with the positive actions at higher levels while avoiding responsibility for the negative decisions of those higher authorities. This process worked out quite well as a defensive maneuver, since the reputation of the department remained untarnished after every evaluation cycle, and an external target was provided against which aggrieved applicants could aim their aggression. As Menzies (1990) notes: "Anxieties about one's capacity to do one's job may be projected downwards into subordinates and their roles. . . . Projection of one's capacities upwards also takes place along with an expectation that one's superiors will take over one's responsibilities, so that anxiety about one's capacity to do one's job properly is relieved" (Menzies, in Trist and Murray, 1990:467).

Organizationally, however, as far as the review committee is concerned, the benefits gained from its defensive posture came at great cost: The group abdicated its authority to work and, as a result, lost its way in the structure of the department and organization while compromising its institutional meaning and legitimacy. For it ceased to be a staff review committee once it began functioning like a staff and public relations committee. Instead of eliminating anxiety, the committee simply functioned to redistribute and load it into those members who could serve as appropriate vessels for unwanted feelings of resentment, inauthenticity, and powerlessness. These individuals were left holding affects that could not be publicly expressed without experiencing, in fact or fantasy, the threat of ostracism or reprisal, or the fear of being seen as disloyal to colleagues. Nevertheless, the group as a whole was stuck with its decision, and the organization made it difficult, if not impossible, for its members to publicly disown it.

This example indicates that the culture, social structure, and mode of functioning of groups and organizations are created in response to the individual and collective needs of their members (Trist and Bamford, 1951). The explanation of what happened in the staff review committee of the accounting department is more appropriately found in the functioning of the group rather than in the motivations of its members. Individual members found themselves unable to behave responsibly when confronted with the will of the group. The apparently rational deliberations and actions of the group's members hid the irrational basis for the cohesiveness of the department as a group. The power of this unconscious bond was given precedence by members over the primary task and over rationality. Something along the lines of what Janis (1982) labeled "groupthink" occurred.

Let us now expand the context of the analysis of the review committee to an organizational level by adding further details to this example.

Case 1 (Continued)

For years, the promotions process at the sales firm had been seen by most members as illegitimate, and the members of upper management were perceived as being motivated in their decisions by political considerations rather than objective criteria. These themes were a dominant part of the organizational culture. The institutional folklore of distrust and illegitimacy included the belief that members who were seen as loyal or "useful" to the dominant upper management subgroup were more likely to be granted promotion than those who were either unfamiliar to them or opponents of their collective aims. However, there was a great deal of ambivalence about these feelings. Also existing side by side with these beliefs was the sense that the higher authorities were capable of acting responsibly when faced with objectively impressive, though not necessarily politically correct, applicants. The latter beliefs were sometimes validated by the fact that several candidates had been promoted over the years who were not likely to be promoted, according to the organizational folklore about political favoritism. Symbolically, these candidates represented hope in an organization where standards of performance were unclear at best.

It must be recalled that the accounting department's review committee was composed of individuals who were also its highest ranking members and, as such, were the product of the organization's promotion processes. Therefore, although the troublesome feelings associated with promotions were widespread, in order to reach their decisions and simultaneously protect their own personal sense of legitimacy, the review committee had to split off and disattend any doubts about the validity of the process. The general institutional ambivalence about its legitimacy facilitated this dynamic and made it possible to export the committee's responsibility for the outcome of its deliberations to higher authorities. In acting as they did, the committee members believed in the hope that all applicants, particularly the meritorious ones, had an opportunity of being recognized by those in later phases of the evaluation process.

The review committee, viewed within this broader organizational frame, permitted itself to behave irresponsibly because it convinced itself that its deliberations would not have a significant impact on the overall proceedings or their final outcome. In effect, it ended up colluding with dominant organizational subgroups to perpetuate irresponsibility and illegitimacy as it undermined its own responsibility, legitimacy, and authority to do work. And, by ranking those members who were not qualified for promotion equally with those who were, it also undermined their achievements and their chances for promotion while discrediting its own ability to acknowledge the competence of colleagues. What is most important for this discussion, however, is that the committee, as a functional part of the organization, acted on its behalf to sustain broader-based organizational anxiety about professional standards.

Another example shows how, by isolating itself from the larger system, an entire organization employed irresponsible behavior to contain anxiety.

Case 2

January 28, 1986, will for a long time remind Americans of one of the worst disasters of the twentieth century. Shortly after takeoff, the "O-rings" of the booster rockets on the *Challenger* space shuttle failed, making the rockets explode and thereby killing the seven occupants of the craft. The report of the Presidential Commission on the Space Shuttle Accident and the news media cited the political pressures faced by NASA to produce a large number of flights. It was felt that a schedule of twenty-four flights per year would move the shuttle program toward the goals of routinization and economy. NASA wanted to present the shuttle program as one that could make space travel not only routine but also economical, profitable, and financially self-sustaining. The focus on schedule was contradictory to an external and internal climate of budgetary constraints and cuts. According to the presidential commission's report, engineers at NASA and at Morton-Thiokol, the manufacturer of the rockets, expressed concern about the integrity of the seals in cold weather even as late as the morning of the launch. However, the seals had been a safety concern since 1982. Middle-level personnel at the Marshall Space Center—not the leaders of NASA—approved the launch of the *Challenger*. According to the testimony, they did so in a way that appeared to contradict conscious deliberations and forethought. As a Morton-Thiokol engineer reported: "We had dealt with Marshall for a long time and have always been in the position of defending our position to make sure that we were ready to fly and I guess I didn't realize until after the meeting and after several days that we had absolutely changed our position from what we had been before. We had to prove to them that we weren't ready. We were trying to prove to them that it wouldn't work" (Report of the Presidential Commission, 92). It was difficult for Marshall Space Center executives to hear the warnings of the Morton-Thiokol engineers given their pressure to maintain a schedule. The middle-level managers who approved the flight were acting as if they were the leaders of the program. According to Hirschhorn (1990:189), "They, rather than their superiors, represented the need to launch and therefore reversed the way they typically considered technical judgments. . . . There was no need to let [their supervisors know] because they were acting as the ersatz heads of NASA." The leadership had been isolated, and important information that could have stopped the flight was not made available.[3]

The relevant question here is: Who was responsible for the shuttle disaster? Was it the middle-level managers who acted beyond the boundaries of their authority? Was it the Reagan administration, which insisted that a teacher be made a member of the flight team and thereby created additional public pressure for the technical and management teams? Were the leaders of NASA responsible for creating an environment of excessive expectations from the shuttle program? Or were the responsible parties the government officials who pushed for American technical superiority over the Soviets at the same time that they insisted on fiscal austerity? Were the engineers at Morton-Thiokol responsible for not insisting more aggressively that their products could present a danger?

Again, the answers are neither simple nor clear. How the questions are answered—that is, who is deemed responsible—depends on the "frame for understanding" (Smith and Berg, 1987) that is used. Smith and Berg argue that "frames that pull one's attention to the parts create very different 'realities' from those focused on the system as a whole" (157).

A *New York Times* article (Broad, 1986) noted that NASA as an organization was "like a close-knit family. Problems stay within; whistle blowers are few." The organization set itself up to become isolated and to behave like a closed system. NASA's problems with high leadership turnover, blocked channels of communication between institutional authorities, and leader abdication created the context in which it was possible for middle managers to make decisions they were not authorized to make and to overlook the fact that the Marshall Space Center was responsible to the larger agency, its staff, and the public.

If the shuttle disaster is framed in a context that focuses on organizational units or individuals, then the responsibility might be located in particular individuals or functional teams. However, when looking at this event from the context of the organization as a whole, not only is it difficult to locate blame but in addition a broader set of relationships and their interconnectedness become available for analysis. Hirschhorn (1990:192), writing about the shuttle disaster, points out:

> When leaders abdicate, lower-level managers are forced to resolve policy issues that should be set by the top. They are unable to focus on technical issues alone, and indeed their technical judgments can be distorted by the confused policy environment in which they work. . . . Lacking policy criteria to guide their design choices, lower-level managers typically face two opposing choices: They can burrow even more deeply into their work, becoming unable to complete their projects, or they can presume to fill the leadership vacuum, perhaps giving play to their fantasy that they can run the organization even if their leaders cannot.

Middle-level managers at the Marshall Space Center confronted a great deal of anxiety in the face of an underbounded organization and persistent problems with the authority of its leadership. In order to manage their anxiety, they improperly crossed the boundaries of their authority and attributed to themselves a degree of responsibility they were not authorized to possess, along with a self-assurance that they had no objective reason to maintain. Manic defenses against anxiety (Hirschhorn, 1990; Jacques, 1953, 1955; Menzies, 1959, 1990) were mobilized in order to deny the pervasive sense of vulnerability they felt within the context of so many contradictory demands and unreliable leadership. As a result, middle-level managers found it easier to split off and to project upward their feelings of uncertainty, and this permitted them to act and feel as they did.

The legal problems surrounding James Beggs—who was NASA's chief administrator and who went on leave after his difficulties while an executive at General Dynamics—compromised the legitimacy of the leadership. Moreover, some accounts claim that even after William Graham, the new acting director, took over, Beggs compromised Graham's authority by continuing to affect the functioning of the agency from a distance.

Given the evidence and testimony reported by the presidential commission and by journalists (much of which is omitted from this chapter because of space considerations), it is reasonable to think that, under a stable and clearly defined hierarchy and leadership, the middle-level managers would not have acted as they did (Jacques, 1990). They expressed in their actions some of the fundamental features and contradictions of NASA's structures of authority and responsibility, as well as the agency's relationship to and anxiety about the contradictory demands made by stakeholders in its environment.

Despite the complexity of these events, however, the investigation into the crash was focused on finding the particular factors or individuals responsible.

"It had the flavor of trying to find an appropriate scapegoat, so that certain parts of the system could be free of blame. There was very little public thinking that sought explanation of the system as a whole" (Smith and Berg, 1987:156).

Recently, however, Diane Vaughan's (1996) impressive and detailed sociological and historiographic study of the *Challenger* disaster has convincingly analyzed the ways in which systemic and organizational arrangements that operate outside the consciousness or volition of participants create contextual preconditions for institutional deviance.

Neither of the illustrative examples provided above resulted directly in criminal indictments. They do, however, represent instances of organizational deviance that result from institutionalized social defenses against organizational anxiety. The *Challenger* disaster example, however, also calls attention to the problem of isolating the sources of irresponsibility. It shows how investigators, by colluding in a frame of understanding that focused on the parts, unconsciously attempted to protect societal and organizational fantasies of self-sufficiency, technological superiority, and nationalism. In the words of Smith and Berg (1987:181): "As we move increasingly into a world of professional and organizational specialization, it becomes more and more difficult for groups and the individuals in them to see the 'larger system' or the critical 'configuration of relationships' to which they belong. This makes it harder for interdependent parts to see the connections between the contradictions that are an inevitable aspect of their relations."

The *Challenger* disaster indicates how powerful contextual influences can be in determining organizational functioning. It also highlights the fact of how difficult it is to neutralize the effects that environmental influences can have on organizational functioning. For example, a *New York Times* article that appeared on December 29, 1986, pointed out that

> some space analysts are concerned that the agency [NASA] still lacks the kind of visionary leadership that can fully revive the floundering space program. Moreover, the clear evidence of progress has not erased fears that the pressures and factors blamed in the *Challenger* disaster will continue.
>
> Even as the nation debates the importance of manned flight in space and shuttles in particular, a pent-up demand for vehicles to loft military and civilian payloads is pushing the agency to fly the shuttles sooner and more frequently than most experts believe is safely possible. (Boffey, 1986b)

Such conditions for action are often not within the control of the organization as a whole, let alone individual members. It would be unfair to accuse the middle managers of the Marshall Space Center of intentionally causing the death of the astronauts. As noted earlier, they were caught in a vector of contradictory organizational and environmental demands and, as such, were enacting NASA's irrational institutional dynamics. Nevertheless, this does suggest the more optimistic question of how management can broaden the scope of its frame for understanding their predicament. And, furthermore, it calls for incorporating what they discover into internal institutional mechanisms for promoting responsible work within existing contextual conditions. That is, how can the organization confront societal conditions that threaten to continue and still remain responsible? These and other questions will be briefly addressed later in the chapter.

Hundreds of people died from burns received in automobile rear-end collisions while driving the Ford Pinto. The events associated with the Pinto case, in addition to having been subjected to the publicity of a long and public trial, represent an incident in which government officials filed criminal charges of homicide against an organization.

Case 3

Volkswagen's strong competition for the small car market in the United States fueled interest within the Ford Motor Company to develop its own equivalent. Championed by Lee Iacocca, the production of the Pinto moved with great speed and expectations of high profits. The Pinto's product objectives aimed to market such characteristics as size, weight, price, low fuel costs, reliability, serviceability, appearance, comfort, performance, ride and handling, and other features—but not safety. Behind the design was the "limits of two thousand," meaning two thousand pounds for two thousand dollars, or a dollar a pound—not a pound over in weight, not a cent over in price. This standard drove the design and production process of the car. According to comments made by an engineer interviewed by Dowie (1977, in Hills, 1987:17), "Iacocca enforced these limits with an iron hand." That same engineer added that "safety was not a popular subject in those days."

The key safety problem with the Pinto was the placement of its gas tank, which was so close to the rear bumper that it was unprotected from impact. *Mother Jones* magazine, where Mark Dowie's article first appeared, claimed possession of internal company documents showing what Ford had denied: that "Ford [had] crash-tested the Pinto at a top-secret site more than 40 times and that every test made at over 25 mph without structural alteration of the car [had] resulted in a ruptured fuel tank" (Dowie in Hills, 1987:15). Ruptured fuel tanks caused gasoline to spill around the vehicle, making it possible for any spark to set the car into flames. Alterations, such as placing a rubber bladder inside the tank or placing a steel baffle between the gas tank and the bumper, had been tried with successful results. However, installing those devices on the Pinto would have broken the ironclad rule of the "limits of two thousand." The cost of such alterations was a matter of only a few dollars per vehicle, but the pressure to put the vehicle into the market quickly and at a price that consumers would find attractive was very high.

According to Dowie's information, the Pinto schedule, from design to production, was set at just under twenty-five months, much faster than the usual period of about forty-three months (Dowie, in Hills, 1987:16). The push was to have the Pinto appear in 1970 along with the other 1971 models. Because the time required to complete certain phases of the process, such as tooling, was fixed, while other aspects, such as design, styling, and product planning were not, it was possible to carry out these phases simultaneously. This state of affairs created conditions that made it difficult to incorporate the results of crash tests into the design of the car. It was not until 1977 that the metal baffle that proved successful in preproduction crash tests was made into a standard feature of the new Pintos. Governmental agencies, however, did not compel the Ford Motor Company to recall previously built Pintos until 1978, although the company at that time, in the face of detrimental publicity, did. Later that year, in August, three women were fatally burned in Indiana when their 1973 Pinto was hit from the back by a General Motors van. That year the state of Indiana passed a statute covering "reckless homicide" that stated that corporations could be held culpable for such an offense. Ford was indicted for three counts of this crime but later acquitted; the "jury chose not to label it criminal" (Ermann and Lundman, 1982:18).

In his award-winning article, Marc Dowie (1977) cited what came to be called the "Pinto Papers"—which consisted of internal company engineering and safety documents. Among them was a 1973 cost-benefit study in which Ford compared the financial cost of monetary settlements for lives lost as a result of safety-related fatalities with the cost of making the necessary technical alterations to improve the safety of the vehicle (see Dowie, 1977). The study found that it would be cheaper to pay settlements on lawsuits against Ford than to make structural alterations that would cost approximately eleven dollars per vehicle. Unfortunately for the prosecution, this and other documents were ruled inadmissible: some because Ford "failed" to authenticate them, others because they referred not to the 1973 Pinto (the car in question at the trial) but to vehicles of other years.

Who was responsible for the approximately five hundred deaths? Were there grounds for a criminal trial against the Ford Motor Company as a whole? Were criminal acts committed by certain individuals within it? Why did Elkhart County, Indiana, choose to initially file criminal charges against the entire company rather than against particular individuals? Was the entire company responsible, given the general adherence to Iacocca's "limits of two thousand" and technical knowledge that indicated safety hazards? Was Ford being responsible by insuring, even at this cost, the company's profitability and the staff's jobs? If so, was Ford responsible to its staff or its consumers?

Although the prosecution made the "chilling, opening allegation that Ford 'deliberately chose profit over human life' and 'totally disregarded' repeated warnings from its engineers" (Fisse and Braithwaite, 1980, quoted in Ermann and Lundman, 1987:249), the jury disagreed in their March 1980 findings, stating that they did not have the necessary resources to pursue a case against individuals.

What happened in this case? Why were so many factors ignored, factors that caused so much harm? Did not the cost-benefit study demonstrate a degree of greed and callousness? Maybe. But greed is not a convincing explanation. It would leave unanswered the question of why so many who were involved, such as managers, engineers, and others, went along with the program. It assumes that most if not all involved benefited in some personal way or could have had some pragmatic reason for knowingly colludingin this program. In my view, such a position ignores the pressures exerted by the organization on its members, and it ignores the interplay between the cultural demands that organizations be socially responsible and their desire to remain profitable (Clinard and Yeager, 1980, especially chapter 9). To put these comments in the context of the terms used in this chapter: What dynamics, organizational and contextual, were members acting out on behalf of the Ford Motor Company?

The organizational goals and the acts of the individuals involved were designed to benefit the organization as a whole and not necessarily themselves individually. Economic competition with Volkswagen for a lion's share of the compact car market mobilized Ford to produce the Pinto. Safety issues were devalued within an organizational mentality and culture that was organized around the production of a competitive and profitable automobile. Iacocca's "limits of two thousand" rule was used to split off and displace anxieties about safety, to direct work activity, and to refocus responsibility. In attempting to manage the tension between the company's responsibility to consumers and its responsibility to make a profit and to perform its primary task of producing automobiles, the organization loaded into the "limits of two thousand" rule the authority to guide institutional behavior.

Externally, Ford Motor Company was operating during a time when the automobile industry was not significantly regulated; it existed within the culture of that industry. Dowie (in Hills, 1987:18) notes that: "Blame for Sandra Gillespie's death, Robbie Carlton's unrecognizable face and all the other injuries and deaths in Pinto's [sic] since 1970 does not rest on the shoulders of Lee Iacocca alone. For, while he and his associates fought their battle against a safer Pinto in Dearborn, a larger war against safer cars raged in Washington."

The fight against government regulation was waged by Ford and other car-makers as well as by companies in other industries. In an environment of de-regulation, Ford and other automobile manufacturers found themselves to be inordinately powerful players in the American economy and, in their own right, self-regulated, self-determined, and in control. To whom, then, would Ford have to be responsible?

We saw a similar compromising of safety standards in the airline industry during the 1980s, a time when airlines, under deregulation, apparently com-promised passenger safety for lower fares, greater passenger volume, and, ul-timately, greater profits. Deregulation also made it easier for more powerful airlines to wage fare wars on smaller ones, to decimate them, and to capture their share of the market.

Ford Motor Company's irresponsibility with the Pinto's design was an en-actment of many of these industrywide dynamics. For example, Ford's dollar estimates of the worth of a human life, found among the "Pinto Papers," expresses symbolically the awesome power over life and death the organiza-tion thought it wielded. The price of a human life was rounded off to $200,000, the result of lobbying efforts, negotiations, and agreements be-tween Ford executives and public officials in Washington who would be mak-ing automobile safety decisions. Dowie (in Hills, 1987:28) notes: "Unfortu-nately, the Pinto is not an isolated case of corporate malpractice in the auto industry. Nor is Ford a lone sinner. . . . The anti-emission control lobby and the anti-safety lobby usually work in chorus form, presenting a well-harmo-nized message from the country's richest industry, spoken through the voices of individual companies."

Internally, the process of determining costs and benefits took on an air of sacredness and rationality. The feeling that rational decisions were being made by which the company increased its profits and simultaneously recom-pensed those who lost family members made it easier to neutralize the shared anxiety about safety for those who were key to the design, development, and production of the Pinto. The "limits of two thousand" rule provided a guide-line that could be used to calculate costs and benefits and to contain and neu-tralize the anxiety generated by the tension between public safety and com-pany profitability.

The Effects of Turbulent Contextual Environments on the Management of Anxiety and Responsibility in Organizations

The concept of responsibility, as used in Western culture, is laden with an individualistic bias, particularly as it applies to criminal law. Rather than fo-cus on legal issues surrounding responsibility, my focus has been on looking at the complexity of this notion as it applies to organizations. Therefore, my focus has been on the various factors that make it difficult for members to behave responsibly within groups and organizations. Responsibility, like other organizational resources, must be managed by members if they are to engage each other productively and meaningfully in work. And how well organizations can manage institutional anxiety and redirect it toward creative and productive, rather than defensive, ends will be determined in large part by the degree to which they have a framework for grasping the systemic aspects of organizational life and the causal texture of environments.

This chapter raises initial working hypotheses on a thorny and puzzling concept and concludes as a work still in progress. I have found that the legalistic perspective on responsibility, with its bias on individual behavior, is not helpful either in understanding the complexity of collective action (and responsibility) or in formulating ways to promote responsible organizational behavior.

The examples presented suggest that the problem of corporate and governmental deviance is much more complex than is assumed by the legal theories that embrace individual culpability. Organizational theory has taught us time and again that an organization cannot be changed by simply removing certain individuals who have "gone bad." "Bad apple" theories, by focusing on the behavior of individuals, ignore the ways in which an organization creates the preconditions (the causal nexus) that compel, facilitate, or encourage the irresponsibility or criminality of its members. Although directly addressing and/or correcting the behavior of certain members may be important, seen from this perspective, such initiatives do little to change the institutional and causal context of the behavior.

Seeing the problem from the vantage point of member-relatedness to the rest of the organization assigns to individuality the problematic character it deserves by acknowledging the endless struggle of individuals to simultaneously maintain the personal boundaries of the self and their membership in something larger (Bensman and Lilienfeld, 1979; Bion, 1961; Shapiro and Carr, 1991). Moreover, this perspective recognizes the depth and consequences of the unconscious connections between the organization as a whole and its members and between the organization as a whole and its sociohistorical context. The actions of individual members who "go bad" may be more fruitfully understood to represent as much the complex unconscious and historical dynamics of and between the organization and its environment as their own personal biographical antecedents.

Similarly, in order to make sense of organizations that "go bad," what Eric Trist calls the "contextual environment" of an organization must be taken into account (Trist, 1977, quoted in Shafritz and Ott, 1994; Emery and

Trist, 1965; 1972). He explains that, from the standpoint of organizational ecology,

> the various organizations which compose the organization-set of a fo-
> cal organization have relations with other organizations which overlap in
> their relations with still others and others still again. The field of these
> interwoven indirect relations constitutes the contextual, as distinct from
> transactional, environment. What goes on in the contextual environment
> influences to a considerable extent, as a set of boundary conditions, what
> goes on in the transactional environment, and thence in the organization
> itself. (1977, quoted in Shaffritz and Ott, 1994:317)

The causal texture of the contextual environments of organizations working within postindustrial societies is replete with turbulence, complexity, and
uncertainty (Emery and Trist, 1965; Hirschhorn, 1990). Corporate and governmental organizations more than ever operate in a context of contradictory
demands, unstable priorities and moralities, a broad diversity of values, and
increasing complexity in and conflict between institutional orders. Societal
definitions of responsibility, morality, and authority will not be spared as they
too become more opaque. Organizations will find it increasingly difficult in
this environment to provide for themselves and their members clear guidelines for managing their roles responsibly. This will likely increase anxiety in
organizations.

Members will bring with them into the organization the contradictions and
uncertainty created by shifting boundaries in other spheres of their lives in
society. Societal anxiety about diversity, economic uncertainty, the dangers of
sexual intimacy, nuclear proliferation, pollution, and crises of confidence in
political and religious institutional orders will further complicate the nature
of the enactments of organizational dynamics. These factors are likely to add
to the existing difficulty for working responsibly unless ways are created to
manage their effects toward productive ends (Gutman, 1988).

At this point in history, the American criminal justice system too finds
itself to be a player in this turbulent contextual environment. In its struggle
with corporate and governmental deviance in a postindustrial sociocultural
context, it directly confronts the opaqueness of its own definitions of criminal
responsibility. On the face of it, this is an expression of the tension between
old ways of framing the problem and current reality. Time and again criminal
justice has been forced to respond to the resulting anxiety by multiplying
existing regulations, making bureaucratic structures and processes more complex, or by punishing organizations that commit deviance while being clearly
aware of the futility of this course of action. This has led to a decline in
public confidence and thus greater public anxiety regarding the effectiveness

of this enterprise as well as the degree to which it is truly committed to the just application of the law. Furthermore, the asymmetrical relationship that exists between the individual and organizations has been increasingly magnified. The growing and awesome power of organizations to influence legislation, as well as economic and public policy, has intensified the uncertainty and turbulence individuals feel by cutting deep into the most significant spheres of their lives. As corporations and governmental institutions have gained prominence in recent years, individuals have found themselves progressively more helpless as they struggle to manage and contain the anxiety that results from this condition.

David Gutman's comments on the decline of traditional defenses against anxiety (1988:22) might well be applied to the United States: "Whether the challenge we face today as a society becomes an occasion for creative innovation or for increased defensiveness depends on all of us. . . . Are we going to defend our old positions and resist change, or are we going to take the risk of learning from each other and perhaps create something new?"

Notes

1. This is a composite case. In order to ensure confidentiality and anonymity, the data from which it is created come from three different organizations studied by the author.

2. Bion (1961) originally defined the term "group mentality" as "the unanimous expression of the will of the group, contributed to by the individual in ways of which he is unaware, influencing him disagreeably whenever he thinks or behaves in a manner at variance with the basic assumptions. It is thus a machinery of intercommunication that is designed to ensure that group life is in accordance with the basic assumptions" (65).

   He did not mean to claim the existence of a group mind but used the term "group mentality" instead to call attention to how groups express their collective will and to point to the dialectical relations between the will of each individual member and the will of the group. He also used it to explain group culture as an emergent from the interplay between the individual interest of each member and the group mentality.

3. For the specifics on the shuttle disaster, see Boffey, (1986a, 1986b); Broad (1986); Report of the Presidential Commission on the Space Shuttle Accident (1986); Sanger (1986a, 1986b); Stuart (1986); Vaughan (1996); and Wilford (1986). For further analyses, upon which much of my discussion relies, see the insightful and relevant work of Hirschhorn (1990); Smith and Berg (1987); and Vaughan (1996).

References

Agazarian, Y. (1988). "Reframing the Group as a Whole." Paper delivered at the Ninth Scientific Meeting of the A. K. Rice Institute.

Agazarian, Y., and R. Peters (1985). *The Visible and Invisible Group: Two Perspectives on Group Psychotherapy and Group Process.* New York: Tavistock/Routledge.

Bensman, J., and R. Lilienfeld (1979). *Between Public and Private: Lost Boundaries of the Self.* New York: Free Press.

Bion, W. R. (1961). *Experiences in Groups.* London: Tavistock Publications.

Boffey, P. M. (1986a). "NASA Soon to Get an Outside Chief, Reagan Aides Say." *New York Times,* February 22, pp. A1, A29.

―――― (1986b). "Rebuilt NASA 'On Way Back' as an Array of Doubts Persist." *New York Times,* December 29, pp. A1, B12.

Broad, W. J. (1986). "Silence about Shuttle Flaw Attributed to Pitfalls of Pride." *New York Times,* September 30, pp. C1, C9.

Clinard, M. B., and P. C. Yeager (1980). *Corporate Crime.* New York: Free Press.

Dowie, M. (1977). "Pinto Madness." *Mother Jones* 2 (September/October):18–32. Reprinted in *Corporate Violence: Injury and Death for Profit,* S. L. Hills, ed. Totowa, N.J.: Rowman and Littlefield, 1987.

Durkheim, E. (1950). *Rules of Sociological Method.* New York: Free Press.

Emery, F. E., and E. L. Trist (1965). "The Causal Texture of Organizational Environments." *Human Relations* 18:21–32.

―――― (1972). *Toward a Social Ecology.* New York: Plenum.

Ermann, M. D., and R. J. Lundman (1982). *Corporate Deviance.* New York: Holt, Rinehart and Winston.

――――, eds. (1987). *Corporate and Governmental Deviance.* 3d ed. New York: Oxford.

Fisse, B., and J. Braithwaite (1980). "The Impact of Publicity on Corporate Offenders: Ford Motor Company and the Pinto Papers." Pp. 51–71 in *Corporate and Governmental Deviance,* M. D. Ermann and R. J. Lundman, eds. New York: Oxford, 1987.

Gutman, D. (1988). "The Decline of Traditional Defenses Against Anxiety." Pp. 5–22 in *The Oxford Proceedings of the Tavistock Institute.* London: Tavistock Publications.

Hirschhorn, L. (1990). *The Workplace Within: Psychodynamics of Organizational Life.* Cambridge: MIT Press.

Jacques, E. (1953). "On the Dynamics of Social Structure: A Contribution to the Psychoanalytical Study of Social Phenomena Deriving from the Views of Melanie Klein." *Human Relations* 6:3–24.

―――― (1955). "Social Systems as a Defence Against Persecutory and Depressive Anxiety." Pp. 478–98 in *New Directions in Psychoanalysis,* M. Klein, P. Heimann, and R. Money-Kyrle, eds. London: Tavistock Publications.

―――― (1990). "In Praise of Hierarchy." *Harvard Business Review* (January/February). Reprinted in Shafritz and Ott, pp. 255–62.

Janis, I. L. (1982). *Groupthink.* Boston: Houghton Mifflin.

Kernberg, O. (1980). *Internal World and External Reality.* Northvale, N.J.: Jason Aronson.

Klein, M. (1946). "Notes on Some Schizoid Mechanisms." Pp. 1–24 in *Envy and Gratitude and Other Works: 1946–1963*. New York: Free Press, 1975.

Menzies, I. (1959). "The Functioning of Social Systems as a Defense Against Anxiety." Tavistock Pamphlet no. 3. Pp. 43– in *Containing Anxiety in Institutions*. London: Free Association Books, 1988.

—— (1990). "A Psychoanalytical Perspective on Social Institutions." Pp. 463–75 in *The Social Engagement of Social Science: A Tavistock Anthology*. Vol. 1: *The Socio-Psychological Perspective*, E. Trist and H. Murray, eds. Philadelphia: University of Pennsylvania Press.

Report of the Presidential Commission on the Space Shuttle Accident (1986). Washington, D.C.: Government Printing Office.

Rice, A. K. (1969). "Individual Group and Intergroup Processes." *Human Relations* 22:565–84.

Sanger, D. E. (1986a). "NASA Photos Hint Trouble Started Right at Liftoff." *New York Times*, February 14, pp. A1, B4.

—— (1986b). "Top NASA Aides Knew of Shuttle Flaw in '84," *New York Times*, December 21, pp. A1, A34.

Shafritz, J. M., and J. S. Ott, eds. (1994). *Classics of Organization Theory*. 3d ed. Pacific Grove, Calif.: Brooks/Cole.

Shapiro, E. R., and E. W. Carr (1991). *Lost in Familiar Places: Creating New Connections Between the Individual and Society*. New Haven: Yale University Press.

Smith, K. K., and D. N. Berg (1987). *Paradoxes of Group Life: Understanding Conflict, Paralysis, and Movement in Group Dynamics*. San Francisco: Jossey-Bass.

Stuart, R. (1986). "Teacher Project Goes On, NASA Says." *New York Times*, February 14, p. B5.

Trist, E. L. (1977). "A Concept of Organizational Ecology." *Australian Journal of Management* 2:162–75.

Trist, E. L., and K. W. Bamforth (1951). "Some Social and Psychological Consequences of the Longwall Method of Coal Getting." *Human Relations* 4:3–38. Reprinted in Shafritz and Ott, pp. 316–28.

Trist, E. L., and H. Murray, eds. (1990). *The Social Engagement of Social Science: A Tavistock Anthology*. Philadelphia: University of Pennsylvania Press.

Vaughan, D. (1996). *The Challenger Launch Decision: Risky Technology, Culture, and Deviance at NASA*. Chicago: University of Chicago Press.

Wells, L. (1990). "The Group as a Whole: A Systemic Socioanalytic Perspective on Interpersonal and Group Relations." Pp. 50–85 in *Groups in Context: A New Perspective on Group Dynamics*, J. Gillette and M. McCollom, eds. New York: Addison-Wesley. [See also *Group Relations Reader*, vol. 2, A.D. Colman and M. H. Geller, eds. Washington, D.C.: A. K. Rice Institute, 1985].

Wilford, J. N. (1986). "Challenger, Disclosure and an 8th Casualty." *New York Times*, February 14, p. B5.

10

Helping Offenders Accept Personal Responsibility

Strategies for Controlling Criminal Behavior

John Rakis

> When anyone commits an act of injustice serious or trivial, the law will combine instruction and constraint, so that in the future either the criminal will never again dare to commit such a crime voluntarily, or he will do it a very great deal less often; and in addition, he will pay compensation for the damage he has done.
>
> —Plato, *The Laws*

In recent years, the criminal justice system has been under mounting pressure to restore public order and prevent innocent people from becoming victims of crime. This growing pressure, along with the enormous growth of the illicit drug industry, has resulted in skyrocketing criminal justice costs. In fiscal year 1990, federal and local governments spent $74 billion for civil and criminal justice, an increase of 21 percent since 1988 (U.S. Department of Justice, 1992). Faced with increased demands on tax revenue, government policy makers have sought to contain costs while simultaneously attempting to satisfy the public's demand for increased security. But the public remains skeptical of government's ability to control offenders and hold them accountable for their crimes. And this skepticism is not without good reason. Consider the following:

• Perhaps the greatest deterrent to crime is the certainty of punishment. But offenders know that the likelihood of being apprehended is very small. And even if an offender is apprehended, the likelihood of conviction and imprisonment is not very great. In New York City, for example, the number of persons sent to prison for a year or more represents less than 1 percent of the million felonies that are committed each year; the chances of committing a felony without being caught and seriously punished are more than sixty to one (Anderson, 1988).

Many types of crimes have been "decriminalized" by the police. Street-corner drug dealing, auto theft, and burglaries are not likely to be investigated by law-enforcement authorities in our nation's metropolitan areas. The neglect of these low-level crimes has not only increased the level of fear and apprehension in communities but has also given the message to offenders that these crimes are "acceptable."

• Plea bargaining, the mechanism by which the most convictions are obtained, is viewed with contempt by both the public and the participants in the criminal justice process. Felonies are routinely reduced to misdemeanors in large cities, and the courts are characterized by a deal-making atmosphere in which offenders use endless adjournments to their advantage. Many will simply jump bail, knowing that they will not be sought for rearrest. In New York City, offenders who are released on their own recognizance are given desk appearance tickets. These documents are commonly known as "disappearance" tickets because many offenders ignore the court's instructions and fail to appear as required.

• The most common sanction imposed by the courts is probation supervision, accounting for more than half of the adults who are serving a criminal sentence on any given day. Probation requires an offender to meet certain conditions while under supervision in the community. The supervision is usually provided by a probation officer who enforces the rules of conduct specified in the sentence. In 1990 the total number of probationers in the United States exceeded 2.6 million men and women, an increase of 5.9 percent over the prior year (U.S. Department of Justice, 1992).

The quality of supervision provided by probation officers has been severely compromised by large caseloads and an offender population with increasingly difficult problems. In large urban areas, it is not unusual for a probation officer to have a caseload exceeding a hundred offenders. A national survey of probation and parole systems conducted by the Institute for Law and Justice in 1986 determined that staff shortage was the dominant problem for all agencies (U.S. Department of Justice, 1988). Large caseloads keep probation officers from closely monitoring the activity of their clients or providing support services. Consequently, many persons placed on probation are rearrested on new charges. A follow-up survey of seventy-nine thousand felons sentenced to probation in 1986 determined that 43 percent had been rearrested for a felony within three years of sentencing (U.S. Department of Justice, 1992). Roughly 18 percent of those arrests were for a violent crime, and 33 percent were for a drug offense. It is not surprising that probation is not held in high esteem by the public.

• The number of offenders under correctional supervision has risen dramatically during the past decade. At the end of 1991, there were more than 800,000 prisoners in federal and state correctional facilities, an increase of roughly 150 percent over the preceding eleven-year period (U.S. Department of Justice, 1992). The rapid rise in the prisoner population has contributed to overcrowding in the nation's prison systems, with more than thirty-four states having prison populations that exceed their capacities (U.S. Department of Justice, 1992). Many correctional facilities are under court order or consent decree to limit their populations or to improve the conditions of confinement.

When conditions of confinement deteriorate in correctional facilities, the quality of rehabilitation services also suffers. Educational and vocational programs may be cut to make room for sorely needed housing space or to provide additional funds for security. Prisoners who want to participate in substance abuse treatment programs may have to delay participation until after their release. In jurisdictions under court order to reduce overcrowding, offenders may never serve time at all or may be released long before their sentences have been completed.

• To relieve overcrowding in prisons, correctional administrators have rapidly expanded the use of temporary release programs. These programs are intended to ease the transition from prison to the community. But when they are used as a safety valve for overcrowded prisons, their effectiveness is greatly diminished. For example, an audit of the New York State Department of Correctional Services revealed that its temporary release program had grown to the point where it placed the public at risk. Over a five-year period, the number of "inmates absconding from supervision or being arrested for new charges increased about tenfold; absconders increased from 101 to 900 and arrests increased from 22 to 247" (State of New York, 1992).

It appears that the criminal justice system has failed or is unable to exercise sufficient control over offenders. This includes the capacity to arrest and prosecute persons who violate the law, to punish convicted offenders, and to offer offenders the opportunity to lead productive lives. The pressures created by the need to restore public order and reduce government deficits have resulted in compromises that have reduced offender accountability and the accountability of criminal justice officials. Some would argue that the United States incarcerates more persons per capita than any other industrialized country and that "widening the net" of social control is an expensive and unwise use of scarce resources. On the other hand, the public's concern about crime and the consequences of ignoring criminal behavior cannot be ignored.

Nineteen percent of the respondents to a recent national survey indicated that crime was the biggest problem facing the country today, and only 29 percent believed that crime would be reduced within several years (Berke, 1994). The reason for this concern is understandable. According to the National Crime Victimization Survey, nearly one in four households was victimized by crime in 1991 (U.S. Department of Justice, 1992). The large number of households affected by crime has caused the public to lose confidence in the criminal justice system and to press for "get tough" legislation that would require mandatory long-term sentences for repeat offenders. Washington State recently enacted legislation that requires life sentences for offenders convicted of three serious crimes. In New York State, Governor Pataki is seeking legislation that would end parole. Similar legislative initiatives are being proposed throughout the country.

While our government has an obligation to ensure that criminal behavior brings sanctions that cannot be easily ignored by offenders, this obligation cannot be met simply by requiring mandatory long-term sentences for repeat offenders. Two points in support of this conclusion can be made:

First, traditional imprisonment is extremely expensive, and its rising costs cannot be left unchecked. Professor John J. DiIulio Jr. of Princeton University has estimated that by the year 2000 the number of persons in the charge of correctional officials will exceed four million and that correctional expenditures will exceed $40 billion annually (DiIulio, 1991). If imprisonment alone is to be relied upon to establish moral imperatives against criminal behavior, valuable resources will need to be diverted from other responsibilities of government, such as education or welfare. This shifting of resources will only contribute to conditions in which crime flourishes.

Second, traditional imprisonment has not demonstrated a capacity for helping offenders accept personal responsibility. Meaningful opportunities for substance abuse counseling, literacy education, and vocational training are the exception and not the rule in most prisons. For example, the General Accounting Office reported that "as of April 1991 only 364 of the 27,000 federal inmates with moderate to severe substance abuse problems were receiving the intensive drug treatment designed for them" (U.S. General Accounting Office, 1992).

The failure of prisons to provide meaningful opportunities for rehabilitation and the detrimental effects of institutionalization have contributed to the nation's high crime rate. Most released prisoners are ill equipped to return to their communities as responsible citizens, and most will return to prison. In a study of 108,580 persons released from prisons in eleven states in 1983, it was determined that 62.5 percent were rearrested for a felony or serious misdemeanor within three years (U.S. Department of Justice, 1989). Clearly, we cannot rely on traditional imprisonment alone to establish moral imperatives against criminal behavior. We must also use alternate punishments that conserve government resources and are effective at changing the lifestyles of offenders.

White and Walters (1989) defined lifestyle criminality as "a life pattern of irresponsible, self-indulgent, interpersonally intrusive, social rule breaking behavior." According to their observations, the lifestyle criminal neglects social and moral obligations to others, lacks self-restraint, ignores the rights and feelings of others, and has a propensity for disregarding societal norms. They argue that the behavior of criminals cannot be changed without focusing on "choice, decision, and responsibility."

It is not uncommon for offenders to deny responsibility for their criminal behavior and see themselves as victims. They may blame their criminal behavior on the easy availability of guns or drugs, the lack of jobs, bad schools, racism, or poverty. They may fault their parents for abusing them as children, their teachers for treating them unfairly, or life as a whole for being unfair. But most persons who are the victims of negative circumstances such as poverty, racism, or unemployment don't resort to crime or violence. What characterizes most offenders is their failure to develop values. They see nothing wrong with hurting others and rarely comprehend the impact of their criminal behavior upon their victims or their community. They do not see the need for working diligently to achieve a goal, and they do not see the reason for settling disputes nonviolently. Their perceptions of responsibility are shaped by distorted thinking processes. And much of this thinking has been shaped by the criminal justice system and the society in which we live.

Our society appears to accept irresponsible behavior as an aspect of everyday life and has removed the stigma formally associated with family breakup, promiscuity, dependency, and illegitimacy. The implications are enormous. Although the social consequences of illegitimacy are well known, out-of-wedlock births have risen sharply among white and black females in the past two decades. The number of persons infected with the AIDS virus continues to grow despite our knowledge of the disease. And drug abuse, a factor highly correlated with criminal behavior, has reached epidemic proportions. Our failure to establish moral imperatives against irresponsible behavior has, undoubtedly, encouraged offenders to view themselves as victims.

If offenders are viewed as victims of circumstances beyond their control, they will be given the message that criminal behavior is acceptable; if they are seen as sick, they will be given the message that they are powerless and not accountable for their antisocial behavior. An alternative view of criminality must be adopted if we are to help offenders obtain a greater sense of moral obligation and personal integration. We must view an offender's propensity to engage in criminal behavior not as an outcome of unchangeable circumstances but as a result of rational choices that can be influenced and modified. The decision to engage in criminal behavior does not occur spontaneously. Rather, it is one step in a long sequence of irresponsible behaviors. To change criminal behavior, therefore, one must change day-to-day irresponsible behavior. The sanctions imposed upon offenders should encourage accountability and help offenders develop a sensitivity to the rights of others. Punishment must instill self-control and a strong sense of interpersonal responsibility. It must help offenders resist destructiveness and lying and teach them to value and respect other people and their property.

Prison and postrelease programs must, therefore, require offenders to conform to recognized standards of accountable behavior. This would include attending school, participating in training programs, working, providing support for dependents, and making restitution to victims. Those requirements should be incorporated into a written contractual agreement that is carefully explained to the offender. Because a contract is meaningless if the offender believes that it will not be enforced, criminal justice agencies must ensure that there is sufficient supervision to know when the rules are broken. Whenever the terms of the contract are violated, the criminal justice system has an obligation to enforce sanctions. It must always assign personal responsibility to offenders for the consequences of their criminal behavior.

The criminal justice system does not, however, have sufficient punishment capacity to hold offenders accountable for their behavior. Punishment capacity could be increased by expanding the system. But a large expansion of the prison system would be enormously expensive and not particularly effective at helping offenders become responsible citizens. Punishment capacity could also be increased by expanding probation or parole supervision programs. But these programs usually do not provide meaningful supervision and are mistrusted by the public. If the criminal justice system is to help offenders accept personal responsibility and control criminal behavior, it must supplement traditional sanctions with punishments that conserve resources and encourage offenders to take responsibility for their actions. The remainder of this paper will examine five strategies that meet these criteria: fines, making offenders pay for their own supervision, restitution and community service, intensive supervision probation and parole, and boot camps.

Fines

Fines encourage accountability by sending a clear message of disapproval for criminal behavior and depriving offenders of illegal gains. Unlike traditional imprisonment and probation, the capacity of this punishment can be expanded without increasing criminal justice costs. Fines can also be combined with other sanctions and easily adjusted to the severity of the offense. This strategy does, however, have a significant shortcoming: Fines cannot incapacitate an offender and are inappropriate for anyone who poses a serious threat to the community.

While this sanction is widely used in this country, it has not been applied to its maximum advantage. Many judges are reluctant to use fines because they believe that this punishment cannot be applied fairly. They would argue that affluent persons can pay their criminal debt more easily than offenders who are poor. Another factor that limits the use of fines is concern about debt collection. Many fines imposed by the courts are never collected. In 1992 the total amount of unpaid criminal debt owed by offenders convicted in federal court exceeded $1.6 billion (U.S. General Accounting Office, 1993). The courts are reluctant to use measures that are difficult to enforce and increase their administrative responsibilities.

It is possible, however, to design a variable fine system that addresses these concerns and ensures that fines are fairly and effectively applied. Day fines are monetary punishments that systematically take into consideration two factors: the offender's economic circumstances and the seriousness of the offense. In the day fine approach, crimes are assigned units of punishment based on their seriousness. These units are usually developed by a planning group of judges, attorneys, and other persons familiar with court practices. The fine is determined by multiplying a percentage of the offender's daily income against the units of punishment assigned to the offense.

Day fines have been used successfully in Europe and South America for many years. In 1988 a pilot day fine system was implemented in Staten Island, New York, and the results of this experiment were encouraging. The project's evaluators concluded that this system permitted fairer punishments, that the process of imposing these fines was not time consuming or onerous, and that fine amounts could be increased without undermining the court's collection rates (U.S. Department of Justice, 1993). Monetary sanctions can be used more frequently and effectively without compromising their fairness.

It can be argued that the increased use of monetary sanctions will give offenders an unintended message: Crime is a business and fines are a necessary business expense. This message would appear to undermine the moral imperative against breaking the law. But the moral imperative against criminal behavior is not established by punishment alone. An offender's arrest, arraignment, trial, and conviction also provide a measure of public censure.

Making Offenders Pay for Their Own Supervision

The rapidly growing cost of supervising offenders has created the need to develop initiatives that defray those expenses without sacrificing public safety. By 1988, legislative statute authorized some form of correctional fees to be paid by probationers in twenty-eight states, jail inmates in twenty-six states, parolees in fifteen states, and prison inmates in thirty-nine states (Parent, 1990). The legislative statutes allow criminal justice agencies to impose fees that are intended to raise revenue for correctional programs. While the ability of criminal justice agencies to collect fees varies widely, some localities have raised a significant amount of money. The state of Texas, for example, collected more than $57 million from probationers in 1990, collecting fees from more than 90 percent of all misdemeanor offenders under supervision and roughly 65 percent of felony offenders (Finn and Parent, 1992). The potential of this practice is enormous. At the end of 1990, over 3.2 million persons were under probation or parole supervision in the United States. If a fee of one dollar a day were imposed on this population, over $1.1 billion dollars could be raised annually.

Although the primary reason for making offenders contribute to their own supervision is financial, the practice clearly encourages offenders to be accountable for their actions and promotes responsible behavior. But the practice is not without potential drawbacks. Many persons on probation are indigent and cannot afford to pay the fees being imposed. Nonindigent offenders may refuse to pay and cause the authorities to spend time and money on collections. The expense of collecting these fees might exceed the revenue raised. Fee collection might also reduce the amount of time a probation officer has for helping a client become responsible. If probation officers are forced to spend much of their time collecting revenues, they will have less time to provide counseling or substance abuse services or to carry out other obligations. Many probationers may refuse to report because they want to avoid a discussion concerning fee payment. A few, perhaps, might even resort to crime to pay the fees. It has also been argued that it is unethical to require offenders to pay for a government service that they are required to receive.

But the courts have upheld the practice of making offenders contribute to their own supervision and have allowed the revocation of probation or parole for failure to pay fees. The experience of several jurisdictions indicates that nonindigent offenders will pay the imposed fees regularly if the system is efficiently organized and well managed. Furthermore, it has been demonstrated that the fees collected can exceed the collection costs and allow the participating criminal justice agencies to enhance their services. The practice of imposing fees has proved to be compatible with the case work services provided by correctional agencies. It requires offenders to become gainfully employed, sharpen their budget skills, and learn how to meet obligations quickly. By motivating a client to develop a plan for fee payment, the probation or parole officer is helping the client become a responsible citizen. The failure to make a fee payment is a clear indication that intervention and assistance are required.

Making offenders pay for supervision is not limited to probation or parole departments. Many correctional agencies bill participants in work-release programs for room and board. And in some jurisdictions, inmates are being billed for the cost of their incarceration. In Michigan, for example, the 1984 Inmate Reimbursement to the County Act allows counties to collect up to thirty dollars a day from inmates for the cost of their incarceration. A reimbursement program initiated under this act by the Macomb County Board of Commissioners in 1985 raised about $2.7 million through June 1993 (Amboyer, 1993).

Restitution and Community Service

The idea that offenders should compensate their victims for material and emotional losses has its roots in ancient times. In his *Laws,* Plato wrote that it is "necessary for the law to aim, like a good archer, at a penalty that will both reflect the magnitude of the crime and fully indemnify the victim." Many courts now impose restitution in an attempt to restore the losses of victims and punish the offender. This type of punishment reflects a recent trend toward restorative justice and is intended to hold offenders accountable for their actions. Although the primary goal of restitution is to compensate victims for their losses, this strategy also promotes the goal of rehabilitation.

Restitution gives offenders an opportunity to restore themselves and to change their behavior. When offenders are required to compensate a victim, they are helped to understand the real consequences of their behavior. Unlike traditional imprisonment, restitution is something that inmates do, not something that is done to them. The process of restitution not only gives the victim redress, it also helps the offender alleviate feelings of guilt that might otherwise interfere with the rehabilitative process.

In addition to providing victims with redress, some restitution programs also require the offender to undertake community service. Community service places convicted offenders in unpaid positions with nonprofit or government agencies to serve a specified number of hours. The work must usually be performed within a given time limit. In the United States, community service orders began as a punishment for persons who violated motor vehicle laws. Offenders convicted of driving while intoxicated, for example, might be required to work in a hospital emergency room where they would witness the consequences of automobile accidents. Community service symbolizes the offenders' responsibility to make amends for their irresponsible behavior. By making reparations to the society they have wronged, the convicted offenders learn that past harms can be compensated for and also that the same is true for past harms committed against them. Community service repairs not only the damage done to the community but also the offenders' view of themselves. It has the potential to teach offenders good work habits and the value of service to others.

In New York City, an experimental community court has been set up in which community service sentences are both handed down and fulfilled in the same courthouse. While it is too early to tell whether the program will be successful, a remark made to a *New York Times* reporter by a woman performing community service in the courthouse reveals its limitations: "Making whores work? I got 49 convictions! You think stuffing envelopes for a few days is going to stop me?" (Hoffman, 1993). It would appear that for some offenders restitution and community service must be combined with other sanctions to be effective.

Despite their limitations, restitution programs have proved their effectiveness at reducing recidivism. The Utah Juvenile Court operates a structured program in which youths make restitution in the form of financial payment or community service. State law allows Utah Juvenile Court to order youthful offenders to repair, replace, or make restitution for victims' property or for other losses. In addition, the court may withhold a portion of fines paid by juveniles to fund a victim restitution fund. If the juveniles are unable to pay restitution, they are permitted to work on a community service project in the public or private sector and their earnings are paid from the fund directly to their victims. Research shows that the use of restitution in Utah is associated with significant reductions in recidivism among certain types of juveniles (Butts and Snyder, 1992).

Do restitution and community service work with adults? There is evidence to suggest that community service is no more successful at changing criminal behavior than traditional punishments. But community service has several advantages over traditional punishments: It is far less expensive, it offers the possibility of providing the victims with compensation for their losses, it gives the offenders a sense of self-worth and self-confidence, and it gives the unemployed offenders work experience that can lead to full-time employment.

Those opposed to restitution and community service have argued that some offenders will resort to crime to compensate their victims. But this outcome can be prevented by setting up a system of controls within the community. These controls might, for example, include the use of curfews or electronic monitoring.

Several localities have enhanced restitution programs by adding a victim-offender reconciliation component. Victim-offender reconciliation programs bring crime victims and offenders face to face under the supervision of trained staff or volunteers. The purpose of these face-to-face meetings is to help the offenders and victims know each other better, to provide a mechanism for exploring and expressing feelings, and to help the offender make amends. Generally, the participation in these programs is voluntary for all parties. The major objectives are healing for the victim and accountability for the offender. Most programs of this type attempt to reduce crime by making offenders aware of the long-lasting emotional and physical damage caused by their criminal activities. Participants in these programs must be willing to accept that they are responsible for their actions and that they are not the victims of society or the criminal justice system. By accepting responsibility for their actions, offenders are given the opportunity for social and moral reconciliation.

Intensive Supervision Probation and Parole

Intensive supervision probation and parole programs provide close monitoring of convicted offenders and impose conditions such as frequent meetings, drug testing and treatment, community service, employment, and education. Curfews and electronic monitoring may be used to control the offender's behavior, and violations of imposed conditions generally result in immediate incarceration. The programs are intended to maintain public safety through heightened surveillance while helping the offender assume personal responsibility and become a productive member of the community. Although these programs cost more than regular probation or parole, they are always less expensive to operate than correctional facilities.

One of the first programs involving intensive supervision was initiated by the Georgia Department of Corrections in 1982. An evaluation involving 2,322 participants in Georgia's Intensive Probation Supervision Program for the period between 1982 and 1985 concluded that the program reduced the flow of offenders to prison, reduced risk to the community, and saved $13 million (Erwin and Bennett, 1987).

A more recent study involving 2,000 adult offenders in fourteen intensive supervision programs in nine states did not, however, reach similar conclusions. The study determined that intensive supervision programs were effective as surveillance and intermediate sanctions but were not good at preventing rearrests and could not show unambiguous cost savings (Petersilia and Turner, 1993). The close supervision received by program participants may explain the apparent failure of these efforts to reduce recidivism. Although program participants may actually commit either the same number of crimes as offenders under regular supervision or fewer crimes, the heightened surveillance provided by intensive supervision programs may increase the possibility of detection and thus increase the rate of recidivism. The failure of these programs to demonstrate unambiguous cost savings is also a matter of debate. If these programs are compared with regular probation and parole, no cost savings are achieved. If, on the other hand, intensive supervision is compared with incarceration, the cost savings are significant.

Because intensive supervision programs have been around for less than a decade, more time is needed to study and develop this approach. Controls may need to be tightened and program requirements may have to be modified. It is possible that some intensive supervision programs encourage dependence in the same way that prisons do. One interesting observation made by Petersilia and Turner is that participants in Texas and California programs who received counseling, held jobs, paid restitution, and performed community service were less likely to be recidivists than offenders who did not. Intensive supervision does have the potential to help offenders become more responsible, and its promise remains to be realized.

Shock Incarceration

During the past decade, shock incarceration, or boot camp programs, have attracted a great deal of interest among criminal justice policy makers in the United States. These programs typically involve a short period of confinement and incorporate rigorous physical activity, intensive regimentation, strict discipline, drug treatment, and other rehabilitative services. Early parole release may be offered upon successful completion of the program. The first prison boot camp dates back to 1983, when the Georgia Department of Corrections initiated its Special Alternative Incarceration program at the Dodge Correctional Institution (Parent, 1989). Since then, boot camp programs have been started by thirty states, ten local jurisdictions, and the Federal Bureau of Prisons (MacKenzie, 1993).

In New York State's correctional system, prisoners are offered a six-month discipline and treatment-oriented program in which they are given the opportunity to develop the life skills needed for a successful return to their communities. Prisoners are involved in the management of the program to the degree that they demonstrate the capacity to make informed, responsible decisions. One method of teaching responsibility is the use of "learning experiences." These are used to make prisoners aware that disruptive behavior or negative habits are not wanted in the community. They could include physical tasks, writing assignments, or wearing symbolic reminders. Or they might involve a process such as socializing with others, changing a habit, or lowering of status. All learning experiences are assigned, approved, and documented by a committee. They are not considered punishments and are not intended to humiliate the inmate. Their primary goal is to encourage behavioral change and to correct mistakes.

Because successful participants can be released before their parole eligibility date, the program has saved money. The first 4,411 shock incarceration graduates were released, on the average, nine months before the completion of their court-determined minimum period of incarceration, resulting in a savings of $84 million in operating costs and $93 million in avoided capital construction costs (State of New York, 1992a). The agency's evaluation of the program shows that shock incarceration graduates were more likely to obtain employment than those offenders who did not participate in the program and were more likely to be successful under parole supervision despite shorter periods of incarceration.

Evaluations of other boot camp programs have yielded more modest findings. The General Accounting Office observed that boot camps were less costly than traditional prisons, but early measurements of recidivism data show only marginal improvement over traditional forms of incarceration (U.S. General Accounting Office, 1993b). A formal evaluation of eight shock incarceration programs was undertaken by the National Institute of Justice to find out if the desired goals of the programs were being achieved. Preliminary findings showed that inmates became more positive about their experience in the program and became less antisocial (MacKenzie, 1993). But the final report on the evaluation concluded that both boot camp inmates and prison inmates became less antisocial during incarceration (MacKenzie and Souryal, 1994). The final report also concluded that while programs can be designed to successfully reduce prison overcrowding, the effectiveness of the programs in changing offenders is less positive. Not unlike intensive supervision probation, shock incarceration continues to evolve, and more time is needed to develop this approach.

Some Conclusions and Possible Directions

The public's demand for increased public safety and balanced government budgets poses a challenging question for policy makers: How can the criminal justice system improve its ability to control offenders and hold them accountable for their crimes without raising the deficit? Most Americans believe that the criminal justice system should have sufficient capacity to arrest and prosecute persons who violate the law as well as sufficient capacity to punish convicted offenders. They also believe that the criminal justice system should offer offenders the opportunity to lead responsible lives. The strategies described in this paper are consistent with these beliefs. They offer government opportunities to increase punishment capacity and offenders opportunities to learn responsible behavior. And they do so without imposing additional burdens upon the taxpayer.

Some would argue that the benefits obtained by incapacitating offenders in traditional prisons outweigh the tax burdens of this punishment strategy. If, however, we depend on traditional imprisonment to hold offenders accountable for their crimes and reduce disorder in our communities, we will contribute enormously to the public debt and be forced to make cuts in areas such as health and welfare. These cuts will inevitably contribute to conditions that promote criminal behavior. Prisons must, therefore, be viewed as a scarce resource that should be used only when no less restrictive form of control will ensure public safety.

The measures described in this chapter do not offer an immediate solution to the problem of crime and disorder. Rather, they provide a range of long-term strategies that are consistent with a democratic vision of justice and offer offenders the prospect of moral development and personal integration. Because these options don't rely on traditional imprisonment, they conserve government resources and offer politically realistic opportunities for changing behavior. Several options discussed in this chapter also promote our obligation to make restitution to victims of crime, a responsibility ignored for many years. The process of making restitution serves a rehabilitative purpose as well, giving offenders an opportunity to understand the impact of their behavior on victims and make amends for past deeds. While rehabilitation is not a goal that is popular in some circles, it cannot be ignored. Punishment without opportunities for rehabilitation will only encourage offenders to continue their irresponsible behavior.

It would be a mistake to believe that the criminal justice system alone can make our communities safe and secure. Ultimately, each citizen bears some responsibility for preventing criminal behavior. Disorder and crime can't flourish in a community organized in opposition to it. The role of the criminal justice system should not, therefore, be limited to apprehending, incapacitating, and rehabilitating offenders. It must also include involving the public in the prevention of crime. This involvement could include participation in community advisory committees, forming neighborhood watch patrols, providing literacy tutoring in the prisons, and supervising evening recreational programs for youthful offenders. If the criminal justice system can involve the public in the prevention of crime and adopt strategies that hold offenders accountable for their criminal behavior, we can restore public order while maintaining the democratic principles upon which our laws are based.

References

Amboyer, Donald J. (1993). "Making Offenders Pay: Michigan County Requires Inmates to Defray the Cost of Incarceration." *Corrections Today* 55:88–90.

Anderson, David C. (1988). *Crimes of Justice: Improving the Police, the Courts, the Prisons.* New York: Times Books.

Berke, Richard L. (1994). "Crime is Becoming Nation's Top Fear." *New York Times,* January 23, sec. A, p. 1.

Butts, Jeffrey A., and Howard N. Snyder (1992). *Restitution and Juvenile Recidivism.* Washington, D.C.: Office of Juvenile Justice and Delinquency Programs.

DiIulio, John J. (1991). *No Escape: The Future of American Corrections.* New York: Basic Books.

Erwin, Billie S., and Lawrence A. Bennett (1987). *New Dimensions in Probation: Georgia's Experience with Intensive Probation Supervision (IPS).* Washington, D.C.: National Institute of Justice.

Finn, Peter, and Dale Parent (1992). *Making Offenders Foot the Bill: A Texas Program.* Washington, D.C.: National Institute of Justice.

Hoffman, Jan (1993). "A Manhattan Court Explores Service-Oriented Sentencing." *New York Times*, November 27, sec. A, p. 1.

MacKenzie, Doris L. (1993). "Boot Camp Prisons in 1993." *National Institute of Justice Journal* 227:21–28.

MacKenzie, Doris L., and Claire Souryal (1994). *Multisite Evaluation of Shock Incarceration.* Washington, D.C.: National Institute of Justice.

Parent, Dale (1989). *Shock Incarceration: An Overview of Existing Programs.* Washington, D.C.: National Institute of Justice.

—— (1990). *Recovering Correctional Costs Through Offender Fees.* Washington, D.C.: National Institute of Justice.

Petersilia, Joan, and Susan Turner (1993). "Evaluating Intensive Supervision Probation/Parole: Results of a Nationwide Experiment." Washington, D.C.: National Institute of Justice.

State of New York (1992a). *Shock Incarceration and Shock Parole: The Fourth Annual Report to the Legislature.* Albany, N.Y.: Department of Correctional Services and the Division of Parole.

—— (1992b). *Inadequate Management of the Temporary Release Program Places the Public at Risk.* Albany, N.Y.: Office of the State Comptroller.

U.S. Department of Justice (1988). *Difficult Clients, Large Caseloads Plague Probation, Parole Agencies.* Washington, D.C.: Bureau of Justice Statistics.

—— (1989). *Recidivism of Prisoners Released in 1983.* Washington, D.C.: Bureau of Justice Statistics.

—— (1992a). *Crime and the Nation's Households, 1991.* Washington, D.C.: Bureau of Justice Statistics.

—— (1992b). *Justice Expenditure and Employment, 1990.* Washington, D.C.: Bureau of Justice Statistics.

—— (1992c). *National Update.* Washington, D.C.: Bureau of Justice Statistics.

—— (1992d). *Prisoners in 1991.* Washington, D.C.: Bureau of Justice Statistics.

—— (1992e). *Recidivism of Felons on Probation, 1986-1989.* Washington, D.C.: Bureau of Justice Statistics.

—— (1993). *The Staten Island Day-Fine Project.* Washington, D.C.: Office of Justice Programs.

U.S. General Accounting Office (1992). *Drug Treatment: Despite New Strategy, Few Federal Inmates Receive Treatment.* Washington, D.C.: Human Resources Division.

—— (1993a). *National Fine Center: Expectations High, but Development Behind Schedule.* Washington, D.C.: General Government Division.

—— (1993b). *Prison Boot Camps: Short-Term Prison Costs Reduced, but Long-Term Impact Uncertain.* Washington, D.C.: General Government Division.

White, W. W., and G. D. Walters (1989). "Lifestyle Criminality and the Psychology of Disresponsibility." *International Journal of Offender Therapy and Comparative Criminology* 33:257–62.

Conclusion

Negotiating Responsibility in an "Age of Innocence"

Jack Kamerman

If there is a theme that runs through the chapters in this book, it is that the assignment of responsibility is never a given—that is, it needs to be explained. It is also clear that certain conditions promote the acceptance of responsibility and others discourage it. While it is not the place of the social sciences to fix responsibility (as tempting as that often is), it is certainly their task to at least try to understand the circumstances under which it is accepted or denied.

C. Wright Mills (1959:7) pointed out that the promise of sociology is to clarify "the intersections of biography and history." More prosaically put, the goal of the social sciences is to see an individual's behavior in its social context. A number of factors define that social context. Many have been discussed in the above chapters.

If it were possible to gauge the volume of avoidance of responsibility in the contemporary United States, this would probably turn out to be avoidance's golden age. Contemporary values, ideologies, organizational structures, and personal defenses elevate explanations into justifications and conspire to create the perfectly blameless individual. In that sense, we live in an "age of innocence."

But, to paraphrase W. S. Gilbert, when everyone is innocent, then no one's really guiltless. As Charles Fethe (in this volume) and Emile Durkheim before him have suggested, the exclusion of responsibility would leave a hole in the social fabric. Ironically, in this age when no one has to look very far for a "good excuse" for bad behavior, the assignment of responsibility to others has become almost an industry. The criminal justice system has assumed the function of assigning responsibility both in criminal and civil cases and in society in general—not as before, as the passive representative of social values and standards, but more as the arbiter of those values and standards. Courts create societal values as much as they reflect them. When the focus is on individual responsibility, this point is particularly clear.

The entitlement of the criminal justice system by society has become clouded. So, in its turn, the criminal justice system has itself become the scapegoat for society's ills. This of course is the ultimate irony because, whether people are aware of the connections or not, the current criminal justice system is simply one of society's more characteristic institutions.

Again, the necessity for examining the kind of society that produces such institutions is obvious. In that spirit, one of the most important artifacts of society involved in the assignment of responsibility is the process of social distance, in particular the way that social distance tends to produce a sense of moral distance.

If social distance is a barometer of moral distance, then it becomes important to note that some societies, in some eras, encourage social distance by the nature of their social structures and by the assumptions of their cultures. In a time when it is almost impossible to hide from exposure to the outside world, it is also a banner period for social distancing. For example, because of extensive coverage by the news media, the similarity between the recent atrocities in Croatia and those in Nazi Europe seemed so unavoidable that it couldn't help but influence the international response. Yet the overall reaction of the world of the 1990s and the 1930s was about the same: This is none of our affair.

If a sense of responsibility is to be restored in people's private and public lives, it will rest in part on the breakdown of social distance. The best approach is to change the circumstances that encourage that distance. The sociological bias is that when social structure is changed the ideas and processes that resonate to it will change also. This is obviously more easily said than done. Social structural change is of course the most difficult to effect. Changing occupations and organizations is somewhat less difficult.

But societies, occupations, organizations, and individuals do in fact change, not necessarily out of conscience, but in response to a redefinition of self-interest and to economic and social pressures. These shifts are often dialectic reactions to the excesses of a prior change. If privatizing government functions, for one example, creates an explosive mixture of public interest and profit motive, the trend may reverse course. The "inevitability" of a social outcome comes clear only in retrospect.

172

What is clear is that a society in which dodging responsibility and distancing oneself from others have been raised to a high art is in serious disrepair.

Reference

Mills, C. Wright (1959). *The Sociological Imagination*. New York: Oxford University Press.

Epilogue
Why Don't They Hit Back?

Paul Neurath

Editor's Note: Paul Neurath's "Why Don't They Hit Back?" is the last chapter of his Columbia University doctoral dissertation, *Social Life in the German Concentration Camps Dachau and Buchenwald.* The study of the social organization and subculture of these two camps was based on his experiences as an inmate in Dachau and then Buchenwald from April 2, 1938, to May 27, 1939. It is, in the grimmest sense, a participant observation study of the first order. In a recent letter to me, Neurath explains that "I wrote this thesis in the present tense about a situation that was still going on, apparently in about the same manner in which I myself had gone through it quite recently."

After his release from Buchenwald, he spent two years in Sweden, one year in school learning to become a metalworker and one year as a lathe operator. He arrived in New York in 1941 and almost immediately enrolled in the graduate school at Columbia University to begin work toward his second doctorate. (He had already received a doctorate in law from the University of Vienna in December of 1937, a few months before he was arrested and sent to Dachau.)

The dissertation was written between 1942 and 1943, and minor revisions were made a year or two later. He successfully defended it in 1943 with the understanding that he would be allowed to polish the writing before final copies were deposited with the university. By the time the final version was completed, the two camps had been liberated by the Allied armies. Neurath's adviser sent the dissertation out to publishers. They weren't interested, because the horrors of the camps had become front-page news by then, and Neurath's work was a sociological analysis rather than a tabloid shocker. In his letter, Neurath quotes the words of one publisher: " 'The public wants more sensational accounts.' " Neurath continues: "At the time when I wrote the thesis, . . . German concentration camps had not yet become annihilation

173

camps. They were essentially . . . places where people were kept out of circulation . . . and forced to do hard work. True enough, the death rate was high compared with that on the outside, but these were essentially 'accidental deaths,' whether from illness or mistreatment."

Although he had completed all of the academic requirements for the Ph.D., it was not actually awarded until 1951. The university had a requirement at that time that 125 printed copies of a dissertation be submitted before the degree could be awarded. Not having the substantial sum required to supply those copies, Neurath waited to apply for his degree until 1950, by which time the university had changed the requirement, allowing a single microfilm copy to suffice. The degree was awarded at the next graduation, in May 1951.

Now, over a half-century after it was written, but with its insights into inmate culture disturbingly timely and fresh, this chapter is published for the first time.

People who listen to reports about the treatment in Nazi concentration camps ask again and again: "If someone mistreated me like that, I would strike back. Rather die than not hit back. Why don't they hit back in concentration camps? Aren't they men?" They don't hit back. Still they are men.

The prisoner is expected to hit back in anger, revenge, self-defense, defense of his honor, and for a number of other reasons. There is a simple explanation why the vast majority don't hit back: The camp is under martial law. The slightest sign of resistance is immediately answered by a bullet through the head. As in so many other situations, the majority of men prefer to live, no matter what they have to suffer. The outsider who asks "Why don't they hit back?" usually realizes that, and what he really means is: "Aren't there any exceptions? Aren't there at least some real men, who don't count the odds and who strike back even in the face of certain death?" There are real men like that in concentration camps. But they don't strike back.

Hundreds of second-termers, after having gone through the hell of a concentration camp once, returned to their underground movement, knowing that if they got caught, they would be brought back to camp and to circumstances under which a bullet through the head would seem like a welcome relief. They certainly are "real men" by any standards. But in concentration camps they don't strike back.

Others, leftists and liberals, sometimes conservatives, fought on against the Nazi regime, under the constant threat of winding up in a concentration camp or getting their head chopped off. But in the camp they don't strike back.

Again others, like most of the people who ask "Why don't they hit back?" have never dealt with politics, have been courageous all their lives, have gone through serious danger, professional and otherwise, without counting the odds. They have developed very rigid concepts of honor, and if anybody in the outside world would dare slap their face, they would strike back immediately and with a vengeance. But in concentration camps they don't.

Nor do the professional criminals, many of whom have brutal and impulsive dispositions, men who have killed and mutilated in anger and excitement. Again, for the majority it is the martial law, the threat of the bullet, that prevents them from striking back. But the question remains: "Aren't there any exceptions?"

I do not know of any exceptions. I have been in two of the largest camps for fourteen months. I have met dozens of people who have passed through practically all German concentration camps.

Still there may possibly be some cases of which I do not know. But it seems that not much would be proven if, among the hundreds of thousands of prisoners who passed through the camps during all these years, finally one or another could be found who was shot because he hit back. The general statement would hold: In concentration camps they don't hit back.

There are cases known of people who hit back at the SS men when they were arrested or during their first hearings at SS or police headquarters. I knew a man in Dachau who hit back at SS men in the famous headquarters in Berlin, Columbia Haus. He was almost torn to pieces. Ernst Winkler, in his book *Four Years of Nazi Torture*, tells about his own similar experience when he struck back during his first hearing (1942:50). But all this happened before these people were brought to concentration camps.

From what knowledge I have from the people who still were in concentration camps when the war broke out, or from reports in the American press after the liberation of the prisoners in the various camps, it seems that even after the beginning of the war there were practically no cases of prisoners hitting back in concentration camps. Not even from the worst annihilation camps, where people were gassed and burned by the thousands and ten thousands, are there any reports so far indicating that the victims resisted their impending death or their general mistreatment.

Detailed newspaper reports of the mistreatment undergone by American and British prisoners of war in German concentration camps—especially in Buchenwald—never mention any resistance on the part of the beaten prisoners. It seems that these men, when put into concentration camps, accepted the situation in a way similar to the way German civilians did, and I am inclined to believe that they did so for the same reasons.

Apparently the reasons for which the camp prisoners refrain from hitting back are not quite the same as those for which a man in the outside world would accept a beating. It is neither simple cowardice nor resignation and indifference, and of course it has nothing whatsoever to do with the prisoner's stolidly accepting what he considers a well-deserved punishment.

One possible way to arrive at an explanation for this behavior seems to be to follow the prisoner step by step on his way from "civilian" society to camp society and watch him go through the metamorphosis from "man" to "camp prisoner."

Individual Prisoners Enter the Camp

Individual prisoners usually come from penitentiaries, prisons, or courts. Ordinarily they are not delivered directly to the camp but, for administrative reasons, have to pass through several prisons, until after several days, sometimes two weeks, they arrive in the city near the camp. On this transport they are guarded by regular police or prison personnel, whose only concern is to deliver their charges safely to the next station. There is practically no pushing or beating on the transport.

From the city—in our case, Munich or Weimar—a prison van is dispatched to the camp once or twice a week, usually with six or eight, seldom with more than ten, prisoners from all over the country.

Up to the moment when they leave the van, the prisoners have been in the hands of civilian authorities, even though legally they already are prisoners of the Gestapo. Now they are handed over to the SS guards of the concentration camp. This is the moment when they lose their status as human beings and become something different: "prisoners under protective custody" (*Schutzhaftgefangene*) or "camp prisoners."

Without any transition they are faced with a completely new world. In the greatest hurry they are chased through an administrative procedure, that, in spite of all the beating, works smoothly, as if it were the most natural thing in the world.

Guards swarm around the prisoners, striking, hitting, beating, shouting that they will teach them how to behave, cursing, swearing, kicking them with their boots, and occasionally threatening them with a bullet from the openly carried gun. It is like being thrown into a witches' cauldron. Nobody understands what is going on, why he is beaten or yelled at, what he has done wrong or how. All he sees is that everybody gets beaten no matter what he does and that the same is the case with other prisoners who apparently have been there for a longer time.

All this time it never happens that an individual prisoner faces an individual guard. Instead, the small group of prisoners simultaneously faces a sort of many-faced and organized mechanism that pushes, shouts, beats, and hits. And not for a single moment does it occur to the prisoner to strike back. He is completely occupied with getting through the procedure, and he is overwhelmed by the smoothness with which it turns. If he needs an additional explanation, he can always get it from the SS man's gun, but ordinarily he grasps the rules of this mechanism by himself.

After evening roll call, the newcomers are led to their barracks, where they get in contact with the old prisoners. During the night they recover to some degree, and in the morning it all looks like a bad dream. The newcomer feels himself a man again, though in a strange world. Perhaps he feels ashamed for having been beaten and having had his face slapped. His desire to keep his status as a man, and if need be to defend it, has not yet been entirely broken.

But it has to be broken. Otherwise the administration could not keep thousands of prisoners together under conditions which, in ordinary prisons, would lead to riot and mutiny every day. The newcomer has to understand that he cannot escape, nor resist, nor attack, nor have any chance to feel himself a man. He has to learn this lesson: Five hundred prisoners at work, guarded by twenty riflemen, are not five hundred men opposing twenty men, with the twenty rifles as the deciding factor. They are five hundred numbers who carry out orders, while the riflemen happen to be around to watch that nobody is lazy or perhaps crazy enough to run off.

They are taught this lesson.

Every morning when the camp marches out to work, the order is given: "Newcomers and retransferred step forward." (The retransferred were camp prisoners who had been away for some time, such as to a court hearing.) Either they are sent to Capo Sterzer in the gravel pit, who will surely knock every thought of resistance out of them, or they are dealt with by a few officers, usually one for every two or three men.

These officers mistreat the newcomers systematically for several days. Each of the poor devils will break down many times during the ordeal. He will faint over his wheelbarrow, topple over under the burden of heavy stones, collapse while being hit over the head with a club. But he will not be allowed to stay down. The officer's boot will bring him to life again, and if that does not do the trick, a jar of water, poured over the head, surely will. Sometimes it won't.

The worst comes when the man says: "I can't go on." Then the officer really crashes down on him and teaches him the lesson for which he has to go through this whole thing: " 'You cannot' means 'you don't want to,' but you must!" He will be trampled upon again and again, he will be beaten and driven, and when he breaks down he will be chased up again, and always he will be told: "Remember, 'you cannot' means 'you don't want to,' but you must!"

It was a dreadful scene when once an officer kept shouting this lesson at a man. The man simply did not get up. The officer taught him more and more, with curses and kicks, with water and boots. But the man did not grasp the lesson. He was dead.

After a few days with the officers or with Sterzer, the new men are assumed to have learned their lesson. They are now expected to do what they are told and not to do what they are not told and to cause no more trouble. They are expected to behave as depersonalized numbers with no more thought of resistance left in them. They are now attached to regular working groups, like the old prisoners. The initiation is over.

Large Groups Enter the Camp

When the prisoners began to arrive by the hundred and by the thousand, this method of careful individual mistreatment to break the personality and resistance of the newcomers could no longer be applied. Something new had to be found, to achieve the same effect in one decisive blow, with no waste of time.

A method was found and the blow was dealt.

Large transports of prisoners are usually brought directly to the concentration camp by train, guarded by one or two companies of SS men, who are sent from the camp for the purpose. These SS men know how to deal with prospective camp prisoners. They know that they have to teach them their lesson in one single night on the train. They do it.

We one hundred and fifty prisoners who went to Dachau on April 1, 1938, were the first Austrians sent to German concentration camps. A few days earlier the two Hohenberg princes and one Hapsburg archduke were sent there. Since then thousands have made the same trip. All of us have seen and experienced scenes of horror, hell at its deepest, with the last idea of humanity dying away under the cries of tortured prisoners and the curses and abuses of their tormentors. And yet we all agree on this—there is nothing like the night on the train from Vienna to Dachau.

In the police prison we had been under the supervision of Austrian police. Although a great number of policemen had already been Nazis before the Anschluss, we were not mistreated, except when some prisoners were taken to hearings before the German Gestapo and SS. But these were rare exceptions. Most of us were sent to concentration camps without any hearing at all.

One evening some of us were taken out of our cells and collected in other cells. The next evening we were ordered out, led through the vast building, over staircases and corridors to a back exit. There we were loaded into prison vans.

I was the last man in the line. In front of me marched Dr. Byck, director general of the Austrian National Library, a tall man of about sixty-five, who walked through the lane of staring and sneering policemen with an admirable calm and dignity. Just before we left the building, a young policeman caught sight of him and said: "Look at him! Looks like the head of a department." And he spat right into his face. Dr. Byck did not turn an eyelash.

We entered the vans, and as soon as I was inside we rolled off. There we sat in the darkness—crowded, sweating, and hardly daring to speak. We tried to guess where we were going. Through the little window we could see that the van was crossing the "Ring," then turning up Mariahilfer Strasse. This is one of Vienna's main thoroughfares, leading up to the Western Railroad Station. Suddenly we realized that were on our way to Dachau. All talk ceased. We were on our way to hell.

At a back entrance of the station the car stopped. The door was thrown open, somebody yelled at us to get the hell out of the van. Half-blind after the darkness in the car, we jumped out and were immediately chased through narrow gauntlets of SS men. They shouted and cursed at us, kicked us with their boots, hit us with the butts of their rifles, tripped us, trampled upon us, kicked us up again, and made us run for the railroad cars.

And we ran for dear life. None of us had time to think about hitting back. All we could do was to try to avoid their rifle butts. With all the hell they raised they might have scared the life out of a hero. Panting for breath and trembling with excitement or fear we climbed the stairs up to the cars. In the corridor there were more SS men, more yelling and beating. Each one of us ran into the first compartment with an empty seat. In came the next man, and the next, and the next, till all eight seats were taken.

After the last man, an SS man stepped into the entrance, in full battle dress, with steel helmet, rifle, sidearms. He gave orders: Sit up straight! Open your eyes! Shut your mouths! Put your hands on your knees! Do this! Do that! Don't move or you will be shot! Don't look out of the window or you will be shot! Don't open your mouth or you will be shot! Don't do this! Don't do that! You will be shot! You will be shot! Do this! Do that! You will be shot! Don't do this! You will be shot!

And each one of us obediently did what was ordered.

This was the moment when the man in us changed into an automaton that carried out orders.

I remember telling myself: "If they intended killing all of us, why should they put us on a train?" I ventured a look at my neighbors. Most of them were old men. I told myself that I was in better physical shape than the others and therefore had probably the best chance of getting through this night.

We heard the order passed through: "Don't let them fall asleep." We were ordered to stare into the eyes of the man opposite us. All night long I stared into Dr. Byck's eyes. When I seemed to be falling asleep, he gently shoved his foot against mine, and I did him the same service.

The torture went on all night long. Exercises, drill, invectives, slaps in the face, beatings with rifles, kicks with boots, interspersed with curious questions about our professions. One of the young hooligans slapped Dr. Byck's face and then asked him what he had been before. Dr. Byck answered in a firm and fearless voice: "Intellectual laborer (*Geistiger Schwerarbeiter*). I have worked sixteen and eighteen hours a day." Only those who know the Nazis' contempt for intellectuals can appreciate the grim humor with which the old man made a fool of the Nazi boy with a rifle in his hand.

In another car Herr Schmitz, fascist mayor of the city of Vienna, had to bear the brunt. A secretary of state, warned by Schmitz's fate, answered that he was a lawyer. He got away a bit cheaper.

One incident seems characteristic to me. A man in my compartment was asked: "What are you?"

"First prosecutor of the state."

Immediately he received a blow. "You are an asshole. What are you?"

"Public prosecutor."

He received another blow. "What are you?"

Now he said it. "An asshole."

Step by step one could follow the change in the man's mind from looking upon himself as the first public prosecutor of the state, and in this capacity defying his enemy, into a poor wretch, trying to keep alive during this hell of a night. He kept alive. He certainly would not have if he had insisted upon his being the first public prosecutor.

Every two hours the guards were relieved. Many of them were drunk. As far as I know, bringing prisoners to the camp is the only occasion when guards are allowed to be drunk on duty. It is part of the system.

For brief intervals sometimes nothing special happened. We simply stared into the eyes of the man opposite. Then it happened again and again, that some passing SS man asked the man on duty why we were "at ease" and whether he thought that we were on our way to a sanatorium. And he started a little celebration of his own.

It seemed as though the night would never end. Beating, shouting, staring, beating, drill, shouting, staring.

We had left Vienna about seven o'clock at night and arrived in Dachau about six o'clock in the morning. We were loaded into SS trucks and ordered to bend our heads down on our knees. He who looks up gets shot.

In the camp we were unloaded amid great yelling and beating. Since we were the first Austrians and many well-known people were among us, Commander Loritz himself came and made a speech. He explained to us that there was corporal punishment in the camp, that we had better behave damned well, that there was no fooling about the lash. He read our names from a list and introduced us to his beloved comrades. Those with resounding titles, like the mayor of Vienna, the secretary of finance, the head of the police department, a consul general, were greeted with a cheer and had to run a little gauntlet.

Then we were lined up and not allowed to move. Snow had fallen overnight. There we stood freezing, at rigid attention. After that horrible night one single man was enough to keep us in order.

The sun came up, rose higher and higher, began to burn our bare heads. Old men fainted. We were not allowed to help them up. They were trampled back to life.

Finally the administrative procedure began. Amid yelling and beating we were rushed through the regular routine and then lined up on the roll call square. All day long SS men swarmed around us, teasing us, beating us. After roll call at night we were led to our barracks, and now we got our first food in thirty-six hours. Then we fell asleep on the straw bags that covered the floor of the otherwise empty barracks. We were dead tired and slept the deep, deep sleep of an overworked horse that simply can't go on any longer.

The next morning we were formed into a special working group with an unusually large number of officers and capos. For weeks we were accorded the camp's "special treatment," until finally the terror ebbed, the old men and invalids were sent to easier jobs, and the rest were attached to ordinary working groups. From then on we were subject "only" to the "ordinary" terror of this hell. We were swallowed by the great mass of the older prisoners, we adjusted ourselves to their way of life. The initiation was over.

I wanted to add lest there be any doubt: I have not tried to describe the horror of the night on the train as such. I have left out everything that might possibly be construed as a manifestation of the guard's own ingenuity. There occurred outrages of sadism that I also consider part of the system but that others might ascribe to individual action. I have only described what is beyond doubt part of a well-planned system to break the spirits of the new prisoners.

Later on, the administration learned that they could save themselves a lot of the breaking-in procedure in the beginning by stepping up the terror of the train. The hundred and fifty men who arrived on May 24 had to keep their hands clasped behind their heads and stare into the electric light all night long. They were more severely mistreated than we had been. But their initiation inside the camp was easier. It is difficult to say which was preferable. But it is important to indicate the system.

The larger the transports became, the more terrific became the terror. When the Viennese Jews were brought in groups of five and six hundred, they were so mistreated and tortured that men went mad and jumped through the closed windows. These men were shot "on attempt to escape." One transport arrived with eight dead. When another transport arrived, one man went mad during the disembarkation and ran in the wrong direction. He was shot to death immediately. Other SS men, hearing the shots, got nervous and also began to shoot. Within a few minutes five prisoners lay dead, others wounded. Incidentally, an SS man was wounded by a bullet.

When large groups arrived, there were not enough tools to keep them busy. But to let the men go idle until the new tools arrived might have given them time enough to recuperate from the shock on the train. So a relay system was organized: A man made a long trip with a heavily loaded wheelbarrow, emptied it, turned it over to a new man, and lined up for his next turn. Officers were placed all along the way and made the men run as they beat them, so that the period at the waiting station became only a short interruption between two long stretches of agony.

Finally there were not enough wheelbarrows even for such a system. The next batch of six hundred men were made to carry heavy blocks of cement on their shoulders over a distance of about half a mile. The stones were not needed, but the men had to be kept busy. Officers along the way made the men with the stones move faster, and those on the return trip they made run. No water or rest was allowed them. Under the blazing sun many of them suffered sunstroke, broke down, were kicked to their feet, broke down again, were kicked up again. Some went mad under the torture. All of a sudden one such a man threw away his stone and ran in wild circles around the roll call square. The circles became rapidly smaller and smaller until finally the man collapsed in the center. Death had put an end to the run. Others were carried in wheelbarrows to the infirmary and suffocated before they arrived. To increase the terror, a few people were shot "on attempt to escape," and the record showed eighteen dead within thirty-six hours.

But the purpose was fulfilled: Any spark of resistance that might possibly have survived in these six hundred men after the night on the train was thoroughly stamped out within a few days.

The same "breaking-in" procedure was applied in a different way to the three hundred Austrian Gypsies. Both prisoners and administration seemed to expect that these "sons of the steppe," famous for being indomitable, for knifing and fighting the police, would behave differently. They might hit back, primarily because they did not understand that this situation was basically different from any other they had faced in "civilian" society. Nobody thought them capable of work and discipline.

All talk about the "free sons of the steppe" proved just so much romanticism. They reacted exactly as we others did. They got the shock of their lives during the night on the train, even more so than the rest of us, because they understood less what it was all about. They forgot completely about their famous indomitability.

The administration let loose at them more than at the others, just in case. On the first day they shot several "on attempt to escape" and that successfully terrorized the rest. Then Commander Koegl proceeded to teach them "regular work" and "civilization." Together with barracks leader Wagner he inspected their working grounds. He picked out a few of them for being lazy and Wagner administered the "twenty-five" on the spot. After this had been repeated for several days, the Gypsies were assumed to have grasped their lesson. And as a matter of fact they had—there was practically no more trouble with them at all.

That all this was part of a carefully planned system and not haphazard mistreatment was confirmed to us very clearly on the way from Dachau to Buchenwald. Again we spent a whole night on the train, guarded by Dachau SS. Yet for most of us the trip was relatively quiet; only in a few cars was there some excitement and beating. Apparently we were considered "old prisoners" who knew the ropes and did not require any special attention.

But in Weimar we were taken over by Buchenwald SS, who thought that they had to break us into our new environment. They were very proud of the hell they kept going up there and kept yelling at us that the "good times in Dachau" were over now. Before we were loaded into the SS trucks, we were lined up in a street tunnel, and there they fell upon us with all the extra cruelty accorded to newcomers.

Later on we learned that the attack in the tunnel was a regular thing for newcomers in Buchenwald, when they came in numbers so large that they couldn't be loaded directly into the trucks. This attack reached its height when, a few weeks after our arrival, the eleven thousand Jews were brought in during the pogroms. Many of them came by truck and car from different parts of Germany and had not yet gone through even the regular night on the train. Thus the whole initial blow had to be concentrated on the short time in the tunnel. Blood flowed in streams, limbs were broken, skulls were smashed; they entered the camp with the most horrible injuries. But the purpose was fulfilled again: With one decisive blow, the very idea of resistance was knocked out of these unfortunates for good.

Why They Don't Hit Back

As has been said before: The vast majority of the prisoners don't hit back because they fear the bullet. What we are trying to answer is this question: "Why aren't there any exceptions? Or at least no more exceptions than perhaps one or two among hundreds of thousands of prisoners?"

One reason why people might hit back is that they could go insane and attack, bullet or no bullet. It is quite possible; that could happen. However, not many men go insane under mistreatment, and of those who do, not many fall into a violent sort of insanity. The chance that a man happens to go insane in a violent way, an SS man happens to be around, and that the madness of the man directs itself against him seems to be rather small. And the question "Why don't they hit back?" is hardly pointed at these cases.

Yet it is often said: "If they beat me, I would get so mad, I would forget what I was doing. I would not think of being shot, I simply would strike back blindly and without a thought. Sure I would."

You would not. Nobody does. It seems inconceivable that the people who make such a statement should be of such exceptional stature that what applies to hundreds of thousands of other men, among whom there are some who have proven themselves to be courageous above and beyond the call of duty, should not apply to them. It seems more plausible to assume that the man indeed would not strike back, just as all the others don't, and for the same reasons, whatever they may be.

The implication of the question is usually not that of self-defense—except perhaps in an unconscious way—because most people will admit that if a man has sense enough to defend himself consciously he also has sense enough not to do so if defending himself might cost him the very life he wants to defend. The implication is usually that the man is expected to be ashamed of being beaten; he is expected to strike back in defense of his honor and dignity as a man. "I would get so mad, I would not care what I did" implies getting angry at the humiliation and shame of having one's face slapped.

To understand why the prisoner does not strike back, we may first ask: Why does the man in civilian society hit back? Which of the reasons that make him hit back do not hold in the camp? At what point on his way from one society to the other does the man realize that the rules that govern his behavior have been changed?

"Honor" is a social concept and so is the necessity of defending it. It cannot, like the necessity for self-preservation, arise within one individual alone, but it has to be seen against the social situation of which it is a part.

To strike back when attacked is one of the basic references in our society. Only a small minority will, in the concrete case of a slap in the face, follow the Christian rule and turn the other cheek.

He who does not strike back is considered a coward, both by other people and by himself. Because the frame of reference of his society has become an integral part of his personality, there is practically no alternative left to him, except when the odds are so obviously unfavorable that he is excused for not striking back. But that is seldom the case. The man who strikes back against heavy odds is admired as a hero. If he has to suffer for it, he is praised as a martyr for his honor. The increased acclaim is in part a compensation for his suffering.

The man who does not strike back loses status in his community. Recognition by the community in which we are living is one of our basic needs. Many a suicide has been committed as a way out from a community in which a man felt he could no longer carry on after having lost status for not striking back when he was beaten.

When a country is occupied and a man is insulted by a member of the enemy's army, he usually has a choice of actions. If he hits back and gets the better of the enemy, he is admired as a hero. If he then receives more mistreatment, is perhaps arrested and executed, he will be regarded as a martyr who died for his country. He knows that his death will be a signal for his friends and he expects them to avenge him. The man who does not hit back will usually not be considered a coward but a victim of the brutality of the enemy. His insult will be glorified as martyrdom. He will not lose in social status.

The man in a concentration camp who gets slapped or whipped on a stand has no choice but to take it, unless he wants to commit suicide. But here is the main difference from civilian life: Nobody expects him to strike back. And if he really does strike back and is immediately shot to death, nobody will glorify him as a hero and martyr. The only comment he can expect from his fellow prisoners is "damned fool." And they may elaborate a little: "Who is he that he thinks himself too good for what we have to endure every day? The hell with him!"

What affects the man's status is the way in which he takes the beating. If he cries and weeps, he is considered a weakling. If he begs for quarter (which is never given anyway) he is held in contempt.

It may be added that men who beg and cry under the lash or on the "tree" get additional blows or have to hang longer, because the guards have the same basic idea: It is dishonorable for a man to cry under torture. They show a little respect (though not much) for the man who takes it the right way.

On the part of the guards this is only the Teutonic image of the redskin at the stake, as they learned it when reading Karl May, author of numerous American Indian stories that were widely read by German youth. But on the part of the prisoners, beyond the redskin image, it is self-preservation, pure and simple. They are faced with this conflict: The ordinary way of gaining and retaining status, namely to hit back, is practically blocked by its absolutely suicidal consequences. If a whole society does not want to commit suicide in consequence of acts that are not a supreme insult, but daily routine, it has to adjust its concepts of honor and social status to this routine.

This adjustment is made by not letting an insult affect a man's status. No social pressure is put upon him to hit back. But on the other hand, terrific social pressure is put on him to take it in the right way, by remaining silent and stolid before, during, and after the beating.

The beating itself becomes a completely impersonal matter, like the weather, or an accident. When the sun burns hot, or when rain and hail fall upon him, the prisoner does not like it. But it does not affect his status. When a worker is injured by a machine, that is his occupational hazard; nobody holds him in contempt for it—except possibly that fellow workers might cast doubt on his craftsmanship. To be slapped and beaten is one of the occupational hazards of the man who happens to have the profession of "camp prisoner." To say of a man "He got 'twenty-five' yesterday" is a sheer factual report, with no value judgment involved. To say of him "Don't know what's the matter with that guy. Every now and then he gets his 'twenty-five'" is a derogatory remark, because it implies that the man, through his carelessness, gets caught and beaten more often than is considered his proper share.

From a man-to-man affair the beating changes into a group-to-group affair. Here are defenseless prisoners. There are guards with rifles and machine guns. Well, there is nothing the individual can do about it.

To the prisoner, the SS guard or officer who slaps him is not so much a man who humiliates him through an insult as a sort of low animal, unpleasant and dangerous. To be bitten by a snake or a mad dog brings many unpleasant consequences. One may even die of it. But it certainly does not arouse the contempt of one's fellow men.

Several parallels come to mind in which people do "get mad" and hit back in situations in which they should not. Children sometimes hit back at their parents and pupils at their teachers, and sometimes prisoners in ordinary prisons at their jailers and civilians in the streets at an arresting policeman. All of these situations have two things in common: To hit back is not identical with suicide, and, to both parties, the concept of honor and defending one's honor is an accepted thing. The individual involved may be punished for violating the law, for hitting back in a situation where it is specifically forbidden to do so, but those who punish him still consider him somebody who ordinarily is encouraged to strike back when attacked.

The citizen who is beaten by a policeman finds himself in a conflict. There is the basic law that tells him to strike back and then there is the exception: but never at a policeman. Against him you can only go and lodge a complaint. Sometimes people do get so angry that they hit the policeman. Then they are sentenced in court, not because the policeman was right, but because the policeman, representing the power of the state, must be protected. The individual policeman may then be sentenced for having beaten a citizen. Occasionally a defendant may plead: "I had to defend my honor. I got so mad I did not know what I was doing. I am sure your Honor would have done the same in my place." Sometimes this kind of defense proves successful.

Our civilian society can afford an occasional exception to the rule that the policeman is sacrosanct. The concentration camp cannot afford a single exception regarding its SS men—the very existence of the camp would be threatened immediately.

The man who hit the policeman is judged by his fellow citizens according to his motives. People who are given long prison terms for having hit back at policemen in political fights never lose and usually gain in social status.

"Getting mad" in situations in which one should not is recognized by the community as a possible form of behavior, though perhaps punishable: The noble outcast who robs the rich and gives to the poor is accepted and glorified by folklore, although he is hanged if caught and that is considered just. If he puts up a terrific last fight against the police, that only adds to his glory. Even the movie gangster who fights for his life receives a lot of admiration for it, although the eventual triumph of justice is almost necessary to absolve society from approving of his defense.

The prisoner in an ordinary prison is of course forbidden to strike back at a guard. But the guard is forbidden to beat the prisoner in the first place, except in self-defense. The relations between prisoner and guard are covered by written laws, which are guaranteed by the justice system. In these rules the prisoner is treated as a man, a member of human society who happens to be in prison and some of whose rights happen to be curtailed or postponed for the time of his stay. Yet both he and the guard—and, in the case of a trial, the judge—know that after his term in prison is up he will return to his community.

Thus the frame of reference of civilian society, of which the guard is a member when off duty and to which the prisoner will return, influences greatly their relations to each other. They may be enemies, but they are, in their relations, a man who happens to be a prisoner and a man who happens to be a guard. And between them is still prevalent the idea that a slap in the face is an insult, and to hit back is the proper reaction, though it may be punished by a week in a dark cell. The fellow prisoners consider the one who strikes back a real man, who does not let "those guards" fool with him, and the fact that he was heavily punished for it, perhaps after an unofficial heavy beating by the guards, does not detract from his status.

The prisoner in a concentration camp is there not for committing a definite crime for which he serves a definite sentence but for his attitude toward the Nazi state or because he belongs to a category of people whom the Nazi state wants to get rid of. By being a Jew, a Jehovah's Witness, or a communist, he has forfeited his membership in Nazi society. He is ejected and outlawed.

There is no time limit set on the period for which he is outlawed. During the first few years, when the pattern of relations between prisoners and guards was set, there were so few releases that release was spoken of as a miracle. But even when, in the fall of 1938, the Nazis began to release masses of Jews on condition that they leave the country (and when they released eleven hundred non-Jews from Buchenwald on Hitler's birthday in 1939), release did not become the logical end of imprisonment but remained something like an accident or gift from heaven.

Thus relations between guard and prisoner are considerably less influenced by the concepts of the outside world than is the case in a regular prison. In the concentration camp both know that the civilian rights of the prisoner are not suspended but abolished. To his guards the prisoner is no longer a man whose personality has any meaning. He no longer has an "honor" that has to be respected. And to the prisoner the guard becomes part of a machine, or a dangerous beast, whose every move he watches and studies carefully in order to get hurt as little as possible, but to whom any concepts of honor simply do not apply.

And so, while the civilian strikes back in order to defend his honor—that is, his social status among his fellow men—the camp prisoner for the same reason takes his beating stolidly: to retain the recognition of his fellow prisoners. Where the civilian reasons, "If anyone dared to slap me like that, I would surely hit him over the head" (which actually means: "I live in a society where to strike back is necessary to retain my status—and I certainly want to retain it"), the prisoner reasons about the man on the stand: "Your turn today, mine perhaps tomorrow. But I'm sure I wouldn't cry out" (which actually means: "If that is the way it is done in this society, then I surely will do it; I wouldn't want to lose my status among the only people for whose judgment I have to care, perhaps for the rest of my life"). The difference between the two societies, that outside and that inside the camp, seems at this point rather one of rules of behavior than basic concepts.

In a situation in which there is no goal worth sacrificing your life for and where there is no one to accept the sacrifice if you make it, sacrificing your life becomes worthless and meaningless. "Sacrifice" is as much a social concept as "honor," and where the society does not recognize an act as a supreme sacrifice the act might, as far as readiness to sacrifice goes, just as well remain undone. And for this reason, in the concentration camp sacrificing one's life for the sake of hitting back is not done.

One question that the outsider often asks is this: "But if they know that so many of them are going to die in the camp anyway, if so many of them have given up the hope of ever getting released, why don't they simply jump at one of these SS men, perhaps snatch his gun from him, shoot one or two of the gangsters, and bring their own life to a more rapid and dignified and perhaps useful end?" This question is aimed particularly at the political prisoners of every party denomination.

The answer is that if they saw the slightest reason for doing so, they would probably do it. Enough of them would be willing to give their lives, if it would serve their cause. But there is not the slightest bit of sense to it: The outside world, to which such an act might be a symbol of the unbroken spirit of its fighters, would never learn of it because nothing would happen spectacular enough to be told. The man would be shot to death while still in the unspectacular act of lifting his arm. His fellow prisoners would not get much satisfaction out of it, because all they could do to carry on his revolt would be to lift an arm again—and be shot, too, for this unspectacular move, before landing the blow. It would not impress the SS either, because for them shooting defenseless prisoners is not a rare sensation anyway. They would not take the prisoner's life as a supreme sacrifice—they would shoot him in the same matter-of-fact way in which they slap his face. Neither would his fellow prisoners, utterly convinced that he had not the slightest chance of success, see any supreme sacrifice in it. They would condemn it as an absolutely foolish undertaking.

To all this is added, for the political prisoner, the political isolation of the camps. No regular contacts are established with the underground movement. The prisoners learn about the still-existing movement through the newly arrested, and the movement in turn learns about its incarcerated members through the few who are released. No messages go to and fro, no encouragement and no promise of help. The political prisoners of the camps, although informed that underground movements still exist, know that these movements are too weak to support them in the case of any attempted uprising.

If perchance once in a hundred thousand cases a man should seriously attack an SS man, because, due to some technical circumstance, he thought that this time he might be able to land at least one blow, the administration would most certainly take the necessary precautions so that such a technical situation could not arise again. We have a good illustration in the case in which two men escaped from Buchenwald and killed an SS man in the process. The day after, in all concentration camps, new orders were given about the guarding of prisoners: The guards from then on carried their rifles not over the shoulder but under the arm, ready to shoot, and with the bayonets attached. The greatest care was taken that one guard was never alone with one prisoner, not even on some special mission such as to get a special tool from a distant tool shed. The distance within which a prisoner could approach a guard without being shot immediately was increased from three to six yards, with the exception of the chain of sentinels, where in any case the guards stand so close to each other that the neighbors to the left and right can always shoot a prisoner while he is trying to approach a guard.

The question remains: When and how does the prisoner realize that the old laws do not hold any longer, that this society has different rules, and that here he is not expected to strike back? Why are there no exceptions, at least among the newcomers on the very first day, before they have talked to anybody?

In my opinion the answer is the shock they receive the moment they are taken over by the SS.

Up to the moment when they leave the prison van, the prisoners have had no occasion in which to make use of their old rule: When beaten, strike back. They have been in the hands of civilian authorities, civilian police perhaps, or prison personnel, who ordinarily did not beat them at all. The change from one society to the other follows with practically no transition.

Out of the dark prison van a prisoner is suddenly faced with this machine that hits, that beats, that yells, shouts, tramples, for no understandable reason, and all in such a hurry that the prisoner has no chance to stop for a single moment or to think about what to do next. He is drawn into this witches' cauldron as though it were a whirlpool so disproportionately stronger than himself that he can do nothing but try to lie still and wait to see whether it will let him loose again. He sees others being beaten like himself and doing nothing about it. When he makes his first contact with old inmates he is told that it is that bad only in the beginning, that after a few days it will let up somewhat, and he will be beaten less than might appear at first glance. As to the shame of being beaten—the old inmate will just laugh at it or dismiss it. Don't take it to heart, don't take it too seriously, it doesn't count. This is not like where you come from. Here it is different. It doesn't matter to us.

Once he has gone through his initiation, he has already learned by his own experience that you can survive having your face slapped and not striking back. And he has learned that he did not have to perish with shame, because nobody takes any notice of it. Having learned in addition about the suicidal nature of any attempt to strike back, he gives up this notion for the time of his stay in camp.

My first idea that a slap in the camp is not the same as a slap outside of it came in a strange way on the train from Vienna to Dachau. Sometime during the night, a young boy of about seventeen or eighteen took over our compartment. For a while he kept silent and did nothing. Then he inquired quietly about our professions. One man answered: "I am an Austrian general." The boy saluted militarily and said: "Yes, General, I know what that means, General." The last man was a "major in the Austrian army during the World War." The boy saluted again, "Yes, Major," and began a quiet conversation with the man. After a short while he said: "Anyone who wants to sleep, do it." We stared at each other in amazement. A miracle. A human being among the devils. He continued to talk to the major in a low voice. I sat next to the major and overheard the conversation. The boy asked the major about his experiences during the World War. Suddenly he said: "One thing I want to tell you, Major. If anybody should beat you, perhaps even slap your face, don't think of it in the same way as if you were free and a major. Here it is different. Just ignore it."

The whole interlude lasted only for a few minutes. One of us really slept for a minute. He was the president of the Vienna Commercial University, a man of almost seventy. Another guard, chancing by, saw the sleeping man and asked the boy whether he was crazy to allow us to sleep. He brought in another SS man, showing him the spectacle of a man who could sleep during that night. They started beating us. Somehow the boy disappeared during the scene.

Having gone through my share of being slapped and beaten both on the train and during the first weeks of special terror, I still wondered whether it would be any different if I should meet an SS man face to face and be beaten by him. The situation soon came up. On a fine spring day I was working with another man in a side street of the camp. We were in an out-of-the-way spot and so began chatting. Suddenly an officer appeared. He shouted at us but soon went away again. Smiling, I said to my companion: "That was luck, wasn't it?" At that moment the officer turned around again: "What are you laughing at? Are you joking about me by any chance?" How could I dare to? I denied it. He came closer. We stood face to face at a distance of a few inches. "You are a damned liar!"—and crash, a blow landed on my face.

Of course there was no choice between hitting back and not hitting back. The only choice I had was whether to take it standing upright or to drop. If you drop, there is always the chance that nothing more may follow than an additional kick with the boot. If you take it on the chin, the guard may feel the resistance and keep on beating until there is no choice left but to go down.

The incident happened to take place in front of my barracks, where I had been moved only a few days before. The barracks senior and my room senior were looking out of the window, curious to see how the new inmate would behave. In addition there was the man with whom I was working, whom I knew from Vienna.

I decided to take it on the chin. I stood straight and stared into the officer's eyes. They can't bear your staring in the eyes. Stare an SS man in the eyes and he will behave like a dog when you stare into its eyes. The dog will bite you or howl at you or pull his tail in and get off. The SS man will either kick and beat you, just to get rid of your eyes, or he will howl at you "Don't you dare look at me! Don't you dare look at me!" *("Schau mich ja nicht an!")*. This one hit once more. I did not move but kept staring into his eyes. A third slap I took in the same manner. Then the dog pulled in his tail and went off.

This one incident I remember better than any beatings I got before or after, because I was so completely aware of my surroundings—in fact I felt more like the observer of a psychological experiment than a victim in the hands of his tormentors. Not for a single moment did I think of the shame of having my face slapped. I only watched myself, curious to see whether I was able to take it and to show the devil that he could not hurt me.

When, on the trip from Dachau to Buchenwald, we were loaded into the SS trucks in Weimar, I looked out of the car to see what sort of people those policemen in the streets were. One of them saw me looking at him and immediately shouted: "Don't you dare look at me!" Here it was again. I turned my head back into the car. An SS man who had seen me looking out of the car, which was forbidden, began to howl at me. That reminded me of my theory about the dogs. I stared into his eyes. The theory proved right. This particular one bit. To get rid of my eyes he gave me a heavy blow over the head with his rifle. Then I kept my head down as had been ordered.

Once, in Buchenwald, when my hand was still bandaged following frostbite and blood poisoning, I was at work carrying water from a garage together with two old men, both about seventy. They always wanted to take time off inside the garage. I kept warning them of Officer Becker and Capo Azzoni.

The two old men kept insisting, "Becker can't be everywhere." Finally I consented to a little rest. We had hardly put down our pails when suddenly the door was flung wide open—Becker and Azzoni entered. Becker gave a mock-surprised "Ahhh!?" and grinned like a boy who is out for a prank. He held a stick in his hand. He had the first of the two old men step forward. "Bend." The man bent forward. Becker walked slowly up behind him, lifted the stick with a wide swing, and let go. The old man lost balance and toppled a few steps forward. When he was back in position, he got another blow. He moaned slightly. All told he got five blows, and that was very cheap. The next man got five blows in the same manner.

While Becker was busy with the old men, I was only angry at the boy for beating these people, each of whom could have been his grandfather. But now, when it was my turn, I felt deeply ashamed—not at the fact of being beaten, although I must confess that the elaborateness of the procedure made me gulp a little—but at the fact of being caught in such a childish manner. It was beneath my dignity as a political prisoner to get a thrashing for such a stupid thing as getting caught in a dark garage that had only one exit.

But here I was, and the best I could do was to take it in a good way. I grinned at Becker, bent, and stood firm as blow after blow fell. Becker, being a relatively decent man within his own standards, made a difference between the two old men and the young one. I received considerably more and harder blows. But it was soon over, and Becker and Azzoni left the scene.

My imagination and feeling of shame had not deceived me. When I told Walter the story, he called me a little boy whom momma can't let take a walk by himself in a concentration camp without having him run into trouble. Jackie added some funny remarks, and then we stopped talking about it. But none of them saw anything shameful in the beating itself. That was an accident. What they teased me for was my stupidity in getting caught.

A good illustration of how a beating does not affect the status of people was an evening in Buchenwald, when all thirty-seven barracks seniors "went over the stand." Discipline had slipped in the camp; relations between seniors and their charges had become very close. To pep up the lax spirits a bit, Commander Roedl gave them first a speech, threatening them with repeated thrashings of "twenty-five" if they did not file reports. Then he had every single one of them receive ten heavy blows, promising them that the missing fifteen would soon follow if they did not tighten up the camp discipline at once.

Each barracks senior was strapped to the stand. The blows echoed over the square. Not one of the men made a sound. And a feeling of admiration ran through the ten thousand men: Aren't they grand, our seniors! Of course when some satan of a senior had his turn, the men of his barracks would smile: Why not, he has given us so much.

The commander hardly achieved what he had wanted. Where the relations between senior and barracks had been bad, they grew worse. But where they had been good before, they grew better now. On coming home from the stand, the senior was treated with the greatest respect; his friends cheered him up and brought the good old home remedies, fat and warm water, and tried their best to get him into shape again.

Another effect was that the esprit de corps of the seniors was strengthened. They were reminded of our common enmity for the administration and again felt themselves more a part of the community than they had before. And as to the shame of being beaten—nobody thought of it as shameful.

Fear and social habit simultaneously tend to form a strong barrier against any conscious attempt at hitting back, either in self-defense or to defend one's honor and social status. The administration may not have been aware of the social implications and may possibly have attributed it to fear only. And in accordance with this, they arranged the terrifying initiation on the train and during the first period after arrival. Their maxim seems to have been: If you want to prevent any riots, you have to break the prisoners' personalities, to knock the spark of resistance out of them at the very moment when they enter the camp. If you are able to crush them with one decisive blow at the beginning, they will never recover.

This pattern has been carefully carried out for years in concentration camps all over Germany. It is planned and carried out in such detail and is so identical from camp to camp that there cannot be the slightest suspicion that these are the incidental sadistic outrages of individual camp commanders.

Reference

Winkler, Ernst (Johannes Wolfgang Mattern). (1942). *Four Years of Nazi Torture.* New York: D. Appleton-Century.

Contributors

William C. Collins, J.D., has worked as an attorney specializing in correctional law for over twenty years. He is the former senior assistant attorney general in the state of Washington, the editor of the *Correctional Law Reporter*, and the author of numerous articles and publications. He has also served as a consultant on legal issues for the National Institute of Corrections, the American Jail Association, and the American Correctional Association.

Charles Fethe, Ph.D., is a professor in the Department of Philosophy at Kean University. He has published articles in major philosophy journals in Great Britain and the United States on medical ethics, social philosophy, religion, and problems related to free will and determinism. He is the recipient of New York University's award for scholarship and has sponsored a series of public lectures on ethics and social policy.

Gilbert Geis, Ph.D., is a professor emeritus in the Department of Criminology, Law and Society at the University of California, Irvine. He is the former president of the American Society of Criminology and has received the Sutherland Award for Research from that organization. He has written more than 350 original articles on matters of crime and some 20 books.

Jack Kamerman, Ph.D., is a professor in the Department of Sociology and Anthropology at Kean University. He has written on the sociology of death and suicide, and his work on training correctional officers has been incorporated into prison service training programs in the United States and Eastern

Europe. He is the author of *Death in the Midst of Life: Social and Cultural Influences on Death, Grief, and Mourning* and a forthcoming book on police suicide.

Robert J. Kelly, Ph.D., is the Broeklundian Professor of Social Science and Criminal Justice at Brooklyn College and the Graduate Center of the City University of New York. In addition to having published numerous articles on organized crime and terrorism, he is the author of *African-American Organized Crime* and the coeditor of *Hate Crimes: The Politics of Global Polarization*.

Alison Liebling, Ph.D., is a senior research associate at the Institute of Criminology in Cambridge, where she received her doctorate in 1991. She has been involved in Home Office funded research since 1986 and is currently studying offending behavior, vulnerability, and incentive-based prison regimes. Her publications include *From Custody to Community: Throughcare for Young Offenders*, *Suicides in Prison*, and *Deaths in Custody: International Perspectives*.

Jess Maghan, Ph.D., is the executive director of the Center for Research in Law and Justice and an associate professor in the Department of Criminal Justice at the University of Illinois at Chicago. Formerly, he served as director of training of the New York City Police Department and as the commissioner for training at the New York City Department of Correction, the world's largest municipal detention service.

Mark Harrison Moore, Ph.D., is the Daniel and Florence V. Guggenheim Professor of Criminal Justice Policy and Management, the faculty chair of the Program in Criminal Justice and Management, and the founding chair of the Committee on Executive Programs at the John F. Kennedy School of Government, Harvard University. His research interests are in public management and leadership and in criminal justice policy and management. Among his publications are *Creating Public Value: Strategic Management in Government* and (with others) *Dangerous Offenders: Elusive Targets of Justice, From Children to Citizens: The Mandate for Juvenile Justice*, and *Beyond 911: A New Era for Policing*.

Paul Neurath, Ph.D., J.D., is a professor emeritus in the Department of Sociology at Queens College of the City University of New York and a visiting professor and honorary professor of sociology at the University of Vienna. He is the author of a number of books on demography and sociological methodology and theory. In addition to other honors in both the United States and Austria, he has been the recipient of three Fulbright grants.

John Rakis is the president and executive director of the South Forty Corporation, a nonprofit criminal justice agency that provides vocational services to prisoners and ex-offenders in New York City. He has served as the director of Health Services Management for the New York City Department of Correction and as the deputy executive director of the New York City Board of Correction. He holds a master's degree in public administration from Harvard University.

William Rentzmann, Cand. jur. (University of Copenhagen), is the general director of the Danish Prison and Probation Service (Ministry of Justice). He is the former president of the European Council for Penological Affairs and has advised prison administrations in several former communist states in central and eastern Europe. He is a member of the boards of the Danish Society of Criminology and the Danish Association of Criminalists and is the president of the Association of Danish Lawyers and Economists. He is the author of numerous articles and the coauthor (with Johan Reimann) of *Community Service and Other Community Sanctions and Measures.*

José E. Sánchez, Ph.D., is a professor in the Department of Sociology and Anthropology and in the Program in Criminal Justice at Kean University. He has published in the areas of criminology, the psychodynamics of organizations, psychopathology, and social interaction. He received his Ph.D. from the Graduate School of the City University of New York and completed postgraduate work in the Program in Organizational Development and Consultation of the William Alanson White Institute of Psychoanalysis, Psychiatry and Psychology in New York City. He has worked as an organizational consultant for institutions in the private and public sectors.